The Cultural and Intercultural Dimensions of English as a Lingua Franca

LANGUAGES FOR INTERCULTURAL COMMUNICATION AND EDUCATION

Series Editors: Michael Byram, *University of Durham, UK* and Alison Phipps, *University of Glasgow, UK*

The overall aim of this series is to publish books which will ultimately inform learning and teaching, but whose primary focus is on the analysis of intercultural relationships, whether in textual form or in people's experience. There will also be books which deal directly with pedagogy, with the relationships between language learning and cultural learning, between processes inside the classroom and beyond. They will all have in common a concern with the relationship between language and culture, and the development of intercultural communicative competence.

Full details of all the books in this series and of all our other publications can be found on http://www.multilingual-matters.com, or by writing to Multilingual Matters, St Nicholas House, 31–34 High Street, Bristol BS1 2AW, UK.

LANGUAGES FOR INTERCULTURAL COMMUNICATION AND EDUCATION: 29

The Cultural and Intercultural Dimensions of English as a Lingua Franca

Edited by
Prue Holmes and Fred Dervin

MULTILINGUAL MATTERS
Bristol • Buffalo • Toronto

Library of Congress Cataloging in Publication Data
Names: Holmes, Prue, editor. | Dervin, Fred, 1974- editor.
Title: The Cultural and Intercultural Dimensions of English as a Lingua Franca/Edited by Prue Holmes and Fred Dervin.
Description: Bristol; Buffalo: Multilingual Matters, [2016] |
Series: Languages for Intercultural Communication and Education: 29 |
Includes bibliographical references and index.
Identifiers: LCCN 2015036352| ISBN 9781783095094 (hbk : alk. paper) | ISBN 9781783095087 (pbk : alk. paper) | ISBN 9781783095100 (ebook)
Subjects: LCSH: Intercultural communication. | Multicultural education. | Lingua francas. | Language and languages—Variation. | Cross-cultural orientation. | Language and education. | Language and culture.
Classification: LCC P94.6 .C693 2016 | DDC 306.442/21—dc23 LC record available at http://lccn.loc.gov/2015036352

British Library Cataloguing in Publication Data
A catalogue entry for this book is available from the British Library.

ISBN-13: 978-1-78309-509-4 (hbk)
ISBN-13: 978-1-78309-508-7 (pbk)

Multilingual Matters
UK: St Nicholas House, 31–34 High Street, Bristol BS1 2AW, UK.
USA: UTP, 2250 Military Road, Tonawanda, NY 14150, USA.
Canada: UTP, 5201 Dufferin Street, North York, Ontario M3H 5T8, Canada.

Website: www.multilingual-matters.com
Twitter: Multi_Ling_Mat
Facebook: https://www.facebook.com/multilingualmatters
Blog: www.channelviewpublications.wordpress.com

Copyright © 2016 Prue Holmes, Fred Dervin and the authors of individual chapters.

All rights reserved. No part of this work may be reproduced in any form or by any means without permission in writing from the publisher.

Typeset by Techset Composition India(P) Ltd, Bangalore and Chennai, India.
Printed and bound in Great Britain by Short Run Press Ltd.

Contents

Acknowledgements	vii
Contributors	ix
Foreword	xiii

Introduction – English as a Lingua Franca and Interculturality:
Beyond Orthodoxies   1
Prue Holmes and Fred Dervin

Part 1: The Interconnections and Inter-Relationships Between Interculturality and ELF

1   Lingua Francas in a World of Migrations   33
Karen Risager

2   Interculturalities of English as a Lingua Franca: International Communication and Multicultural Awareness in the Greek Context   50
Richard Fay, Nicos Sifakis and Vally Lytra

3   Culture and Language in Intercultural Communication, English as a Lingua Franca and English Language Teaching: Points of Convergence and Conflict   70
Will Baker

Part 2: Grounding Conceptual Understandings of Interculturality in ELF Communication

4   Talking Cultural Identities into Being in ELF Interactions: An Investigation of International Postgraduate Students in the United Kingdom   93
Chris Jenks

5 Conflict Talk and ELF Communities of Practice 114
   Anne Kari Bjørge

6 Intercultural Misunderstanding Revisited: Cultural Difference
   as a (non) Source of Misunderstanding in ELF
   Communication 134
   Jagdish Kaur

7 Finnish Engineers' Trajectories of Socialisation into Global
   Working Life: From Language Learners to BELF Users and
   the Emergence of a Finnish Way of Speaking English 157
   Tiina Räisänen

8 The Local Purposes of a Global Language: English as an
   Intracultural Communicative Medium in China 180
   Eric S. Henry

Part 3: Commentary

9 Intercultural Communication and the Possibility of English as
   a Lingua Franca 203
   John O'Regan

   Index 218

Acknowledgements

The inspiration for this book came from a conversation with Professor Emeritus Michael Byram during a Cultnet seminar at Durham University in April 2011. We appreciate his insights, encouragement and support in undertaking this exploration of the intercultural and cultural aspects of English as a lingua franca. We also acknowledge the commitment of the authors who have contributed to the book, and thank them for their revisions and patience during the publication process. Finally, we thank series editors Michael Byram and Alison Phipps for supporting this publication, the reviewers for their helpful insights in the final stages of completing the manuscript and Multilingual Matters for bringing the edited collection to publication.

Contributors

Will Baker is a Lecturer in Modern Languages at the University of Southampton, United Kingdom, where he teaches and supervises doctoral students in Global Englishes, Intercultural Communication and Applied Linguistics. He is a founding member and Deputy Director of the University's Centre for Global Englishes. He is co-editor of the book series *Developments in English as a lingua franca*. His current research interests include ELF, intercultural communication, culture and language, e-learning, English medium instruction and ELT. He has published and presented internationally in all these areas.

Anne Kari Bjørge is an Associate Professor in the Department of Professional and Intercultural Communication (FSK), NHH Norwegian School of Economics. Her research interests include ELF with particular focus on email correspondence and negotiations discourse, corporate communication in multilingual workforces and corporate values discourse. Other contributions concern textbook chapters on the role of linguistic issues in cross-cultural management contexts such as language management and discourse strategies for cross-cultural communication. Publications journals include *Applied Linguistics* and *International Journal of Applied Linguistics*. Her present teaching interests focus on cross-cultural management practice and professional English.

Fred Dervin is a Professor of Multicultural Education at the University of Helsinki. He also holds professorships in Canada, Luxembourg and Malaysia. Prof Dervin specialises in intercultural education, the sociology of multiculturalism and student and academic mobility. He has widely published in international journals on identity, the 'intercultural' and mobility/migration. He has published more than 30 books and is the series editor of *Education beyond borders* (Peter Lang), *Nordic studies on diversity in education* (with Kulbrandstad & Ragnarsdóttir, Cambridge Scholars Publishing) and *Post-intercultural communication and education* (Cambridge Scholars Publishing).

Richard Fay is a Lecturer in Education (TESOL and Intercultural Communication) at The University of Manchester where he also is a programme co-ordinator for the MA Intercultural Communication, the Manchester Global Award, and the PhD in Education. Since the mid-1990s he has been researching the functions of English and related pedagogical implications for an era of increasing transnationality. His connections with Greece and Greek English language teaching cover a similar period. He is Co-Investigator on the AHRC-funded project 'Researching multilingually at the borders of language, the body, law and the state' (http://researching-multilingually-at-borders.com/)

Eric S. Henry is an Assistant Professor of Anthropology at Saint Mary's University in Halifax, Canada, where he teaches courses in linguistic anthropology, sociolinguistics, Asian studies and semiotics. Based on ethnographic fieldwork in Shenyang, his research concerns the role of contemporary speech practices and foreign languages in China's developing sense of itself as a modern, cosmopolitan nation.

Prue Holmes is a Reader in the School of Education at Durham University. She teaches masterate and doctoral students in languages education, intercultural communication, intercultural education, internationalization, and student mobility; she also publishes in these areas. Prue is Co-Investigator on the AHRC-funded project 'Researching multilingually at the borders of language, the body, law and the state' (http://researching-multilingually-at-borders.com/) and the EU-funded project 'Intercultural resources for Erasmus students and their teachers' (IEREST) (http://ierest-project.eu/). She chairs the International Association of Languages and Intercultural Communication (IALIC).

Chris Jenks is an Assistant Professor of English and an Intensive English/TESOL Coordinator at the University of South Dakota. He is the author and co-editor of several books, including an edited collection on second language learning that was runner-up for the 2011 British Association for Applied Linguistics (BAAL) Book Award. He is currently working on a book that examines race and ethnicity in the English language teaching profession in South Korea.

Jagdish Kaur is a Senior Lecturer in the Faculty of Languages and Linguistics, University of Malaya. In her main research interest, the microanalysis of interactions in English as a lingua franca, she uses conversation analysis procedures to establish how speakers of ELF communicate and to identify the kinds of competences they rely on to achieve success in communication. She has published her findings on ELF in journals such as *World Englishes, Journal of Pragmatics, Intercultural Pragmatics* and *Text & Talk*.

Vally Lytra is a Lecturer in the Department of Educational Studies at Goldsmiths, University of London. She studies multilingualism in schools, homes and communities in cross-cultural urban contexts. She is the author of *Play Frames and Social Identities: Contact Encounters in a Greek Primary School* (John Benjamins, 2007) and the editor of *Multilingualism and Identities across Contexts: Cross-Disciplinary Perspectives on Turkish-Speaking Youth in Europe* (with J.N. Jørgensen, Copenhagen Studies in Bilingualism, 2008), *Sites of Multilingualism: Complementary Schools in Britain Today* (with P. Martin, Trentham, 2010) and *When Greeks and Turks Meet: Interdisciplinary Perspectives on the Relationship Since 1923* (Ashgate, 2014). Her new edited book *Languages, Literacies and Identities: Religion in Young Lives* with Dinah Volk and Eve Gregory will appear in 2016 (Routledge).

John O'Regan is a Senior Lecturer in Applied Linguistics at UCL Institute of Education, University College London, where he is also a doctoral supervisor and leads the MA programme in Applied Linguistics. He specialises in World Englishes, intercultural communication and critical discourse analysis, and is the author of articles on a wide range of topics in applied linguistics and cultural studies. He has published in several journals, including the *Journal of Applied Linguistics, Language and Intercultural Communication, Critical Discourse Studies,* and the *Journal of the Royal Asiatic Society, Hong Kong*. He is currently researching a book on global English and political economy.

Tiina Räisänen (née Virkkula) is a post-doctoral researcher in the Department of Languages, University of Jyväskylä, Finland. She received her PhD in 2013 with a study titled 'Professional communicative repertoires and trajectories of socialization into global working life'. She co-edited *Dangerous Multilingualism: Northern Perspectives on Order, Purity and Normality* (w. Blommaert, J., Leppänen, S. and Pahta, P.) and has published in *International Journal of Applied Language Studies, Sociolinguistic Studies* and *Journal of Business Communication*. She is interested in sociolinguistics, business and engineering communication and intercultural communication.

Karen Risager is a Professor Emerita in Cultural Encounters at Roskilde University, Denmark. She has published widely on language, culture and migration from transnational and global perspectives. Her areas of empirical research include the cultural dimensions of foreign language teaching and learning, the cultural dimensions of second language learning among migrants and multilingual policies at the international university. Publications include *Language and Culture: Global Flows and Local Complexity* (2006, author), *Language and Culture Pedagogy: From a National to a Transnational Paradigm* (2007, author), and *Researching Identity and Interculturality* (2015, co-edited with F. Dervin).

Nicos Sifakis is an Associate Professor in the School of Humanities at the Hellenic Open University (HOU) and the Director of the MEd in the TESOL programme. He holds a PhD in language and linguistics from the University of Essex. He is Editor-in-Chief of *Research Papers in Language Teaching and Learning* (http://rpltl.eap.gr/). He has published extensively on intercultural communication and pedagogy, teaching and researching English as an international lingua franca, language teaching methodology, distance education, adult education and teacher education.

Foreword

As the editors and authors of this book repeatedly emphasise, identities and identifications are important. They have always been so but perhaps were less noticed in those apparently stable societies which, through colonisation, dominated the world of the last few centuries. Let us not forget, however, how George Eliot analyses instabilities, marginalisations – what today would be called 'fluidities' – in the 19th century world of *Daniel Deronda*, which happens to be my parallel reading to the manuscript of *The Cultural and Intercultural Dimensions English as a Lingua Franca*.

Let me say, then, that I write this Foreword as an editor of the LICE series but also as a colleague of the book's editors. It was in the former capacity that three or more years ago, I wanted to fill an obvious gap in the literature. It was in the latter capacity that I knew it would be good to encourage Prue and Fred to take on the task. I and my fellow series editor, Alison Phipps, are delighted with the outcome. It is a challenging book because it questions orthodoxies. It is a highly readable book because it brings contributions from a wide range of geographical places, and social and educational contexts. It may also turn out to be controversial, as the editors hint in their introduction – and all the better so.

I also write in my own right as someone who has been involved in 'foreign' language teaching for many years and who is still mindful of and influenced by my attempting to teach 'French' and 'German' to 'English' adolescents in a secondary school in the 1970s. Today I have to put scare quotes around 'foreign', 'French', 'German' and 'English' because we are all aware of the essentialisation so much criticised in recent writings and the fluidities that have become more evident in contemporary societies, although we must be equally careful not to assume that societies are homogeneous in their fluidities – another kind of essentialising. I write this Foreword from a village in France which is certainly not 'post-modern' and there are many such villages and small towns in most if not all countries. China is the unavoidable reference today, and is often thought of as an industrial giant, where people live and work in cities, some of them very rich. Yet there are many parts of China which outsiders do not often see and which resemble my French village. Even if the majority of people in the world now live in cities – and have done so since the crucial moment in the 1950s when, as Eric Hobsbawm often said, the world changed from majority agrarian to majority industrial and now post-industrial – nonetheless, the minority experience must not be ignored.

Thus the starting point for my suggestion to Prue and Fred was my concern for the vast numbers of teachers of English as a foreign language whether they live in small towns and villages or modern metropolises. The editors explain how they considered extending the scope to other lingua francas and how this proved to be difficult. There is no doubt that English is dominant, and different. For example in a recent Norwegian education policy paper, the language curriculum is described as comprising 'Norwegian, English and foreign languages', leaving the precise nature of English undefined but placed somewhere between the national language(s) and foreign languages. Whatever we academics may think, language users are aware of the reality and – in a cycle which we may call vicious or virtuous – learners, and just as importantly their parents, wish to learn 'English'. At the same time, English teachers, wherever they are, are realising that the subject, or 'object', they ought to teach is changing rapidly. They are faced with a change from the object 'English as a foreign language' to 'English as a lingua franca', and a change from the object of linguistic/grammatical competence to communication competence, a richer concept than 'communicative competence' as it has been understood hitherto. Can we help them deal with such changes?

The purpose of our LICE series is 'to publish books which will ultimately inform learning and teaching, but whose primary focus is on the analysis of intercultural relationships', as Alison Phipps and I wrote more than a decade ago. The editors and contributors to this book have fulfilled that purpose admirably, and we are grateful to them for doing so. The process has been longer than the editors – and we series editors – expected, but it is worth emphasising that, despite contemporary pressures to publish ever more and ever faster, the quality of the text is more important than the speed of production. That quality will be determined in years rather than months, and I hope and believe that the quality of this book will be revealed over a long time as it stimulates discussion and debate, and controversy.

The editors end their introduction with an agenda for future research where there is 'still much theoretical, methodological and pedagogical work to be done'. This book does much already to address theory and methodology. My enduring identity as a French and German teacher means that I hope we can find a way through to a pedagogy which will be accessible and feasible for teachers of English or 'Englishes as lingua francas', but also be useful to all language teachers, whether the languages are labelled 'first', 'second', 'foreign', 'world', or whatever. As Prue and Fred say, this is the beginning and I am grateful to them and their contributors for meeting the challenge of making the first steps.

Mike Byram

Introduction – English as a Lingua Franca and Interculturality: Beyond Orthodoxies[1]

Prue Holmes and Fred Dervin

ELF and Interculturality: Two Different Fields that Have Much in Common

When we started working on this book project, we envisaged a publication about the links between the use of lingua francas and interculturality in our post-national and 'glocal' (both global and local) worlds that would, in a sense, follow up on Byram's (2008) idea that language – including lingua franca language – is somehow detached from culture and contexts of interaction. As the project advanced, however, we attracted very few contributions that dealt with lingua francas other than English. Although the world is 'full' of lingua francas used within and across national and many other types of borders, English as a lingua franca (ELF) as a field of research has attracted a lot of attention worldwide (Bowles & Cogo, 2015; Jenkins *et al.*, 2011; Mauranen & Ranta, 2009; Seidlhofer, 2011). We therefore decided to concentrate on ELF, hoping that the discussions provoked by the chapters in this book might also trigger debates in relation to other lingua francas such as Arabic, Chinese Mandarin, Spanish and French, but also Esperanto – or any other language, for that matter, as all can serve as lingua francas today. The need for these languages to be examined is dire (Dervin, 2010). Interculturality is not exclusive to English. Thus, just as O'Regan in his commentary chapter at the end of our book aims to 'open a new reading' of the term 'ELF', we too aim to open up discussion of the cultural and intercultural in lingua franca communication.

It is of course obvious that English is today's lingua franca *par excellence*, with 375 million people speaking it as their first language and one in four of the world's population speaking it as a second/foreign language (Crystal, 2012). Although many aspects of the use of ELF have been researched, interculturality seems to have been neglected, or at least discussions on interculturality in relation to ELF do not appear to be in line with current perspectives on and understandings of the term in fields such as language education, applied linguistics, inter-/multicultural education and intercultural communication. For example, earlier attempts to examine lingua francas have tended to focus more on the linguistic, syntactic, phonological and pragmatic elements of a language, as well as intelligibility and other sociolinguistic features (see for example McGroarty, 2006, in the special issue of *The Annual Review of Applied Linguistics*; although the work of Canagarajah (2006) in that special issue begins to assert the need to address historical associations of lingua francas, discussions are largely framed within applied linguistics theoretical approaches). Jenkins *et al.* appear to make a move into the field of interculturality when they discuss how ELF talk is used for a range of purposes 'including the projection of cultural identity, the promotion of solidarity, the sharing of humor' (2011: 296) or when Jenkins examines the position of English as a lingua franca in the international university (2014). More recent work on metrolingualism by Otsuji and Pennycook (2010) challenges common frameworks of language by investigating contemporary urban language practices that accommodate both fixity and fluidity in understanding language use, albeit more in the realm of plurilingualism than lingua franca use.

In this volume, our aim is to attempt to link for the first time research on ELF and 'renewed' interculturality as put forward by e.g. Dervin, 2012; Dervin & Risager, 2014; Holliday, 2010, 2013; Holmes, 2014, 2015; Machart *et al.*, 2013; Piller, 2011 and their predecessors such as Abdallah-Pretceille, 1986 and Sarangi, 1994. All of these scholars represent a coherent understanding of interculturality, as we also present in this introduction. As intercultural communication and education scholars, we believe that any exploration of languages – including lingua francas – in intercultural communication must explore and seek to understand, both interpretively and critically, how language – and its problematic associated term 'culture' – are constructed and reconstructed, negotiated and renegotiated through communication in intercultural encounters. We are interested in exploring how languages are shaped and constructed in interactions and intercultural encounters as well as how the (inter)subjectivities of individuals' multiple realities and identities inevitably influence how and why people engage with one another, and their understandings of those encounters. Using and understanding language in communication thus goes beyond static, reified, normative and discrete forms of language and interaction to account for individuals' (inter)subjectivities, which in turn are influenced by history, geography, languages, culture, religion, multiple identities, social class, economics, power, belonging, etc. Reference to this aspect of research on interculturality is often absent from studies of ELF.

We are also interested in how historical, political, economic and organisational structures can assert and/or require preference for one language, or language form, over others. Some examples, in the case of English, would be cultivating a 'correct' English accent, understanding the norms of communication in and through English and knowing the cultures of English-speaking countries – in other words, understanding the reified, structuralist, idealised, unauthentic and unrealistic meanings of communication in Englishes and in languages more generally. Many of these notions of 'good' or 'correct' English are perpetuated by state and private language regimes such as language schools (Henry in his chapter discusses the proliferation of English schools in China); language testing systems such as IELTS that require a certain level of English for study in English-language universities or schools; opportunities for study abroad to acquire 'native-like' proficiency (again, usually determine by economic status); state and regional educational policies (e.g. the Common European Framework of Reference which delineates 'levels' of competent language knowledge and use); and examination systems that favour grammatical proficiency and linguistic knowledge (e.g. College English – CET 4 – which all university students in China must pass to obtain an undergraduate degree). These historical and pragmatic features of English language learning are captured perfectly in Tawona Sithole's (2014) poem 'Good English'. Although good at English at school, and although told by all who heard him speak English that 'you have such good English', Sithole's choices in life were pre-ordained, prescribed, and pre-judged according to the linguistic features of his language use; structures of class, race and economics; his place of birth and country in which he was educated (Zimbabwe). In short, the intercultural aspects of his English-language identity and communication in English appear to inscribe a fixed identity. It is these much more nuanced and situated aspects of lingua franca communication that the authors explore herein.

To this end, we have put together chapters that seek to invoke and provoke further discussion and research on the complex, multitudinous and multifarious forms of languages more generally, and Englishes in particular – pidgins, creoles, 'Chinglishes', regional, colonial and popular forms – the innumerable Englishes that people have used and are using around the world in their daily encounters. In doing so, we open up the possibility of thinking about Englishes as lingua francas, as they are shaped by both the interculturality that speakers bring to the encounter and the sociocultural-economic-historical (etc.) aspects of the context of the interaction, and not in some 'hypostatized' form which, as O'Regan argues in his chapter, has emerged in recent thinking about ELF.

The literature on ELF that has attempted to tackle issues of intercultural communication tends to remain at a basic level, e.g. at the simplistic and uncritical levels of 'cultural difference', 'tolerance' and 'respect for other(s')' (cultures)' (see Ya-Chen Su, 2014). Moreover, the lack of interdisciplinary and multilingual discussions on these issues requires attention – a task that most interculturalists feel is necessary when working on, for example, identity, community, culture, etc. as these concepts have been imported from anthropology, cultural studies and sociology, among others. An overemphasis on pragmatic competence (House, 2010; Murray, 2012) in the field of ELF as a marker of interculturality illustrates these problematic issues. Exceptions are increasing; many of the authors in this volume have already taken steps to relate both fields (e.g. Baker, 2012, 2015; Dervin, 2013; Fay *et al.*, 2010; see also Gu *et al.*, 2014).

Indeed, during the development of this book, research on both ELF and the intercultural have been the scenes of internal and external debates, particularly around orthodoxies. For example, O'Regan (formerly a co-editor of the influential intercultural journal *Language and Intercultural Communication*) published in 2014 a Marxist critique of how ELF is being conceptualised, which led key figures from the field to react and attack him for misinterpreting ELF and even for not representing 'outstanding scholarship' (Baker *et al.*, 2015; Widdowson, 2015). In putting this volume together, we too received similar comments when we approached some ELF scholars for cooperation, and we also lost a few authors who chose to remain 'faithful' to their ELF 'territory' (Becher & Trowler, 2001). However, our aim here is not to create a polemic, or to nurture or perpetuate spurious disciplinary boundaries, but rather to explore and build interdisciplinary understandings about interculturality and lingua francas, including ELF, and to initiate a research agenda. In our book proposal some three years ago we noted that ELF is a new field of research that accounts for an empirically based and theoretically informed understanding of how English is used today in an increasing number of contexts. However, O'Regan reminds us that this kind of lingua franca communication, even some 500 years ago, was characterised by culturally – and interculturally – nuanced features. Dervin also remarked that lingua francas 'have always existed and have enabled interaction and communication, business negotiation, agreement, debate, love and hate' (2011: 3, our translation from French). Acknowledging O'Regan's invitation in his final commentary chapter, we would like to open up exploration of the notion of lingua francas more generally, in order to look for and invite 'a new reading'.

We note that current trends in research on ELF appear to be different to those in the field of interculturality. Whereas the latter is represented by different lines of thought, both theoretically and methodologicially, ELF scholars appear to share understandings about the definition of the concept and ways of analysing ELF interaction. By contrast, both outside of ELF and in the field of intercultural communication, many scholars still wonder about who is included and excluded from the label 'ELF' and what constitutes a context of ELF interaction. For example, a recent definition of ELF, which now includes 'native speakers of English' who were initially excluded from ELF communication, specifies 'any use of English among speakers of different first languages [including English] for whom English is the communicative medium of choice, and often the only option' (Seidlhofer, 2011: 7).

Since the notions of 'native speakers' and 'mother tongues' have been abandoned because of their Eurocentric and essentialist characteristics which tend to remove individuals' agency, one must ask if the label 'ELF' is still viable. (For example, O'Regan in this volume prefers 'lingua franca Englishes'.) Considering that speaking a language is always influenced by our identity markers – the ones we (wish to) project, and the ones that are imposed on us – gender, social class, status in society, regional origins that mark out accents, dialects, discourses, etc. – then are not all situations of interaction in English ELF? Again, we must ask who has the right to decide, and for whom. Who among the interlocutors is able to defend his or her status as a 'native' or 'non-native' speaker?

Skin colour, for example, can easily lead to people being classified as ELF speakers. In the 'I, too, am Oxford' project, through which students of colour demanded a discussion on race to be taken seriously at Oxford University, many participants complained about the fact that their skin colour often led people to tell them, for example, 'Wow your English is great', even though most of them were born in England. For the anthropologist Marc Augé, people who share a same language do not always 'speak' the same language and do not always understand each other. He adds: 'A volatile and mobile, fluid and invisible, frontier can separate those who seem near and unite those whose language and culture seem to separate' (2010: 17, our translation).

All these questions could resemble the questions of 'Who is normal? Who is not?'. Moreover, as Lemke (2010: 20) asserts: 'Normality is always a mystification of normativity, a social lie that succeeds in part by introducing simplistic, low-dimensional category grids for pigeon-holing us, and in part by sanctioning any too public display of mismatched qualities'. This is one of the most important messages of the form of 'renewed' interculturality that is suggested in this volume: not only power relations, identity and agency but also work on representations should be the most important elements in discussing these issues. The over-emphasis on 'cultural difference' and (national?) 'culture' in the 'intercultural', as discussed below, is increasingly becoming a thing of the past.

But similar questions might be asked about the intercultural. Who is considered intercultural? Who decides? Isn't 'intercultural' a viewpoint? For example, two friends from different countries who use ELF to speak with each other may not consider what they do as ELF. Is it appropriate that we, as researchers, straitjacket them into this label? What impact can such labeling have on the kind of interculturality they 'do' in front of us if we start from this premise? And what about our readers? How do they perceive these two individuals in our accounts of their relations?

Next, we discuss current critical perspectives on interculturality and how these can help us to reflect on the relationship between interculturality and the notion of ELF.

Making sense of interculturality

The concept of interculturality is a complex one which has been defined and understood in many different ways. Because of its complexity, it can easily be used as an intellectual simplifier or a simplistic slogan, which contributes to pinning down and labelling. The fact that it is used, overused, and sometimes abused by decision makers does not help. Many approaches to interculturality rely on a deficit framework in which someone needs to learn to think and behave like the other in order to interact with her. The contested ideas of misunderstanding and non-understanding often lie behind certain conceptions of interculturality (Dervin et al., 2015).

The notion itself contains the old, tired and biased term 'culture', which many fields of research have begun to problematise and even discard. Culture has always been part of the intercultural orthodoxy, but in order to make sense of the intercultural in relation to ELF we propose to review the problems the concept poses – and, potentially, to get rid of it. We ask: What does the concept refer to? Is this still a valid concept for such complex worlds as ours? Does it refer to the global, the national, the regional, the local? Does it include references to gender, social class, power, language, religion, etc.? Is it possible to determine the boundaries between cultures when cultures exist because they have been interacting with other cultures (or rather, because people have interacted with people across borders)? For Moghaddam (2011: 19): 'There is no such thing as a coherent Western or Islamic civilisation that could/would clash. Civilisations are not tectonic plates that move against each other'. We thus need to be careful not to put people into 'little boxes of disparate civilisations' (Sen, 2005: 4), or to reify culture. So when we speak of ELF, we must ask: What are the interlocutors' cultures that should/could be borne in mind? And what are the implications when we do so? (See for example the chapters by Baker, Henry, O'Regan and Räisänen in this volume.)

Our first argument is that culture is not a *thing* but a *concept*. Adichie (2014: 127) reminds us, 'Culture does not make people. People make culture'. In the following excerpt, found randomly on the internet and reprinted verbatim, the fear of the other's culture – rather than fear of the Other as such – is clearly expressed:

> I'm in China and one friend invited me to visit her house. If I bring some pears as a gift into her house, she and her family would get embarrassed and I'd wonder what's wrong. It's the cultural misunderstanding. I know pears has the meaning "goodbyes" in China, but not in Korea. If you're in Korea, you would be surprised at the fact that Korean people split pears when they eat it. Korean pears are really big, you can never eat one pear all yourself. (http://www.italki.com/question/40081?answer-sorting=1)

This sort of fear of 'cultural misunderstanding' is common and has been highly 'commodified' since the late 1930s (Dahlen, 1997: 174). The problem with the above assertions is that the individual expects the Chinese family to behave in a certain way, not to be flexible and to be thus guided/commanded by their culture, as if it were their destiny, as if they were helpless. We thus agree with Sen:

> Even though certain basic cultural attitudes and beliefs may influence the nature of our reasoning, they cannot invariably determine it fully. There are various influences on our reasoning, and we need not lose our ability to consider other ways of reasoning just because we identify with, and have been influenced by membership in a particular group. Influence is not the same thing as complete determination, and choices do remain despite the existence—and importance—of cultural influences. (2006: 34–35)

For Holliday (2010: 4) there is danger in adopting a 'destiny' approach to culture. He calls this danger 'essentialism' and defines it as an approach that 'presets people's individual behaviour as entirely defined and constrained by the cultures in which they live so that the stereotype becomes the essence of who they are'. Of course such discourses of culture are very practical, as they give us the impression that we can explain everything. Yet in many cases culture is used as a dangerous proxy for something else. Prashad (2001: xi), for example, explains that culture can easily be used to camouflage discourses of race – which are taboo in many parts of the world. So instead of uttering racially incorrect discourses, by means of culture one can turn such discourses into acceptable discourses about interculturality, cultural difference, norms, etc. Also in this introduction, Prashad observes that discourses of culture can also contribute to placing ourselves on pedestals, leading us to pathologise and consider the Other as less civilised, modern and cosmopolitan, even if these discourses can be accompanied, contradictorily, by discourses of tolerance and respect.

Our second argument relates to the definition of the Other. Again, this is a very unstable category. Pieterse (2007: 139) argues that 'the Other is no longer a stable or even meaningful category'. People may share a current nationality, place of birth, a language, a religion, a profession or a neighbourhood and still be very different from one another. Breidenbach and Nyiri problematise for example the current homogenising discourses on Muslims:

> If for instance a journalist tries to convince you that the 200 lashes of the whip to which a twenty-year old rape victim was sentenced in Saudi Arabia in 2007 has to do with 'Muslim culture', ask yourself how likely it is that [Muslim] men and women, grandparents and teenagers, workers, lawyers, writers, residents of Mecca, Tangiers, Cologne, and Detroit all share the same values and will behave alike in similar situations. (2009: 343)

Our world is obsessed with difference, especially difference across – and rarely within – in relation to interculturality and imagined fictions such as the East versus the West, speakers of French versus speakers of English, Us and Them (Laplantine, 2012), which establish purist/homogenising boundaries between outsiders/insiders, as well as between 'Our' culture and 'Their' culture. In the current glocal era, this obsession is highly questionable. Kureishi (2011), for example, explains that defining British culture as a list of distinctively English cultural elements such as Derby Day, Henley regatta, or Wensleydale cheese – as marketers of cultures want us to believe – ignores the global mélange which has made 'yoga exercise, going to Indian restaurants, the music of Bob Marley, the Hare Krishna temple as well as the films of Sylvester Stallone, therapy, hamburgers, visits to gay bars, the dole offices and the taking of drugs' (56) into essential characteristics of Britishness.

This pervasive bias of cultural difference – without considering similarities among people – tends to be the entry point into interculturality in ELF research, as it is also in some 'intercultural' research. People might share similar values, opinions, interests and so forth across borders; for their part, researchers must investigate these elements and what they do to ELF interaction. The following example, taken from the British television comedy series *Mind Your Language* (1977) (Allen, 1978) offers an interesting example. The show, which was set in an adult education college in London in the 1970s, focuses on a class of English as a Foreign Language. All the students are from different parts of the world and have to use ELF throughout the programme. In one of the episodes, a new student (Speaker 4 in Excerpt 1), who does not speak English, is trying to interact with the other 'foreign' students. An Italian student (Speaker 3) starts a conversation with the new student by using words he assumes he knows and which are related to football:

Excerpt 1
1: Hey, you not speak nothing?
2: He is not knowing the English as well as what we are knowing
3: I speak with him
1: Blimey, he speak Hungryarian
3: Sure I speak Hunarian... Football
4: Football
3: Puskas
4: Pele
3: Kepkens
4: Beckenball
3: Bobby Lee Shutkan
4: Bobby Lee Moor
3: You see I told you I speak the language. (Series 2, Episode 2: 'All present if not correct')

Although these students do not have a language in common, their references to football and the names of famous international players allow them to enter into a dialogue, which is limited of course, but could be the first step towards friendship.

As a first step toward joining forces with the intercultural, ELF research should problematise and potentially rupture the cultural cul-de-sac. ELF users do not meet cultures, but complex subjects who 'do' identity and culture with each other. (The chapters of Räisänen, Henry and Jenks, for example, are illustrative of this move.)

Identity and interculturality as a way out?

Work on interculturality now requires reversing the usual direction of thought, which has been 'polluted' by essentialist and culturalist approaches to self and other. Like Wimmer (2013: 3), we must find a middle ground between the Charybis of essentialism described above and the counter-reactive Scylla of hyperconstructivism. In what follows, we make some suggestions for research on ELF.

As previously asserted, it is important for researchers and practitioners of ELF to work from a diverse diversities approach (Dervin, 2008), i.e. an approach that attempts to 'complexify' the way one observes, problematises and analyses ELF interaction. The concept of intersectionality, an analytic framework that allows the interrelating of dimensions such as gender, ethnicity, race, class, status, disabilities, language, sexuality, etc., is a fruitful path to diverse diversities. If, when working on interculturality, ELF encounters are considered from the perspective of national culture only, then many identity markers that could help us to understand certain phenomena not only might be ignored but also might be detrimental to research participants. On the contrary, if researchers complexify their analyses by such a process, they may be able to empower their participants to exit the minuscule and biased box of culture that is imposed on them. Some of the chapters in this volume attempt to challenge this position. For example, the Finnish engineers in Räisänen's study realised the limitations of calling upon a so-called Finnish linguistic identity to assert themselves as reasonably competent speakers of English in the face of their German English-speaking counterparts whom they had initially considered as worse speakers of English than they themselves. In other words, such categories were not helpful. By contrast, Kaur found no trace of national culture-based misunderstanding in the interactions of her international students in a Malaysian university; instead, she found misunderstanding that might also be found in 'intracultural' communication.

Other aspects of identity and interculturality that could enrich research on ELF are presented here. The following dimensions are in interaction with one another: discrimination, inequalities, power relations and social justice. Too often, whether in language education or analysis of intercultural encounters, researchers have refrained from entering the muddy terrain of politics (with either a small or capital 'p'). It is important to examine, though ELF interactions, how (for example) power relations connected to discourses of culture are expressed, co-constructed and enacted, as well as how hierarchies are created and what their consequences are for people. Such examinations should help researchers to complexify their studies and also help practitioners and ELF speakers themselves to feel empowered and also to note instances of inequality (for example) and to act upon them. It should not be denied that ELF does contribute to unbalanced power relations; thus, educators, researchers and decision makers have a duty to help ELF users defuse such situations and to provide them with the tools to do so. Intercultural pedagogies, for instance, should encourage ELF users to take action and to be ethical/responsible communicators.

We conclude by discussing the position of the researcher in examining interculturality in ELF contexts. Krumer-Nevo and Sidi (2012) note that a lot of research contributes to othering research participants. As subjective beings, researchers cannot pretend to be absent or invisible from their field. They have an impact not only upon interaction but also upon their participants who are 'doing' identity and culture. Therefore, as Krumer-Nevo and Sidi observe, it is important for researchers to try to avoid the following in the research process: (i) objectification (turning the participant into an object of research rather than recognising the participant as an agent of discourse and actions); (ii) decontextualisation (ignoring the micro- and macro-contexts of interaction, research and identity); (iii) dehistorisation (emphasising the present and ignoring the past); and (iv) deauthorisation (imagining the subjective subtext of what participants claim to be objective about). All of these tasks require honesty, ethicality and reflexivity from researchers.

Further, researchers need to acknowledge and harness their own linguistic resources as well as those of their participants when undertaking their research; additionally, they should challenge the ideologies of the linguistic regimes embedded in the research site, including assumptions about the role of English (as a lingua franca) (Holmes et al., 2013).

Before moving to the contributions of this volume to these discussions and to linking up ELF and the 'intercultural', we review the main points made hitherto. Within the ELF scholarship, research on interculturality seems to lag behind work in the intercultural communication field; moreover, the way the notion of interculturality is used does not always match the discussions in the latter field. These discussions put into question certain orthodoxies that are deemed to be counterproductive and of the past (uncritical use of the concept of culture, obsession with cultural difference, the straitjacketing of individuals, etc.). We therefore maintain that research and practice of Englishes as lingua francas would benefit from a perspective that examines how users of these forms of English construct, reconstruct, negotiate and renegotiate culture, methodological nationalism or geographicality (e.g. East vs. West), their identities, the context of interaction, power relations and so forth in intercultural encounters.

The interconnections and inter-relationships between interculturality and ELF

The key objectives of this edited collection are to investigate the interconnections and inter-relationships among the broader concept of interculturality (and its related elements or dimensions of language, culture, identity, etc.) and English as a lingua franca, and to consider the possible pedagogical implications of such investigation. The chapters explore these relationships in a range of different ways by (i) discussing how interculturality can be understood, theorised, constructed and researched in ELF contexts and within the domain of ELF more generally; (ii) exploring how the notions and concepts of not only 'interculturality'/'the intercultural' and 'culture' but also 'identity' and 'intersection' are discussed and understood in relation to ELF-oriented learning and teaching; and (iii) investigating the intercultural implications (ideological, political, religious, historical, etc.) and modes of ELF pedagogies.

These aims are addressed by several authors through empirical investigations in various contexts (ELF interactions in interpersonal and inter-/intracultural communication and negotiation, educational settings, etc.), and through examinations of how far existing theoretical approaches in the fields of intercultural communication, applied linguistics and language/intercultural education can be productively applied to such investigations. Through conceptual analyses and empirical research, the chapters offer implications for new directions in ELF research – theories, methodologies, and pedagogy – thus illustrating a diversity of approaches and understandings within the field of ELF. We deal with each of these domains, follow with a summary of chapters and finish by suggesting an agenda for research into lingua franca communication as well as the cultural and intercultural in these encounters.

Theoretical standpoints

This collection increases awareness of a number of emergent theoretical standpoints or positionings for scholars to consider when researching the intercultural dimensions of ELF. As previously discussed, the first standpoint concerns the treatment of the omnipresence of the term 'culture'. Most authors problematise the term and highlight its socially constructed nature, specifically how it is (re)constructed through communication in multilingual and plurilingual contexts. Risager, in the introductory chapter, claims that no language is culturally neutral – including English used as a lingua franca. All languages, even when functioning as lingua francas, (re)produce culture in the sense of meaning in human society through complex language-related cultural flows via people over time, which she calls 'linguacultural' and 'discursive' flows. Baker notes that culture is not congruent with nations or ethnic groups, but instead should be considered a resource for constructing flexible and hybridised forms of identity. For Henry, culture is understood not as a fixed set of attributes, but as a larger sociocultural-political context that allows interactants to bring into being 'intracultural imaginings' of who they are. O'Regan, who questions its usefulness even as a concept, notes how it is situational and dependent upon the contexts in which concrete interactions occur.

The empirical studies by Jenks, Bjørge and Kaur all highlight the deficiencies of a differentialist paradigm of culture (i.e. of misunderstanding and miscommunication based on cultural difference) in understanding ELF encounters. As they view the matter, culture – and, by implication, the corollary term 'national identity' – become relevant only when they are talked into existence, for example in the context of food preparation, or in academic interactions between student and supervisor (as in Jenks' study). Bjørge points to the need to recognise the cultural hybridity at play in ELF interactions, argues that social constructionist approaches may shine brighter light on the nature of this hybridity and draws on Bhabha's 'third space' (1994) as a potentially useful locus at which to explore such interactions.

A second theoretical focus concerns the notion of identity. The chapters, both directly and indirectly, allude to a range of ways in which interlocutors express, negotiate and enact identity through ELF. Henry introduces the term 'indexicality'; that is, how interlocutors index their communication and identity in intracultural interactions to demonstrate membership in a class of globally competent Chinese citizens as signified through English fluency. As first-language Chinese speakers, they index their use of English to enact a particular identity (or 'intracultural imaginings' as Henry puts it), such as, for example, bringing into being modern or cosmopolitan identities. Henry argues that in intracultural interactions of this nature, questions of indexicality can illuminate undercurrents of power, inequality, or ideology among the speakers using that lingua franca. He draws on Holliday's (2010) view that cultural description is never a neutral practice, but rather is one bound up in political discourses from which individuals negotiate the meanings and boundaries of self and other in society.

To some extent, without making this explicit, Räisänen alludes to this indexicality – of linking English-speaking ability to Finnish culture and education. Her Finnish engineers draw on a discourse of Finnishness to (re)construct understandings of their own identity, positionality and power as Finnish speakers of business English with German and other colleagues in their workplace in Germany. How they define themselves (and others) as speakers of English is indexed to being Finnish and to having studied English as a foreign language in Finland, including the high status attributed to such education internationally. Citing Piller, Räisänen reminds us that access to discourses is unequal among different individuals and that this inequality of access inherently characterises intercultural communication, which is 'typically between people who have starkly different *material, economic, social and cultural resources* at their disposal' (Piller, 2011: 173, italics added).

The final chapter, by O'Regan, draws on critical theory to challenge the legitimacy of ELF as a 'new' field of study and on Marxism to highlight the limits of its reach. First, drawing on Spivak (1976), O'Regan places the term 'ELF' under erasure in order to question its legitimacy in the complex sociolinguistic terrain of the global and local uses of English. By crossing out the term (i.e. using a strikethrough to 'delete' it), he alludes to Derrida's (1976: 19) understanding of the inadequacy of a concept – 'that ill-named thing' – as inadequate in that it has taken on 'an hypostatized form – reified, settled, resolved, fixed, sedimented, cemented, and finally stamped onto the page: an inked sign in a white landscape' (see O'Regan, Chapter 9). He is also critical of more recent ELF research that positions ELF as a new field. By tracing the development of the use of Englishes for communication, O'Regan shows that from the time of the voyages of discovery, beginning around the 1600s, Englishes were being developed and shaped by their use as a common form of communication – hence the emergences of his preferred term, 'lingua franca Englishes'. Second, taking a Marxist theoretical stance, he argues that ELF focuses on certain groups, such as global elites that are involved in international business and education, research and tourism/leisure even as they ignore the poor, the disenfranchised, the ethnically marginalised and the exploited. O'Regan reminds us that people, throughout the world and throughout history, have been 'accommodating and cooperating in the marginalisation, oppression and annihilation of one another' using (Englishes as) a lingua franca in (citing Phipps, 2007) 'the human struggle to make meaning'. In her chapter, Risager too notes that ELF research could widen its empirical basis to address all groups.

Methodologies

The chapters present a range of methodologies for exploring ELF interactions. All of them indicate the importance of understanding the macro- and microcontextual features of an interaction as well as how those features influence forms of talk and identity construction. Where ethnographic approaches are not central, researchers acknowledge how culture and context, and at times even a certain idea of national identity (e.g. Jenks, Räisänen) can influence ELF communication.

Henry applies an ethnographic approach to observe classes taught by multiple teachers in China and takes note of teacher-student interactions, pedagogy, methods, textbooks, technology and other teaching materials. He interviewed English language teachers (both foreign and Chinese), students, parents and school administrators to ascertain their understandings of English, the role it plays in Chinese society and their own relationship to it. From the linguistic choices of Chinese ELF users and the meanings they ascribe to those choices, he accessed their intentions and interpretations in order to illustrate the discursive production of identity.

Räisänen adopts a discursive approach to understand ELF users' identity construction. She argues that such an approach is necessary for exploring the cultural and intercultural aspects of language use because it is often by going beneath the surface that researchers can witness the kind of reality participants construct, reject, embrace and reconstruct, i.e. the layers of hidden discourses (Dervin, 2011). By uncovering these discourses, Räisänen states, the researcher can 'trace the ways in which individuals construct identities in relation to intercultural encounters and their linguistic and discursive choices when talking about their experiences'. Her own subjective engagement in the field (as a former doctoral researcher) facilitated a fine-grained understanding and analysis of her participants' (Finnish engineering students on work placement in Germany) intercultural ELF interactions.

Jenks and Bjørge also adopt a corpus-based discourse analysis approach: Jenks to understand how international students in the United Kingdom talk into being national identity and culture around food, and Bjørge to explore her students' uses of mitigated and unmitigated disagreement strategies in business negotiations using ELF. Kaur uses conversational analysis to analyse her data derived from participant observation of student classroom and conversational events, as well as interviews with teachers, students, and administrators. Kaur believes that for culture or nationality to be made relevant or acknowledged in any analysis, participants must be seen as attending to such elements in their talk. Analysing participants' conversations in context therefore prevents the researcher from applying any preconceived notions of a causal relationship between misunderstanding and cultural difference to the data.

Contexts

Most of the studies described in the chapters orient their discussion to a particular macro- and microcontext which makes interculturality salient. Risager shows how Danish – like most languages – operates as a lingua franca in communities worldwide, through the flow of (Danish) immigrants as they construct new diaspora/communities; thus, Danish becomes both a lingua franca and an international language. Similarly, other languages, through the global linguistic flows enacted by people, also operate as lingua francas. Fay, Sifakis and Lytra's study discusses contemporary debates around English language education – and the viability of ELF – in the context of contemporary Greek society under reconstruction in the face of linguistic flows resulting from economic, refugee and asylum immigration. Traditional understandings of English and the native speaker model are being challenged by the hybridised forms of English in the new Greek landscape that is linguistically and politically fractured. For teachers, this situation raises questions about what English to teach and what pedagogy to use. Baker draws on the communication in English between two speakers – one Thai and the other French – in a café in Bangkok as they discuss their cultural understandings of the game of pétanque. He uses this ELF scenario to highlight the multifarious nature of intercultural communication and the situated, emergent relationship between language and culture.

Jenks, Bjørge, Kaur and Räisänen focus on international students' ELF experiences. Jenks locates his research in the kitchen of a hall of residence at a university in the United Kingdom to analyse how postgraduate international students invoke personal understandings of their own and others' nationhood and identity as they discuss aspects of their lives such as doctoral supervision, food preparation food cultures. Bjørge analyses the interactions of 118 international master's-level students, from 28 countries, who are studying business English in a Danish university. By investigating how they deal with mitigated and unmitigated disagreement in negotiations through a shared language learning exercise, she shows that nation-based, cultural traditions may not be automatically transferable to an ELF context in which cultural hybridity may come into play. In Kaur's study, which is situated in a university in Kuala Lumpur, Malaysia, she investigated the naturally occurring spoken interaction (discussion of group assignments and casual conversations) in ELF outside the classroom among graduate students from 15 different linguacultural backgrounds. Finally, Räisänen draws on her lived experience in a student hall of residence in Germany with Finnish engineering students on work placement to gain an insider's perspective of the communicative situations they encountered with German, Greek, Chinese and Indian students living in the same hall of residence as well as with work colleagues, who were mostly of German or Portuguese origin. The ELF interactions of these research subjects were both intercultural and potentially plurilingual.

Henry's study, which is divergent from the others but still complementary, focuses on intracultural communication among Chinese speakers of English. Henry drew on his teaching and research experience in educational institutions in Shenyang, where his subjects at two universities, one middle school, two elementary schools, three private adult language education centres and eight private children's schools show how Chinese L1 speakers use ELF to index their status and power. Like Henry, Fay *et al.* in the contemporary Greek context point to the need for an intercultural stance open to the international and intranational English-medium needs of, and possibilities for, speakers of English in and from Greece.

O'Regan, by contrast, provides an historical context by reminding readers that the concept ELF has been erroneously constructed – invented almost – as a late-20th-century phenomenon. He contextualises this discussion through examples of writings that show the use and development of Englishes dating from the 1600s and the time of the voyages of discovery, when Englishes developed and spread through trade and pirateering. Fay *et al.* also review the various types of Englishes that have been the focus of English language teaching since the mid-20th century in the 'Taking stock' section of their chapter.

The contexts foregrounded in these chapters show how Englishes, when used as lingua francas by speakers of Englishes and other languages, are shaped and constructed by multiple contexts; these include the historical, geographical, political, economic, cultural, religious, educational, gender, social location, class, etc. as well as the dispositions of the speakers themselves. In fact, according to Hall (2013), in a plurilithic view of languages, how individuals learn and use languages is determined by individuals' local experiences and the extent to which they adopt the social practices around them, rather than to some abstracted, monolithic and imposed supranational variety of experience. In summary, the chapters illustrate how context is central to not only how languages develop and flow, but also how culture, communication and (power) relations invoke meaning in ELF interactions.

The pedagogical implications of ELF

The studies in our collection point to some key features that are not specific to ELF but may overlap with language and intercultural pedagogies more generally. Risager suggests a pedagogy that encompasses multiple languages as lingua francas. This pedagogy involves the decentring of 'target-language countries' (in the traditional and narrow national language paradigm of language teaching) in order to focus on the 'interrelationships [of language(s) and culture(s)] with other countries in a global historical perspective'. Baker, too, critiques the Anglocentric positioning of much ELT and argues for a dynamic and fluid approach that recognises the multifarious nature of intercultural communication, particularly in ELF scenarios, as well as the situated, emergent relationship between language and culture.

Risager reminds us that language pedagogy, including any lingua franca pedagogy, should consider the broader goal of developing learners' understandings of global citizenship and their critical awareness of cultural and linguistic complexity. Baker suggests a pedagogy that acknowledges the inherent variety of communicative practices and cultural characterisations embodied in ELF communication, the variety in teachers' experiences (in terms of teacher training) and the needs of different learners according to their learning contexts. He thus emphasises the importance of teaching about intercultural awareness (skills, knowledge and attitudes).

Bjørge's study shows that international students do not necessarily call upon cultural references or cultural identity in their handling of unmitigated disagreements in business negotiations. Her findings point to the dangers of business communication textbooks that rely on national cultural differences as a basis for business English lingua franca (BELF) communication. Similarly, Kaur's study highlights the need to avoid a differentialist approach in teaching about culture and instead to focus on intracultural similarities and differences.

Despite the pedagogic implications of the studies in this volume, O'Regan reminds researchers and teachers that preoccupation with native-speaker models are 'aggressively promoted' by governments and examinations systems in universities and schools, and within international testing systems such as IELTS, TOEIC and TOEFL. He also notes that in some cases, the native-speaker model appears to be the preferred model of parents who believe their children, in acquiring native-speaker English, will then have access to the capitalist world of global elites (the world upon which, as previously mentioned, current empirical ELF research is focused). This situation calls into question, for language learners, not only the status but also the linguistic and even economic potentials of learning a non-native-speaker form of English.

Fay et al. exemplify this contention in their analysis of English language education in contemporary Greece. Through their analysis of Greek educational documents, they identify possibilities and obstacles in developing interculturality in English language education, e.g. developing both learners' language awareness towards the multiplicity of Englishes available and their generic cultural awareness through intercultural skills development (rather than the mastery of 'cultural' topics). To this end, Fay et al. propose a pedagogy they call MATE (multicultural awareness through English), which is intranational and multicultural in character as well as alert to the increasing diversity evident within many schools and within Greece itself. Such a pedagogy acknowledges English as a significant language of communication in diverse societies and among non-native speakers of English (both in the classroom and playground), and entails extensive 'culture-work' in learners to develop their multicultural awareness and skills.

It would seem from the above implications that a(n English as a) lingua franca pedagogy would have to account for what we have previously described as 'interculturality' as well as for the discussions and complexities the term engenders.

Synopsis of the chapters

The nine chapters of this book all enrich contemporary understandings of (English as a) lingua franca studies by shedding light on and articulating insights into the interconnections and inter-relationships between interculturality and ELF in ways that previously have been little foregrounded. The volume is divided into three interrelated sections: 1. The Interconnections and Inter-Relationships between Interculturality and ELF; 2. Grounding Conceptual Understandings of Interculturality in ELF Communication; and 3. Commentary. Below we provide brief synopses of each chapter which may be read in any order, or by following the thematic structure.

First section

Risager's chapter, 'Lingua Francas in a World of Migrations', sets the scene for the book by forging the links between interculturality and lingua francas. She discusses the importance of concepts such as linguacultures, linguistic flows and discursive flows as well as their implications for the study of lingua francas. She argues that, as language users transport their language resources for use in new cultural and migratory contexts, these concepts transcend unitary and monolithic understandings of language, culture, and nation. She reminds us that language is not culture-neutral; speakers bring to an encounter their personal linguacultural profile acquired from the language(s) they learned as children, at school, later in life and in different places connected to their lives; such language(s) and language uses are imbued with cultural complexity. Linguacultural and discursive flows are also subjected to hierarchisations, depending on who is speaking, who is listening, and upon the contextual rules and constraints as well as the purposes of the communication. Linguacultures and discursive flows are always 'intercultural', Risager argues, because they are both individual (personal) and collective; the former are shared by others and the latter represent a perspective taken either in response to something else or as an assemblage of various perspectives. She concludes by raising an important question that requires further investigation: 'Are there discourses, topics and areas of knowledge that are preferred or evaded in ELF communication simply because English is the common language – with its specific semantic potentials and constraints' or 'because participants do not share the relevant knowledge in some depth?'.

Chapter 2, by Fay, Sifakis and Lytra, 'Interculturalities of English as a Lingua Franca: International Communication and Multicultural Awareness in the Greek Context', captures the complexity of the intercultural in ELF as the authors historically chart the development of Englishes in the world. They also offer a conceptualisation and pedagogy of the interculturalities of Englishes as explored within the context of the post-TEFL era of English language education in Greece. They begin by outlining the development of approaches to English language education and pedagogies from the 1950s (e.g. through the work of Larry Smith) and the development of the need for competence (citing Baxter, 1983). They then describe the myriad of ways in which English users can use English in ELF interactions and the interculturalities of Englishes across this varied and complex English language user spectrum. This description highlights how Englishes are fused, shaped, refashioned and reinscribed with other forms of world Englishes, alongside the other languages speakers use and amidst the transnational and local flows of people. These contextual, theoretical and pedagogical concepts offer a complex historical lens for exploring the intercultural in ELF, hitherto largely undiscussed in current ELF literature (see also O'Regan in this volume). In the second part of the chapter they highlight the need for an intercultural pedagogy in English language teaching in Greece, as multiculturalism and native-speaker English language models for teaching and speaking English begin to be questioned. They propose an approach that consists of multicultural awareness for teaching English (MATE), combined with recognition of international dimensions (as in teaching English as an international Language or TEIL), which introduces cultural awareness and interculturality into English language education pedagogy and foregrounds world Englishes in the context of contemporary multicultural Greece.

Chapter 3, Baker's 'Culture and Language in Intercultural Communication, English as a Lingua Franca and English Language Teaching: Points of Convergence and Conflict', focuses on the convergences and conflicts within and across the fields of English as a lingua franca (ELF), applied linguistics research in intercultural communication, and English language teaching (ELT). Baker argues for a conceptualisation of intercultural communicative competence wherein language and culture are viewed as emergent resources in intercultural communication that need to be approached critically. He draws on data from Thailand, where two communicators using

ELF (one Thai and one French-speaking Belgian) discuss the game of petanque without reference to binary notions of culture and language. The example serves to illustrate how the relationship between language and culture is contingent and emergent and not 'between' any particular communities. Thus, he argues for more ELF research from a postmodernist perspective that not only illustrates fluid, dynamic and multiple viewpoints in exploring the relationship between language and culture but also explores how interlocutors draw on their knowledge, skills and attitudes during a communication episode. To this end, he believes that ELF researchers who take a postmodernist stance and eschew cultural categories are better able to offer understandings of what is necessary for successful intercultural communication and its related concept of intercultural competence. He refers to Kramsch's (2009) notion of 'symbolic competence', a dynamic, flexible and locally contingent competence, in order to inform his concept of intercultural awareness which 'recognises the context-specific nature of our communicative practices and that they are temporal and negotiable'. He concludes that a critical perspective for understanding intercultural competence through ELF requires further exploration and implementation in both theory and practice.

Second section

Five chapters provide empirically informed discussions to ground their conceptual understandings of interculturality in ELF communication.

In Chapter 4, 'Talking Cultural Identities into Being in ELF interactions: An Investigation of International Postgraduate Students in the United Kingdom', Jenks draws on conversational data among international students from three or more nations or regions in the kitchen space of a hall of residence in a UK university. Using conversational analysis and membership categorisation analysis of these students' discussions of their academic and personal issues, Jenks shows how national identity and culture are used as interactional resources to manage talk-based activities in ELF encounters. Jenks' study builds on earlier work that demonstrates how national identities are used as discursive resources and thus highlight the 'complex, collaborative interactional work that is involved in the co-construction of Self and Other' (p. 96). Further, through the three interactional episodes (discussing a supervisor–supervisee relationship, the use of spices in cooking, and food preparatory practices), Jenks' analysis offers a counter to House's (2003) claim that ELF interactions are culturally neutral; he proposes instead that ELF encounters are potentially intercultural encounters.

Like Jenks', Bjørge's corpus-based Chapter 5, 'Conflict Talk and ELF Communities of Practice', draws on a discourse analytical perspective to investigate how expressions of unmitigated disagreement (e.g. using direct disagreement responses such as 'no') impacted the negotiations process among ELF users in a business English class. The participants, master's-level students, demonstrated that their national identities did not appear to influence how they approached unmitigated disagreement and thereby negotiated theories of national cultural differences. That is, participants who supposedly came from so-called direct communication cultures (Hall, 1976) did not necessarily use this kind of communication when negotiating disagreement. Indeed, Bjørge found that negotiators did not appear to be disrupted by unmitigated disagreement in their negotiations and continued on with the negotiation process. She suggests that some cultural hybridity may be at play in participants' communicative exchanges, although she does not elaborate because this would require further investigation.

In Chapter 6, 'Intercultural Misunderstanding Revisited: Cultural Difference as a (non) Source of Misunderstanding in ELF Communication', Kaur revisits an earlier study that examined the sources and nature of misunderstanding in intercultural communication of international students engaged in ELF communication in a Malaysian higher education context. From her data she discerned no trace of culture-based misunderstanding; instead, misunderstandings appeared to stem from reasons no different from those contributing to misunderstanding in intracultural communication (e.g. mishearing, ambiguity and lack of world knowledge). Her findings, although ELF-focused, have pedagogic implications that highlight the need for understanding how multilingual speakers display linguistic and communicative skills and strategies in both successful and unsuccessful intercultural communication encounters; such skills and strategies are not necessarily grounded in a paradigm of cultural or national difference. Overall, her findings provide evidence to support an alternative approach to intercultural communication – one which accepts understanding, rather than misunderstanding, as the default.

Chapter 7, Räisänen's 'Finnish Engineers' Trajectories of Socialisation into Global Working Life: From Language Learners to BELF Users and the Emergence of a Finnish Way of Speaking English', explores how identity work and processes of 'enregisterment' change among Finnish student engineers who shift their understanding of their English-speaking abilities (linked to their Finnish schooling and the Finnish education system) as they are socialised into new ways of speaking with their German and other international peers during work experience in Germany. Participants discuss their feelings and emotions that emerge during intercultural interactions as they begin to both foreground the relational aspects of intercultural communication and question stereotypes and assumptions about nationalities. Unlike the participants in Bjørge's study, culture and nationality become increasingly important to these students as they make sense of lingua franca interactions and of themselves as users of English. Räisänen concludes that a mere linguistic identity, i.e. that of a language learner or language user, is too narrow for conceptualising identity when ELF is used. Instead, her study suggests that ELF speakers embody different communicative repertoires (Räisänen, 2013) and linguacultural backgrounds (Risager, 2010) and that these repertoires and backgrounds are (re)constructed in intercultural communication. Her research raises further questions about the influence of a stay abroad on identity construction, the intercultural dimensions of identity work, and the processes of acquiring and developing intercultural competence. She suggests that future ELF research should explore whether participants foreground stereotypes or move beyond 'Us' and 'Them' dichotomies to challenge their own views about culture, as well as how they manage intercultural encounters and how they project a communicator identity (as proposed by Gao, 2014). Echoing Gao (2014), Räisänen notes that individuals' identities can contain variations and combinations for different situations and that these are determined in interactions between the social and the individual.

Chapter 8, by Henry, 'The Local Purposes of a Global Language: English as an Intracultural Communicative Medium in China', shifts the focus from intelligibility and the intercultural to indexicality and the intracultural. English use in the northeastern Chinese city of Shenyang is adopted to demonstrate how ELF can be used among speakers of the same first language (here, Mandarin), not for the purpose of intelligibility but to index and perform cosmopolitan or global identities. For example, Chinese speakers use English with other native speakers of Chinese to express localised discursive concerns such as producing cultural capital, negotiating status, establishing authority and signalling identity. Henry draws on sociolinguistic indexical components, e.g. the way varied forms of referential (demonstratives, pronouns, tenses) and non-referential (accent, stance, style, etc.) content may suggest particular forms of speaker identity, as well as how particular choices about register, style, accent and lexical usage signal to other speakers desirable identities, stances, attitudes and forms of belonging. His ELF research in an intracultural context suggests that the concept of indexicality may have wide application in studies of ELF to illustrate links between cultural frameworks and individual choices. As this study shows, it may also be an arena for intracultural imaginings of, for example, modern or cosmopolitan identities.

Third section

Chapter 9, 'Intercultural Communication and the Possibility of English as a Lingua Franca' by O'Regan, contains commentary which invites a 'new reading' of ELF. As he reflects upon the positionings and stances of the various contributors to this book, as well as other researchers working under the ELF label, O'Regan challenges the legitimacy of the concept of ELF. He then embarks on a critical analysis (drawing on Marx, Spivak and Derrida) of the concept and its implications for intercultural communication. Following Spivak, he places the concept of ELF under erasure 'so that its provisional and sociolinguistically inadequate nature can be clearly signalled and explored'. He contests the existence of ELF as a contemporary monolinguistic construction and instead argues for the term 'lingua franca Englishes' (LFEs):

> We may say then that *lingua franca* Englishes when used in intercultural communication encounters are historical, contemporary, personal and often messy, and that the linguistic pragmatics of LFEs are created anew from one context to another, and not according to an *a priori*, emergent or incrementally-evolving plan.

Indeed, in his Prolegomena he sets out examples, dating back to the 1600s and the start of the voyages of discovery, of intercultural communication using lingua franca Englishes; these remind readers that the theoretical and empirical foundations of ELF that portray it as a concept which has been in existence since 1995 are erroneous. His analysis, which is both critical and social constructionist in its reference to historicity, situatedness, power and social interaction, alludes to the cultural and contextual features that underpin the positioning of each speaker in intercultural communication encounters.

Adoping a Marxist perspective, O'Regan criticises contemporary ELF research for its focus on global, mostly White, elites (in international business, education, diplomacy, research contexts and tourism/leisure) while ignoring those who are economically deprived, politically oppressed and dispossessed, war ravaged, marginalised and exploited. His new reading invites ELF researchers, teachers and (English) language learners to think of lingua franca Englishes in all their varieties and types, and as used by speakers of Englishes everywhere – irrespective of class, race, gender, economy, religion, geographical location, etc. To this end, he argues for a redistribution of language resources and capital away from these global elites and towards those who are linguistically and economically disadvantaged by ELF in its current state and status.

Where to Next? An Agenda for Research into ELF, Lingua Francas and Intercultural Communication

The rich variety of theoretical and methodological approaches, contexts and pedagogical implications discussed by the researchers in these nine chapters open up a new agenda for ELF in particular, and for lingua franca research and pedagogy more generally as well. The studies prompt several questions. By including interculturality, how can lingua franca research be (re)conceptualised? What critical and interpretive theoretical frameworks allow researchers to explore the complexities of ELF encounters? How can researchers look beyond methodologies in, for example, applied linguistics and ELF, to include intercultural communication and account for the intercultural? How can complex understandings of intercultural identities inform lingua franca communication? How does the context of an interaction (in all its historical, social, religious, economic, etc.) complexity impact lingua franca encounters? How can interculturality, critical intercultural awareness, multicultural awareness (Fay et al.'s MATE), ethical communication, etc., be incorporated into lingua franca pedagogies?

Although the chapters in this volume begin to address these questions, much theoretical, methodological and pedagogical work remains to be done to address these questions and others not formulated herein. Despite recent efforts to establish a corpus of ELF communication, e.g. the VOICE corpus at the University of Vienna, and the University of Helsinki's corpus of English as a Lingua Franca in Academic Settings (ELFA) and corpus of Written English as a Lingua Franca in Academic Settings (WrELFA), the ability to name what ELF communication is, as well as its underlying rules, structure, cultural/intercultural dimensions, etc., remains somewhat elusive. According to the research discussions in these chapters, these goals may be both unlikely and undesirable. To this possibility we might add that recent critiques of the limitations of the theoretical concepts of intercultural competence and intercultural dialogue also open up new lines of investigation towards capabilities (rather than competences) and towards ethical and responsible communication. (For theoretical discussions of these concepts and their development, see for example, Crosbie, 2014; Ferri, 2014; Guilherme et al., 2010; Holmes, 2015; Phipps, 2014. For pedagogical examples, see for example Porto, 2014 and Santos et al., 2014).

The Marxist critique offered by O'Regan, and the various approaches and outcomes highlighted in this volume, point strongly to the limitations of much contemporary ELF research. O'Regan offers a jarring reminder that we should be ever vigilant of the dangers of words – in their rigidity, sedimentation and fashion. These terms which underpin much of our theoretical, methodological and pedagogical discussions of intercultural communication and applied linguistics – 'English', 'culture', 'ELF' (under erasure, crossed out) – appear with uncertainty, contradiction, inconsistency and incongruity. The challenge, then, for researchers and teachers, is perhaps not to seek solid, stable answers, but to continue to question and investigate in order to appreciate and understand the uniqueness of human interaction in whatever lingua franca encounters.

In closing, we prioritise a research agenda that adopts a broader exploration of the role lingua francas play in intercultural encounters, not just among global elites and those economically advantaged (to refer again to what Tawona Sithole calls a 'good English' and all its entrapments, which are well illustrated by the 'good English' of Christine Lagarde in O'Regan's chapter). Instead, we suggest the examination of lingua franca experience among people in the majority of the world – that is, the poor, the oppressed, and those disadvantaged, disenfranchised and disowned through wars, religious oppression and persecution, and economic transformations inflicted upon them by global, powerful and privileged elites in the developed world. We particularly wish to promote such examination among those people who, for whatever reasons, constitute and contribute to the transnational, linguacultural, migratory flows of people across borders and who (re)construct new linguacultures and communities. Currently, much of the research published in the name of ELF ignores and erases from discussion such other speakers of English as a lingua franca.

Further, a focus on borders and border crossings (whether geographical or metaphorical) – as places where people congregate and exchange, enact, (re)construct and (re)negotiate linguistic and cultural forms, practices and identities – offers rich opportunities for understanding the importance of lingua franca communication beyond ELF as well as the interculturality it entails (see for example, the AHRC project 'Researching multilingually at the borders of languages, the body, law and the state' http://researching-multilingually-at-borders.com/).[2] These works in progress illustrate that lingua francas are characterised and shaped by complex cultural, social, economic, political, religious, historical, etc. forces. These research agendas, and others like them, along with the chapters in this volume, challenge the limitations of extant ELF research and open up new possibilities that necessitate a variety of theoretical, methodological and ontological research approaches and tools – those which also prioritise the concept of interculturality entailed in such encounters. We hope that this volume will be the first of many to come, and that it will allow scholars and practitioners – and others – involved in researching and teaching about ELF and interculturality to come together, enter into dialogue and break away from the orthodoxies described in this introduction and the chapters.

Notes

(1) 'A belief or a way of thinking that is accepted as true or correct' (Online Merriam-Webster).
(2) See also the linguistic complexity at play within established communities whose linguistic spaces are constantly under (re)construction (see for example, Blommaert, 2013; and the current AHRC project 'Translation and translanguaging: Investigating linguistic and cultural transformations in superdiverse wards in four UK cities', http://www.birmingham.ac.uk/generic/tlang/index.aspx)

References

Abdallah-Pretceille, M. (1986) *Vers une Pédagogie Interculturelle*. Paris: PUF.
Adichie, C.N. (2014) *We Should All Be Feminists*. New York: Vintage.
Allen, S. (1978) All present if not correct (Episode 14). *Mind Your Language*. London: London Weekend Television.
Augé, M. (2010) *La Communauté*. Paris: Éditions Payot et Rivage.
Baker, W. (2012) From cultural awareness to intercultural awareness: Vulture in ELT. *ELT Journal* 66 (1), 62–70.
Baker, W. (2015) Research into practice: Cultural and intercultural awareness. *Language Teaching* 48 (1), 130–141.
Baker, W., Jenkins, J. and Baird, R. (2015) ELF researchers take issue with 'English as a lingua Franca: An immanent critique'. *Applied Linguistics* 36 (1), 121–123.
Baxter, J. (1983) English for intercultural competence: An approach to intercultural communication training. In D. Landis and R.W. Brislin (eds) *Handbook of Intercultural Training* (Vol. 1) (pp. 290–324). Oxford: Pergamon Press.
Becher, T. and Trowler, P. (2001) *Academic Tribes and Territories: Intellectual Enquiry and the Culture of Disciplines*. Oxford: Oxford University Press.
Bhabha, H. (1994) *The Location of Culture*. Abingdon: Routledge.
Blommaert, J. (2013) *Ethnography Superdiversity and Linguistic Landscapes: Chronicles of Complexity*. Bristol: Multilingual Matters.
Bowles, H. and Cogo, A. (eds.) (2015) *International Perspectives on English as a Lingua Franca: Pedagogical Insights*. London: Palgrave.
Breidenbach, J. and Nyiri, P. (2009) *Seeing Culture Everywhere: From Genocide to Consumer Habits*. Seattle and London: University of Washington Press.
Byram, M.S. (2008) *From Foreign Language Education to Education for Intercultural Citizenship*. Clevedon: Multilingual Matters.
Canagarajah, S. (2006) Negotiating the local in English as a lingua franca (Special Issue). *Annual Review of Applied Linguistics* 26, 197–218.
Crosbie, V. (2014) Capabilities for intercultural dialogue. *Language and Intercultural Communication* 14 (1), 91–107.
Crystal, D. (2012) *English as a Global Language* (2nd edn). Cambridge: Cambridge University Press.
Dahlen, T. (1997) *Among the Interculturalists*. Stockholm: Department of Social Anthropology, Stockholm University Press.

Derrida, J. (1976) *Of Grammatology*. Baltimore: John Hopkins University Press.
Dervin, F. (2008) *Métamorphoses Identitaires en Situation de Mobilité*. Turku: Humanoria.
Dervin, F. (ed.) (2010) *Lingua Francas. La Véhicularité Linguistique pour Vivre, Travailler et Étudier*. Paris: L'Harmattan.
Dervin, F. (2011) A plea for change in research on intercultural discourses: A 'liquid' approach to the study of the acculturation of Chinese students. *Journal of Multicultural Discourses* 6 (1), 37–52.
Dervin, F. (2013) Politics of identification in the use of lingua francas in student mobility to Finland and France. In C. Kinginger (ed.) *Social and Cultural Aspects of Language Learning in Study Abroad* (pp. 101–126). Amsterdam: John Benjamins Publishing Company.
Dervin, F. and Risager, K. (2014) *Researching Identity and Interculturality*. New York: Routledge.
Dervin, F., Layne, H. and Trémion, V. (2015) *Making the Most of Intercultural Education*. Newcastle upon Tyne: Cambridge Scholars Publishing.
Fay, R., Lytra, V. and Ntavaliagkou, M. (2010) Multicultural awareness through English: A potential contribution of TESOL in Greek schools. *Intercultural Education* 21 (6), 581–595.
Ferri, G. (2014) Ethical communication and intercultural responsibility: A philosophical perspective. *Language and Intercultural Communication* 14 (1), 7–23.
Gao, Y.-H. (2014) Faithful imitator, legitimate speaker, playful creator and dialogical communicator: Shift in English learners' identity prototypes. *Language and Intercultural Communication* 14 (1), 59–75.
Gu, M., Patkin, J. and Kirkpatrick, A. (2014) The dynamic identity construction in English as lingua franca intercultural communication: A positioning perspective. *System* 46, 131–142.
Guilherme, M., Keating, C. and Hoppe, D. (2010) Intercultural responsibility: Power and ethics in intercultural dialogue and interaction. In M. Guilherme, E. Glaser and M.C. Mendez-Garcia (eds) *The Intercultural Dynamics of Multicultural Working* (pp. 77–96). Bristol: Multilingual Matters.
Hall, C. (2013) Cognitive contributions to plurilithic views of English and other languages. *Applied Linguistics* 34 (2), 211–231.
Hall, E.T. (1976) *Beyond Culture*. Garden City, NY: Anchor Press.
Holliday, A. (2010) *Intercultural Communication and Ideology*. London: Sage.
Holliday, A. (2013) *Understanding Intercultural Communication: Negotiating a Grammar of Culture*. London: Routledge.
Holmes, P. (2014) Researching Chinese students' intercultural communication experiences in higher education: Researcher and participant reflexivity. In J. Byrd-Clarke and F. Dervin (eds) *Reflexivity in Language and Intercultural Education: Rethinking Multilingualism and Interculturality* (pp. 100–118) New York: Routledge.
Holmes, P. (2015) Intercultural encounters as socially constructed experiences: Which concepts? Which pedagogies? In N. Holden, S. Michailova, and S. Tietze (eds) *The Routledge Companion to Cross-Cultural Management* (pp. 237–247). New York: Routledge.
Holmes, P., Fay, R., Andrews, J. and Attia, M. (2013) Researching multilingually: New theoretical and methodological directions. *International Journal of Applied Linguistics* 23 (3), 285–299.
House, J. (2003) English as a lingua franca: A threat to multilingualism? *Journal of Sociolinguistics*, 7 (4), 556–578.
House, J. (2010) English as a global lingua franca: A threat to multilingualism? In S. Shiyab, M. Gaddis Rose, J. House and J. Duval (eds) *Globalization and Aspects of Translation* (pp. 11–35). Newcastle upon Tyne: Cambridge Scholars Publishing.

Jenkins, J. (2014) *English as a Lingua Franca in the International University*. London: Routledge.
Jenkins, J., Cogo, A. and Dewey, M. (2011) Review of developments in research into English as a lingua franca. *Language Teaching* 44 (3), 281–315.
Kramsch, C. (2009) *The Multilingual Subject*. Oxford: Oxford University Press.
Krumer-Nevo, M. and Sidi, M. (2012) Writing against othering. *Qualitative Inquiry* 18 (4), 299–309.
Kureishi, H. (2011) *Collected Essays*. London: Faber and Faber.
Laplantine, F. (2012) *Une Autre Chine. Gens de Pékin, Observateurs et Passeurs des Temps*. Paris: De l'incidence éditeur.
Lemke, J.L. (2010) Identity, development and desire: Critical questions. In C. Caldas-Coulthard and R. Iedema (eds) *Identity Trouble* (pp. 17–42). London: Palgrave MacMillan.
Machart, R., Lim, C.B., Lim, S.N. and Yamato, E. (2013) *Intersecting Identities and Interculturality: Discourse and Practice*. Newcastle upon Tyne: Cambridge Scholars Publishing.
Mauranen, A. and Ranta, E. (2009) *English as a Lingua Franca*. Newcastle upon Tyne: Cambridge Scholars Publishing.
McGroarty, M. (2006) Introduction: Lingua franca languages (Special Issue). *Annual Review of Applied Linguistics* 26, vii–x.
Moghaddam, F.M. (2011) The omnicultural imperative. *Culture & Psychology* 18, 304–330.
Murray, N. (2012) English as a lingua franca and the development of pragmatic competence. *ELT Journal* 66 (3), 318–326.
O'Regan, J. (2014) English as a lingua franca: An immanent critique. *Applied Linguistics* 35 (5), 533–522.
Otsuji, E. and Pennycook, A. (2010) Metrolingualism: Fixity, fluidity and language in flux. *International Journal of Multilingualism* 7 (3), 240–254.
Phipps, A. (2007) *Learning the Arts of Linguistic Survival: Languaging, Tourism, Life*. Clevedon: Channel View Publications.
Phipps, A. (2014) 'They are bombing now': The meaninglessness of 'intercultural dialogue' in times of conflict. *Language and Intercultural Communication* 14 (1), 108–124.
Pieterse, N.P. (2007) *Ethnicities and Global Multiculture: Pants for an Octopus*. London: Rowman & Littlefield.
Piller, I. (2011) *Intercultural Communication*. Edinburgh: Edinburgh University Press.
Porto, M. (2014) Intercultural citizenship education in an EFL online project in Argentina. *Language and Intercultural Communication* 14 (2), 245–261.
Prashad, V. (2001) *Everybody Was Kung Fu Fighting: Afro-Asian Connections and the Myth of Cultural Purity*. Boston: Beacon Press.
Researching multilingually at the borders of languages, the body, law and the state (2015) Arts and Humanities Research Council-funded project. University of Glasgow. See http://researching-multilingually-at-borders.com/?page_id=46 (accessed 31 January 2015).
Santos, M., Araújo e Sá, M.-H. and Simões, A.R. (2014) Intercultural education in primary school: A collaborative project. *Language and Intercultural Communication* 14 (1), 140–150.
Sarangi, S. (1994) Intercultural or not? Beyond celebration of cultural differences in miscommunication analysis. *Pragmatics* 4 (3), 409–427.
Seidlhofer, B. (2011) *Understanding English as a Lingua Franca*. Oxford: Oxford University Press.

Sen, A. (2005) *The Argumentative Indian*. London, England: Penguin Books.
Sen, A. (2006) *Identity and Violence: The Illusion of Destiny*. New Delhi: Penguin Books.
Sithole, T. (2014) Good English (blog posting 19 June 2014). See http://researching-multilingually-at-borders.com/?page_id=795&paged=3?page_id=795
Su, Y-C. (2014) The international status of English for intercultural understanding in Taiwan's high school EFL textbooks. *Asia Pacific Journal of Education* (published online). DOI: 10.1080/02188791.2014.959469.
Translation and translanguaging: Investigating linguistic and cultural transformations in superdiverse wards in four UK cities (2015) Arts and Humanities Research Council-funded project. University of Birmingham. See http://www.birmingham.ac.uk/generic/tlang/index.aspx (accessed 31 January 2015).
Widdowson, H. (2015) Contradiction and conviction: A reaction to O'Regan. *Applied Linguistics* 36 (1), 124–127.
Wimmer, A. (2013) *Ethnic Boundary Making: Institutions, Power, Networks*. Oxford: Oxford University Press.

Part 1
The Interconnections and Inter-Relationships Between Interculturality and ELF

1 Lingua Francas in a World of Migrations

Karen Risager

Introduction

In this chapter I focus on transnational mobility and the ensuing linguistic and cultural flows in the world. I emphasise the importance of the field of ELF for studies of other languages as well, and look specifically at the cultural/intercultural dimensions of ELF and their relevance for other languages. I want to add that I am using the term 'ELF' as a shorthand for English as it is used in lingua franca situations. The concept of lingua franca situation is much debated (see for example Jenkins *et al.*, 2011), but here I will define it as a communicative situation dominated by people who don't have the language in question as their first or early second language (the term 'early second' is treated below). The chapter argues for the following points:

(1) English is the language that is used most as a lingua franca today. But at the same time a large number of the world's other languages are used as lingua francas as well. English and many other languages are used as lingua francas not only in settings like international business and international higher education, but also between immigrants of diverse origins living in the countries where the languages in question are national or official languages.
(2) No language is culturally neutral, and that includes English in lingua franca use. All languages, whether they function as a first language, a foreign language or a second language for the individual, and whether they are used in a lingua franca situation or not, (re)produce culture in the sense of meaning. The culturality of language may be analysed at two different levels: linguaculture, which is bound to specific languages, and discourse, which is not necessarily bound to specific languages.

(3) The learning and teaching of English for lingua franca use can, and should, contribute to the development of global citizenship and critical awareness of cultural complexity. Such a pedagogical goal is immediately relevant for ELF, but it is also relevant for all other language learning and teaching because we have to transcend the traditional national paradigm of one nation, one language, one culture.

The Growth of the Lingua Franca Phenomenon

Transnational mobility and linguistic flows

A large number of the languages of the world are spread by transnational mobility. I would like to start with the concrete example of Danish, my first language: Danish is spoken in Denmark, but not only there. There are Danish-speaking people all over the world as a consequence of all kinds of mobility such as, for example, tourism, job-related and educational travels and sojourns, and regular emigration. There are Danish-speaking doctors, businesspeople, students, diplomats, sports people, journalists, artists, pensioners, etc. in most countries of the world, and Danish is taught on all continents in Scandinavian departments in higher education. Danish is also spoken, of course, in other parts of the Danish kingdom: Greenland and the Faroe Islands. Thus, one can encounter Danish-speaking people all over the world who can, in principle, communicate in Danish via the internet. They can use email, Skype and social media, look at Danish TV, read online newspapers, etc., provided they have access to relevant infrastructure.

I am thinking not only of people having Danish as a first or native language, but also as a second language or a foreign language. People may, as immigrants from, for example, Egypt, have learnt Danish as a second language in Denmark, and then moved on to another country and maybe back to Egypt. Or people may have learnt Danish as a foreign language in, for example, Russia, and then moved to Denmark to conduct further studies. Or people may have acquired Danish as a first language as members of a Danish-speaking family working in, for example, Kenya. Danish is used in many kinds of communicative situations; current researchis focusing on Danish as a language of internationalisation at universities in Denmark (Haberland, 2011).

Danish can therefore be said to be a world language – not on the basis of the number of its speakers, but on the basis of the global range of its use. Of course, exactly the same thing can be said of a large number of the world's other languages. The spread of English has a global scope, but so has that of Polish, Farsi, Somali, Cantonese, Turkish, Italian, Filipino, Hindi, Swahili, Swedish, etc.

This dynamic picture of the languages of the world rests on a sociological theory of language that focuses on language practices (in specific 'languages', including pidgins, creoles and other language mixings) in social networks of different scales, from the micro-level of interpersonal communication in real and virtual space to macro-levels of mass communication and the global spread of information through social media (Risager, 2006). Seen in the light of this theory, inspired by social anthropologist Hannerz's theory of global cultural flows and cultural complexity (Hannerz, 1992), people who move or migrate, change the patterns of social networks, leaving some of them behind, creating new ones in new locations, 'stretching' old ones, etc. They take their personal language resources with them to new environments and put them to use there in relevant settings. Thus, languages are not seen as territorially bound, they are seen as mobile to the extent that their users are mobile (see also Blommaert, 2010; Pennycook, 2007; Piller, 2011).

Local linguistic complexity

The flows of a large number of languages across national borders give rise to local complexity in all countries, especially in the big cities with a multitude of linguistic minorities and recent newcomers (Blommaert, 2010; Canagarajah, 2007; Jørgensen, 2008; Otsuji & Pennycook, 2010; Rampton, 1995). Several hundred languages may be spoken. In a small country like Denmark, for instance, about 120 languages are spoken by various groups of immigrants (Risager, 2006).

The local linguistic complexity is characterised by language hierarchisations in both practice and representation (Risager, 2012a). Language hierarchisation in practice happens all the time as people choose languages for verbal interaction and writing in specific situations and contexts. Codeswitching and crossing are among the phenomena that show the interplay of different power positions, symbolic functions and identities of languages in interaction (Otsuji & Pennycook, 2010; Rampton, 1995). But language hierarchisation is also carried out via language representation. For example, government authorities may produce a language policy document outlining the use and learning of a certain number of languages in education. Or a local radio station may organise a discussion of the use of various languages in the media. Language representations may also be used in identity politics, as for example when a group of people fight for recognition of their language, and thus for a change of language hierarchies.

One of the achievements of ELF studies is the emphasis on innovative language practices and the creation of local and situational norms in everyday communication between people with different language backgrounds. But it is also important to be aware of power issues in the linguistic landscape, for example in relation to norms. Certain norms are more dominant than others, and certain models (real or imagined language users) are more dominant than others. When people communicate in informal settings and just want to get themselves understood, there may well be openness as to norms and models, which offers a great freedom for instant experimentation and innovation. But in some situations people have to conform to other people's norms if they want to be taken seriously, such as when they seek a job or want to publish an academic article. At such times it is in their own interest to conform to these organisational norms and conventions, particularly if they are not in a position to change them.

The concepts of first, second and foreign language, and of lingua franca use

All these languages in the local setting may have different functions for the individual, according to the context in and age at which they were learnt. Four ideal-typical cases may be distinguished: (1) it can be a first (or native) language, i.e. a language (or maybe two or even three) learnt in early childhood in the family; (2) it can be an early second language, i.e. a language that is the national or official language of the country of residence, and which is learnt in childhood outside the family, for instance in the neighbourhood and/or for use in school as a medium of learning; (3) it can be a late second language, i.e. a language that is the national or official language of the country one lives in as an immigrant, and which is learnt upon arrival in order to be able to live as a new citizen, with all that this entails; or (4) it can be a foreign language, i.e. a language that is not the national or official language of the country of residence, and which is learnt in school or later in life for more limited and well-defined reasons such as being able to communicate with other people who also know the language, or being able to read texts in the language (see Risager, 2006, which includes a discussion of changes among these functions in the light of transnational migration).

What I want to emphasise here is that these concepts relate to the individual (or more precisely the subject; see for example Kramsch, 2009), whereas the concept of lingua franca use relates to communication in real-time in specific settings. An individual participating in a lingua franca situation may be a first-language speaker, or an early second-language speaker, or a late second-language speaker, or a foreign-language speaker.

And, according to his or her language-learning background, the speaker may have a more or less dominant position in the situation with more or less control over emergent forms in the course of communication.

The distinction between English as a lingua franca (ELF) and English as a foreign language (EFL), which is characteristic of much research in ELF (Jenkins *et al.*, 2011: 283ff), is problematic because it mixes these two perspectives: the social and the individual. The social perspective deals with language practice in communicative situations; as I noted in the introduction, I define a lingua franca situation as a communicative situation dominated by people who don't have the language in question as their first or early second language (i.e. they have it as a late second or foreign language). The social perspective is about the communicative situation or event, whereas the individual perspective is about the role of the language in the individual's life and learning. When an individual is taught a language that is a foreign language for him or her, the teaching can focus on uses of the language in non-lingua franca situations (i.e. situations that are dominated by participants who have the language as first or early second language); prototypically, the teaching would focus on communication with native speakers in target-language countries. I would characterise such teaching as drawing on the traditional national paradigm in language and culture pedagogy. Alternatively, the teaching of the foreign language can focus on (or at least include) uses of the language in lingua franca situations and thus favour a more transnational approach to language and culture pedagogy by drawing attention to the fact that the target language may be used in many kinds of situations all over the world (Risager, 2007).

Lingua franca use between immigrants of diverse origins

Linguistic complexity is of course also the general situation in the countries where English is the national or official language (Inner Circle and Outer Circle countries; Kachru, 1986). There are hundreds of different linguistic minorities, including indigenous communities and/or communities identifying with heritage languages. Moreover, there are all the different types of newcomers and travelers referred to above (tourists, students, expatriates, refugees, etc.). Those who can communicate in English do it every day or from time to time. Therefore, why not describe the use of English between immigrants of diverse origins as lingua franca communication? Here I would like to expand on Canagarajah's historical comment:

> There are at least two major senses in which English has served as a lingua franca, in relation to historical developments. When English

spread to the colonies from English beginning from the 16th century, it served as a contact language between the colonisers and the colonised. It also served as a contact language *between* the colonised. However, after decolonisation in the 1950s and, more significantly, in the recent forms of globalisation marked by new technology, transnational economic and production relationships, and the porous nature of nation-state boundaries, English has become a contact language for a wider range of communities (outside the former British empire). (Canagarajah, 2006: 197, italics in the original)

What I would add here is that English has also, by the very same processes of globalisation, become a contact language between immigrants and 'natives' in the countries where English is a national or official language, and has also become a contact language between immigrants of diverse origins. Seen in this light, English is being used in lingua franca situations in all countries of the world, including Inner and Outer Circle countries, as well as in virtual space. The same can be said of all other languages that are spread by transnational mobility, including for example Danish, which is used for communication between people of diverse linguistic origins living in Denmark if Danish is their only common language.

Thus with the worldwide increase of transnational migrations and mobility in general, and with the increase in the learning and use of a large number of languages as second languages in host countries, the lingua franca phenomenon is gaining importance as a mode of verbal communication among a multitude of diverse groups and networks. This also means that for many languages, ethnolectal variation and innovation are probably on the increase.

The geographical basis of the field of ELF would widen if it included the use of ELF within countries where English is the national or official language. For example, take two imagined communicative events, one in London and one in Kraków in Poland: in London, a British-Greek immigrant and a British-Russian immigrant talk with each other in English in a restaurant because English is their only common language. Compare this to the other event: in Kraków, the same two people talk with each other about the same topics in English in a restaurant because English is their only common language. Although the larger cultural contexts are different, the course of communication may be very similar. Yet the second case is seen as an instance of ELF communication, whereas the first is not.

ELF could also widen its empirical basis to social domains other than elite domains such as communication in transnational business companies or communication among international students in higher education

(Preisler & Fabricius, 2011). Transnational mobility concerns all age groups, all social groups and probably most professions. Thus the field of ELF, as it is now and also with the potentially larger geographical and social scope described above, could in fact have very positive functions because it could give new impulses to lingua franca studies related to other languages. The latter is a field that is under-researched at the moment (but see McGroarty, 2006, for a number of interesting surveys on Lingala, Esperanto, Chinese, French, Quechua, Spanish, Russian and German; also see Dervin, 2011).

The Culturality of Language: Linguaculture and Discourse

Linguaculture within linguistic flows

I now turn to the question of the culturality of language, beginning with the concept of linguaculture (Risager, 2006, 2011b). I am among those who maintain that language is never culturally neutral. Language is not just a code; it is a system for the production and reproduction of meaning in human society. And meaning is culture – as per the title of the above-mentioned book by Hannerz (1992): *Cultural Complexity: Studies of the Social Organization of Meaning*. Any language carries meaning, and in this sense any language carries culture (see for example Crozet & Liddicoat, 2000, who do not use the term 'linguaculture', but rather the expression 'culture in language').

To capture this fundamental aspect of human language, I find the term 'linguaculture' convenient. It enables one to maintain two premises at the same time: (1) Language is never culturally neutral, it carries linguaculture; and (2) Language (with its linguaculture) can be disconnected from one cultural context and reconnected to another as a consequence of linguistic flow, i.e. language users moving about in the world.

In the field of ELF there is a tendency to use the term 'linguaculture' in another way in order to describe people's backgrounds when they are using English as a lingua franca, for example: '...when English is chosen as the means of communication among people from *different* first language backgrounds, across linguacultural boundaries, the preferred term is "English as a lingua franca..."' (Seidlhofer, 2005: 339, emphasis in the original). Moreover, '...they [features of ELF] have been found to occur frequently and extensively with features most often being produced by numerous speakers from a wide variety of *linguacultural backgrounds*' (Jenkins *et al.*, 2011: 289, emphasis in the original).

The view expressed in these quotations seems to presuppose that an individual's first language is tied to the local culture and that one can talk about a single territorialised 'linguaculture' which comprises both first language and 'first' culture. This idea of linguaculture (or languaculture) as a single universe of language and culture has been theorised by Agar (1994) in an anthropological discussion of the cultural dimensions of conversation between people of diverse social, cultural and ethnic backgrounds. But although Agar's approach is very sensitive to complexity and a good inspiration for studies of the cultural dimensions of ELF, he does not take up the idea of linguistic flows.

From the perspective of linguistic flows it is possible to say that when language users move across countries, they take their language resources with them – including the linguaculture they have developed. As they move from one cultural context to another, they also more or less maintain their linguaculture. Thus language and culture do not form a single universe; instead, a language can be disconnected from one cultural context and reconnected into a new one. For example, a (Mandarin) Chinese-speaking person who has learnt Chinese (as a first or second language) in China, but moves to Germany, takes the Chinese language with him or her and puts it to use in the new cultural context. (Note that the languages involved may change in the process.) In principle, a language can be used in any cultural context in the world, although more or less easily depending on its particular lexicalisations and other structural characteristics. This is of course also the case with English.

Three interrelated dimensions of linguaculture

I propose that the concept of linguaculture should be seen as encompassing three interrelated dimensions: a semantic-pragmatic dimension, a poetic dimension, and an identity dimension. These three dimensions have all been investigated by well-established linguistic fields that have not, however, so often been brought together. (One very interesting exception is Kramsch, 2009, although she does not use the term 'linguaculture' as such.)

The semantic-pragmatic dimension is that explored by Agar, and by many others interested in intercultural pragmatics and contrastive semantics. It has also been a longstanding focus of interest for linguistic anthropology since Boas, Sapir and Whorf. This dimension is about constancy and variability in the semantics and pragmatics of specific languages: More or less obligatory distinctions between (in English) 'forest' and 'wood', between 'he' and 'she', between 'red' and 'orange', between 'hello' and 'how are you', between 'nature' and 'culture', etc. – and the social and personal variability that is found in concrete situations of use. It is also being investigated in the field of ELF by such scholars as Meierkord (2002) and Pitzl (2009). One can expect a wide range of interesting linguacultural differences in lingua franca communication, not only in everyday situations at work places etc. but also in cross-national political communication. Dovring (1997), for example, deals with the political consequences of semantic diversity in the English language and shows how important it is to analyse the language dimension of international conflicts: What does 'crusade' imply for different people? What counts as an 'excuse' in international relations?

The poetic dimension is related to the specific kinds of meaning created in the exploitation of the phonological and syllabic structure of the language in question, its rhymes, its relationships between speech and writing etc. – areas that have for a long time interested literary theorists focusing on literary poetics, style, literariness and the like. This dimension has been been studied for example by Pennycook (2007) in his investigation of interrelationships between hip hop and the English language in the perspective of global linguistic and cultural flows (although in this work he deals only with flows of English; see also Otsuji & Pennycook, 2010).

The identity dimension is also referred to as social meaning by some sociolinguists. It is related to the social variation of the language in question; by using the language in a specific way, with a specific accent (for instance), you identify yourself and make it possible for others to identify you according to their background knowledge and attitudes. Linguistic practice is a continuing series of 'acts of identity' (Le Page & Tabouret-Keller, 1985) in which people project their own understanding of the world onto the interlocutors and consciously or unconsciously invite them to react. This dimension has been explored by those scholars within sociolinguistics who are interested in language identity and language ideology. As regards the field of ELF, Jenkins (2007) has for example conducted a major study of identities related to the English language and to English language teaching.

Personal linguacultural profiles

Linguaculture, in its configuration of the three dimensions described above, has both collective and personal aspects. On the one hand, the individual's linguaculture is shared with other people's linguacultures in the sense that all share the same structural constraints and potentials of the language in question, for instance related to the difference (in English) between 'forest' and 'wood'. On the other hand, the individual's linguaculture is embodied and tied to his or her personal life history under specific social, cultural and historical circumstances: What role does the word 'forest' and the concept of a forest have in your life experiences – how has it been embodied, what significance does it have for your emotions, what place does it take in your imagination? How does it colour your use of other languages? (See Kramsch, 2009, on language and subjectivity).

One's linguaculture is first and foremost tied to the language (or languages) one learnt first in life – in childhood and in the formative years of youth. Learning other languages later in life means building on the linguaculture of the first language(s). Personal connotations to and memories of words and phrases are transferred, and a kind of language mixture develops, where the new language is supplied with linguacultural matter from the first (and early second) language(s). One can say that every person develops his or her own personal linguacultural profile. For example, when I travel around in the world, I carry my linguaculture with me, which is primarily based on my life experiences expressed in the Danish language and mostly related to my life in the Copenhagen area, but it also influences my use of English, French and other languages I know. Thus, with regard to English for example, I contribute to both the very large ethnolectal variation and the particularly composite linguacultural space of the English language.

Translingual discursive flows

I now turn to the second level of meaning related to language: discourse. In my view it is fruitful to distinguish between linguistic/linguacultural flows on the one hand, and discursive flows on the other. Linguistic/linguacultural flows concern the use and meaning potentials of specific languages, such as English, Danish, Swahili and Esperanto, as well as pidgins and creoles and any other language mixtures. Discursive flows concern what is communicated about. I here propose to draw on the field of critical discourse analysis such as that of Fairclough (1992) and others. This concept of discourse is content-oriented. Discourse carries and forms themes, positions and perspectives. It structures all kinds of ideas, ideologies and knowledge.

Discourse is mainly linguistically formed (though often incorporated in wider semiotic practices), but it is in principle not restricted to any specific language or language community. This means that discourses may carry content from one language community to another. Discourses spread translingually from language to language by processes of translation and other kinds of transformation. Discourses on nationalism, on agriculture, on citizenship, on Islam, on education, on culture, on human relations, on food and drink, etc. spread transnationally all over the world. But any discourse is at any time embodied in a specific language and consequently formed by the linguacultural potential of that language. Thus one can say that there are two levels of meaning in language: linguaculture (bound to the use of specific languages), and discourse (not necessarily bound to specific languages) (Risager, 2006).

Certain discourses may circulate within a specific language community and never leave it because they are never translated or referred to in other languages. They may for example be discourses of resistance in dominated groups, or they may be pieces of literature that are not translated because of lack of resources. But otherwise the world situation is mostly marked by an enormous translingual exchange of discourses among many different languages, especially the national or official languages that are used in national media and publishing houses.

One example could be the flow of information from international news agencies (in English, French, Spanish, Arabic or other languages) into the national media around the world and therefore into diverse national languages. In national media offices we see day-to-day translations of all kinds of news items and thus a constant discursive flow from language to language. Another example could be the flows described by Pennycook (2007), where hip hop is shown to be spreading all over the world – not least expressed in the English language, but also expressed in many other languages (seen as local languages in their local settings) and in mixtures between these languages and English. The example of hip hop illustrates a combined flow of discourse and other, nonverbal, forms of culture: music, dance, dress, etc. (see also Otsuji & Pennycook, 2010, on metrolingualism).

Discursive flows give rise to local discursive formations of great complexity characterised by internal struggles and hierarchisations similar to what is going on in the local linguascapes referred to above. All societies, communities and institutions are characterised by struggles over discourses and social practices, as emphasised by Fairclough (1992).

Lingua franca communication, and indeed any communication, can in principle be about any topic. Any discourses may be touched upon and any discourses may be combined, irrespective of the specific language(s) used. Discourse is primarily translingual meaning. But some discourses may be easier to express in certain languages than others, as for example in English. It would be interesting to carry out research on this question: Are there discourses, topics and areas of knowledge that are preferred or evaded in ELF communication simply because English is the common language – with its specific semantic potentials and constraints?

A related but somewhat different question would be: Are there discourses, topics and areas of knowledge that are preferred or evaded in lingua franca communication because the participants do not share the relevant knowledge in some depth? Do they have to deal with more general, de-localised knowledge? Take for example an ELF communication taking place in Taiwan, dealing with schooling and school life: Would this communication be quite superficial because participants know nothing about each other's school systems? Or what strategies are used, if at all, in order to remediate this problem?

Finally I want to add that linguistic/linguacultural flows and discursive flows are only parts of the many different cultural flows described by Hannerz (1992), flows that are also more or less independent of each other: the spread of classical European music, the spread of food traditions and innovations, the spread of new technologies and designs, etc. What I have been focusing on in the preceding sections are the language-related cultural flows. That is, I have expanded on what constitutes the cultural dimensions of language, with a certain focus on language in lingua franca use. In the next section I will focus on the field of language teaching and learning as such.

The Cultural Dimensions of the Learning and Teaching of Languages, Taking into Account Their Use as Lingua Francas

The terms 'cultural' and 'intercultural'

In my various writings I have lingered between 'cultural' and 'intercultural'; in this chapter I have decided to use the term 'cultural'. Cultural studies and cultural analysis, and also culture teaching and learning in relation to languages, are fields that are to a large degree influenced by hermeneutical and social constructionist methodologies. These fields tend to draw on approaches in which different perspectives, voices or positions are made visible and reflected upon. As explained above, I use the word 'culture' in the sense of 'meaning', following Hannerz (1992). Linguaculture, in the sense I give to it, is meaning related to specific languages, and discourse is also a kind of meaning-production formed by language.

So, in a way, everything that can be described as 'cultural' within this frame of understanding is always 'intercultural'. Linguaculture is always 'intercultural' because the personal linguaculture that is developed throughout life is both individual and collective – that is, shared with others to some extent. The personal linguaculture constitutes a language-related and subjective perspective on the world. Discourse in the general sense employed by critical discourse analysts is always 'intercultural' because it represents a perspective, or maybe a contradictory assembly of perspectives.

In the following section I will distinguish between three aspects of culture pedagogy in relation to languages (see also Risager, 2012b).

Linguaculture: Exploring the great variability of linguacultures

In language teaching there is a long tradition of dealing with the semantics and pragmatics of words and phrases, but mostly related to first-language speakers ('native speakers') in target language countries, typically without consideration of the great potential variability within a population (e.g. consideration of what words like 'work' and 'leisure' mean for different people speaking the same language). In both second and foreign language teaching, more attention should be directed at the larger semantic and pragmatic variability within ethnically diverse populations. Teaching should deal with both the meaning of words in the target language used by immigrants who speak different first languages, as well as with differences of meaning related to single individuals among them – differences that are related to personal life histories, associations and memories (e.g. What do 'beer' or 'nature' mean to me? What do I think 'beer' or 'nature' means to him or her?). For reflections on such linguacualtural differences, work with personal mindmaps and other creative graphics will probably be illuminating.

Another area covered by the linguaculture concept is the poetic dimension of language. One example could be the very different poetic potentials between languages such as English and Mandarin Chinese. Some may be related to differences in semantics, idiomaticity and metaphoric traditions; others may be related to differences in the relationship between pronunciation and writing/script (Pitzl, 2009).

The identity dimension of linguaculture is especially interesting in lingua franca communication and should also be explored in language teaching: What does it mean to use the target language as a lingua franca – to me and to the others present? Can I form my identity more freely when I use the target language in a multiethnic group? A book that deals mostly with this dimension of linguaculture, but also relates to the other two dimensions, was written by Kramsch (2009). Although it does not specifically adopt a lingua franca perspective, it could be a good inspiration for language teaching with a wider transnational perspective. The book deals with the subjective aspects of language learning with a focus on the multilingual subject and his/her language-learning biography and practices from a semiotic/symbolic perspective, including links with identity, memory, emotion and imagination. The data are mainly spoken and written data from individual language learners, including online data from, for example, electronic chatrooms, as well as published testimonies and memoirs of former language learners.

Discourse: Working with topics, texts and media that do not only focus on the national

As regards language teaching and learning, a greater emphasis on language used as a lingua franca implies a greater emphasis on a transnational paradigm (Risager, 2007). With the growing interest in transnational mobility and migration, and the use of languages, especially English, for communication between people with more or less different linguistic life histories, we must give up the idea of focusing only on a target language country/countries, their native speakers and their national culture (e.g. national geography, history, literature, discourses, norms and values, everyday practices). The movement towards a less national approach has been evident for some years in the teaching of English as a foreign language, but it is also relevant for the teaching of English as a second language (for immigrants and linguistic minorities) as well as for many languages other than English. As emphasised above, many languages are 'world languages' and all countries are *de facto* multilingual, at least in parts of civil society.

It may be relevant to deal with national institutions and discourses of national identity, and in fact the instructional guidelines may require this to be done. In any case, the relative abandonment of the national paradigm offers large opportunities to choose and work with topics, texts and media that are totally different from the ones students are working with now or have worked with until recently. As I said above, in principle all communication and language learning can take place in relation to any topic, discourse and genre. It is only within the national paradigm that there is a conviction that language learning and teaching can take place only on the basis of work with certain kinds of texts and discourses drawn from the national literature and national 'culture'.

Furthering global citizenship and critical awareness of cultural complexity

There have been attempts to define more globally oriented goals for language teaching – goals that may also have an influence on the choice of topics, texts and media. Among the goals proposed are multilingual and multicultural awareness, critical intercultural citizenship, and education of the world citizen (Byram, 2008; Guilherme, 2002; Holliday, 2011; Houghton, 2012; Risager, 2007; Tsai & Houghton, 2010; see also the research timeline in Risager, 2011a). All these goals are well suited for preparing and training students to participate constructively in lingua franca communication; in addition, they are relevant for other languages. They may contribute to orienting the choice of topics, texts and media more towards issues of cultural complexity, including linguistic complexity, in all societies and communities – for example categorisations and identity constructions, collaboration and understanding, hierarchies and inequalities, discrimination, domination and resistance. They may lead to more work with issues of transnational mobility and migration – traveling, life trajectories, worries about forced displacement or barriers to free mobility. And they may try to further a sense of world citizenship by introducing reflections on colonial and post-colonial histories and global inequalities. In my view, an important point would be to try to decentre 'target-language countries' and to see them in their interrelationships with other countries in a global historical perspective. This task is especially relevant for the teaching of languages with a view to their more or less widespread use as lingua francas, but also for language teaching in general in order to overcome the ideological limitations inherent in the national paradigm.

Conclusion

The field of ELF is part of a much larger and continually expanding field: lingua franca communication, which in itself is related to transnational mobility and migration, both of which are considerable today. Lingua franca communication involves all age groups, all social groups and most professions, and it also concerns a large number of languages. Languages flow across national borders and continents to the extent that their users move or migrate. Most countries in the world have immigrants and other residents from many different parts of the world, a situation that results in communities in which hundreds of different languages are spoken. Lingua franca studies should include the study of communication among all kinds of linguistically diverse groups in our societies, including immigrant groups.

Lingua franca communication is not culturally neutral; on the contrary, all languages carry linguaculture (culture in language), and all human beings develop their own linguacultural profiles. Lingua franca communication can therefore be expected to be, linguaculturally, quite diverse. Another level of culture in language is (content-oriented) discourse, which is not bound to specific languages but rather flows from language to language via translation and other kinds of transformation.

Language teaching that aims at preparing and training students to take part in lingua franca communication is not necessarily required to focus primarily on national institutions and discourses on national identity. Other more transnationally oriented goals are becoming more important, for example global citizenship and critical awareness of cultural and linguistic complexity. Such goals are also relevant for other languages since all language teaching must transcend the traditional national paradigm of one nation, one language, one culture.

References

Agar, M. (1994) *Language Shock: Understanding the Culture of Conversation*. New York: William Morrow.
Blommaert, J. (2010) *The Sociolinguistics of Globalization*. Cambridge: Cambridge University Press.
Byram, M. (2008) *From Foreign Language Education to Education for Intercultural Citizenship: Essays and Reflections*. Clevedon: Multilingual Matters.
Canagarajah, S. (2006) Negotiating the local in English as a lingua franca. *Annual Review of Applied Linguistics* 26, 197–218.
Canagarajah, S. (2007) Lingua franca English, multilingual communities, and language acquisition. *The Modern Language Journal* 91, 923–939.
Crozet, C. and Liddicoat, A.J. (2000) Teaching culture as an integrated part of language: Implications for the aims, approaches and pedagogies of language teaching. In A.J. Liddicoat and C. Crozet (eds) *Teaching Languages, Teaching Cultures* (pp. 1–18). Applied Linguistics Association of Australia, Melbourne: Language Australia.
Dervin, F. (2011) *Les Identités des Couples Interculturels: En Finir Vraiment avec la Culture?* Paris: L'Harmattan.
Dovring, K. (1997) *English as Lingua Franca: Double Talk in Global Persuasion*. Westport, CT: Praeger.
Fairclough, N. (1992) *Discourse and Social Change*. Cambridge: Polity Press.
Guilherme, M. (2002) *Critical Citizens for in Intercultural World: Foreign Language Education as Cultural Politics*. Clevedon: Multilingual Matters.
Haberland, H. (2011) Local languages as the languages of internationalization: Internationalization and language choice. *Intercultural Education Review* (Tokyo) 9, 37–47.
Hannerz, U. (1992) *Cultural Complexity: Studies in the Social Organization of Meaning*. New York: Columbia University Press.
Holliday, A. (2011) *Intercultural Communication and Ideology*. London: Sage Publications.
Houghton, S.A. (2012) *Intercultural Dialogue in Practice: Managing Value Judgment through Foreign Language Education*. Bristol: Multilingual Matters.
Jenkins, J. (2007) *English as a Lingua Franca: Attitudes and Identity*. Oxford: Oxford University Press.
Jenkins, J., Cogo, A. and Dewey, M. (2011) State-of-the-art article: Review of developments in research into English as a lingua franca. *Language Teaching* 44 (3), 281–315.
Jørgensen, J.N. (2008) Polylingual languaging around and among children and adolescents. *International Journal of Multilingualism* 5 (3), 161–176.
Kachru, B.B. (1986) *The Alchemy of English: The Spread, Functions and Models of Non-Native Englishes*. Oxford: Pergamon Press.
Kramsch, C. (2009) *The Multilingual Subject*. Oxford: Oxford University Press.
Le Page, R. and Tabouret-Keller, A. (1985) *Acts of Identity: Creole-based Approaches to Language and Ethnicity*. Cambridge: Cambridge University Press.

McGroarty, M. (2006) Editor's introduction: Lingua franca languages. *Annual Review of Applied Linguistics* 26, vii–xi.
Meierkord, C. (2002) 'Language stripped bare' or 'linguistic marsala'? Culture in lingua franca conversation. In K. Knapp and C. Meierkord (eds) *Lingua Franca Communication* (pp. 109–133). Frankfurt am Main: Peter Lang.
Otsuji, E. and Pennycook, A. (2010) Metrolingualism: Fixity, fluidity and language in flux. *International Journal of Multilingualism* 7 (3), 240–254.
Pennycook, A. (2007) *Global Englishes and Transcultural Flows*. New York: Routledge.
Piller, I. (2011) *Intercultural Communication: A Critical Introduction*. Edinburgh: Edinburgh University Press.
Pitzl, M.-L. (2009) 'We should not wake up any dogs': Idiom and metaphor in ELF. In A. Mauranen and E. Ranta (eds) *English as a Lingua Franca: Studies and Findings* (pp. 298–322). Newcastle upon Tyne: Cambridge Scholars Publishing.
Preisler, B., Klitgaard I. and Fabricius A. (eds) (2011) *Language and Learning in the International University: From English Uniformity to Diversity and Hybridity*. Clevedon: Multilingual Matters.
Rampton, B. (1995) *Crossing: Language and Ethnicity Among Adolescents*. London and New York: Longman.
Risager, K. (2006) *Language and Culture: Global Flows and Local Complexity*. Clevedon: Multilingual Matters.
Risager, K. (2007) *Language and Culture Pedagogy: From a National to a Transnational Paradigm*. Clevedon: Multilingual Matters.
Risager, K. (2011a) Research timeline: The cultural dimensions of language teaching and learning. *Language Teaching* 44 (4), 485–499.
Risager, K. (2011b) Linguaculture and transnationality. In J. Jackson (ed.) *The Routledge Handbook of Language and Intercultural Communication* (pp. 101–115). New York: Routledge.
Risager, K. (2012a) Language hierarchies at the international university. *International Journal of the Sociology of Language* 216, 111–130.
Risager, K. (2012b) Intercultural learning: Raising cultural awareness. Introduction. In M. Eisenmann and T. Summer (eds) *Basic Issues in EFL Teaching and Learning* (pp. 143–155). Heidelberg: Universitätsverlag Winter.
Seidlhofer, B. (2005) Key concepts in ELT: English as a lingua franca. *ELT Journal* 59 (4), 339–341.
Tsai, Y. and Houghton S. (eds) (2010) *Becoming Intercultural. Inside and Outside the Classroom*. Newcastle upon Tyne: Cambridge Scholars Publishing.

2 Interculturalities of English as a Lingua Franca: International Communication and Multicultural Awareness in the Greek Context

Richard Fay, Nicos Sifakis and Vally Lytra

Looking Back

In the original proposal for this book (Holmes & Derwin, 2011), the editors noted that although lingua francas 'have always existed... [nonetheless] the cultural and intercultural aspects, so much a part of research in intercultural communication, international business and (foreign language) education, have only recently begun to be addressed in some detail in ELF research'. We would agree that ELF research has tended to focus on linguistic aspects (i.e. phonology, lexis and lexico-grammar, and pragmatics) and less so on the educational and (inter)cultural aspects. However, it could be argued that the seeds for these previously under-discussed aspects were sown in part during the late 1950s in the discussions (admittedly outside the current applied linguistics home for much ELF research) of English's function in international scientific debate. For example, writing in the *Observer* in 1958, the Cambridge astronomer Fred Hoyle reflected on his recent experiences of English use at an international conference in Moscow. As discussed by Close (1959, 1981), Hoyle identified two sorts of English, native English and international English, each character-ised by the speaker's relationship with (the complexities of) English:

> Th[e conference participants] who were neither British nor American were handicapped in the sense that their repertoire of English

vocabulary, syntax, and idiom was limited. On the other hand, the British and Americans were handicapped by not *being* handicapped in that sense. They could draw fluently from a far wider range of vocabulary, syntax, and idiom, and had free access to a wealth of allusion, of quotations and sayings that a native speaker would resort to without thinking. (cited by Close, 1981: 7)

Although the cultural and intercultural aspects of English in such an international setting are not explicitly invoked in this quotation, the native/ international distinction does foreshadow later ELF debates. In contrast, the educational aspects were more explicitly addressed. In his 'English as World Language' (1959) and in later work (1981), Close used Hoyle's reflections to underpin the rationale for his English for specific purposes (ESP) materials (Close, 1965). In doing so, he established a line of thinking subsequently taken up by major researchers of English as an international language, e.g. Widdowson, who later argued that 'English as an international language is English for Specific Purposes' (1997: 144). Thus, while ELF research has tended more towards linguistic than pedagogical aspects, the pedagogically oriented ESP arena has, over many years, frequently asserted a pedagogic implication that flows from the international and intercultural use of English, one that we have also dwelt upon previously (e.g. Fay, 1997; Sifakis & Sougari, 2003).

Although some aspects of Hoyle and Close's discourse (e.g. the negative connotations we now read into 'handicapped') are unappealing for our contemporary sensibilities, nonetheless they were among the first to argue for lingua franca use of English – rather than native-like use – for international scientific discussion, and they were also pioneers in raising some educational considerations of this lingua franca usage. Their discussion also acknowledged some of the native/non-native politics and challenges of English used internationally. For example, Hoyle noted how 'complaints [by conference participants] against speakers in English were all directed against Americans and British', and Close remarked that

It is not easy for an educated man to restrict the use of his mother tongue. However, even if we do not do so for the sake of making our contribution to science more accessible to foreign readers, we may be forced to by the fact that our language has ceased to be our private concern. English is already a world language – a *lingua franca* in science as in other fields – perhaps, in science, to a special degree. But the English that is a world language is not the English that takes the native speaker of it years to master; and it is becoming less and less that. (1959: 116–117)

The issues raised in these discussions from over half a century ago are now commonplace in ELF debate. They include the focus on linguistic forms and the concern for international intelligibility in English, the emergence of international-user practices and the challenge these pose to the continued use of English native-speaker norms in such international communication. In his related teaching materials, Close developed various pedagogical responses to this developing, specific purposes, lingua franca usage – for example, the pedagogic value of using authentic texts. However, perhaps unsurprisingly in this 'culture-free' era of ESP, the cultural (and intercultural) dimensions of such international English learning and use were rejected: 'students of highly-specialised sciences must ignore many aspects of language that would delight linguists or literary critics' (Close, 1965).

Further, in the mid-1970s Larry Smith promoted several terms, including English as an international auxiliary language (EIAL; 1976); English as an international and intranational language (1978); English as an international language (EIL; e.g. 1983), and world Englishes (e.g. 1987, 1997). He, too, had concerns with the distinctive features of the user-driven worlds of international English, but was keen to point out that EIL 'refers to the functions of English, not to any given form of the language' (1983: vi). He also extended the EIL remit to include intranational communication (a point to which we will return). With regard to pedagogy, he questioned whether some parts of English language education might be better positioned as EIAL classes rather than as ESL, EFL, ESOL or one of the other variants under the umbrella term TESOL. However, perhaps most importantly for our present purposes, he linked these discussions to communication, and to cross-cultural communication in particular (Smith, 1981; Smith & Rafiqzad, 1979). This concern is also evident in his argument that EIL requires changes from both international users and native speakers regarding their attitudes towards and assumptions about English. In particular, for the non-native speakers, intercultural competence rather than English language competence, is invoked: 'The Japanese businessman will not be very successful with an Indonesian if he expects him to do business as an American just because he is using English' (1983: 9). Smith also robustly addresses assumptions (e.g. as often held by foreign language educators) about the inextricable link between language and culture, arguing that 'no one language is inextricably tied to any one culture and no one needs to become more like native English speakers in order to use English well' (1983: 10).

Some of the contributions in the British Council (1978) volume entitled *English as an International Language* speak directly to contemporary debates despite the passage of so much time and the even more transnational and multicultural/multilingual contexts in which Englishes are now used. For example, Lester notes that 'A naive view of international English held by some native speakers .... [is that] any sophisticated communication between two non-native speakers of English would of necessity have to take place through the medium of common core, educated norm native speaker English .... [rather than accepting that] a perfectly satisfactory level of communication can take place between, say, Greeks and Japanese through the shared medium of English as an international language' (1978: 9). Of relevance for intercultural debates regarding foreign language learning and use, he notes that: (a) communicational needs usually predominate over native-like detailed knowledge of the idiosyncrasies of the linguistic system; (b) even if native-like linguistic performance is attained, native-like cultural performance is not guaranteed nor especially sought after; and (c) that 'the vast majority of English learners around the world have no wish to detach themselves from their own cultural/national identity and form a new identity with the people and culture of a specific English-speaking country' (1978: 10). Even though this final point does not fundamentally challenge the native/non-native distinction, it does question the assumption that native-norms have validity for most non-native learners/users of English.

As a final example of these earlier debates, we can mention Baxter's (1983) chapter – which, interestingly, was the only language-oriented chapter to appear in the first edition of the *Handbook of Intercultural Training* and which was not replaced in the later editions of this work. Baxter's starting point is that linguistic fluency in English does not ensure effective intercultural communication (1983: 290). He also sought to bring methodological debates about English language teaching and intercultural communication training out of their respective silos (and, in some ways, we might say that this current book some thirty years later revisits this objective vis-à-vis ELF and intercultural communication). Baxter's thinking is encapsulated in his proposal for a new approach to English language education, namely English for intercultural competence (EIC). Further, he noted (1983: 295) the increasing awareness at that time that teaching English to speakers of other languages (TESOL) should also be viewed as teaching English to speakers of other cultures (what might be termed TESOC); with regard to the language-culture debate, he argues that 'although the use of English is always culture-bound, the language itself is not bound to any specific culture' (1983: 295).

Baxter was writing at a time characterised by major discussion of the move from linguistic competence to communicative competence in language teaching circles. However, he notes that this discussion did not fully explain '*whose* social rules of speaking learners [were] supposed to acquire' (1983: 297) but he accepts that, implicitly, the assumed target was native-speaker communicative competence. He critiques the assumptions – e.g. conformity to native-speaker models and exclusion of non-native speakers' cultural backgrounds – underpinning native-speaker defined communicative competence in a foreign language (e.g. English), and argues that intercultural communicative competence would be a more appropriate reference point for English language learning and use (1983: 304). He then reviews EIL as an alternative to EFL but notes that this simply shifts the model-provider from the educated native-speaker of a standard variety of English to an educated non-native-speaker of English and does not address the pressing issue of how one speaks (uses) English interculturally. It is this gap which his EIC approach seeks to fill and it is an approach targeting both native and non-native speakers of English as they face up to the challenge of using English not just, for example, American-ly and Japanese-ly, but also effectively in and for intercultural communication.

Taking Stock

The above retrospective reminds us that discussions of the educational, cultural and intercultural aspects of ELF are perhaps less recent than it may first seem. Those early works have been followed by a rapid increase in works related to ELF, especially but not solely with regard to its spoken forms. As Figure 2.1 indicates, this literature makes use of a variety of similar, sometimes but not always synonymous, terms.

These terminological possibilities are underpinned by earlier and current discussions of related issues which can also be associated with the work of particular scholars (see Figure 2.2).

Some Interculturalities of Englishes

This chapter builds out of our earlier work regarding English vis-à-vis intercultural awareness, intercultural and international communication, and intercultural competence (Fay, 1996, 1997; Fay & Hyde, 1999; Sifakis, 2004) and continues our current explorations of post-TEFL possibilities for the Greek TESOL context (Fay et al., 2010; Sifakis & Fay, 2011). That body of thinking is informed by our appreciation of the value of the earlier debates for the contemporary complexities of English(es). For example, Smith's (1978: 10) classification of EIL situations in terms of the participants involved in the communication involves three main patterns of EIL interaction (Figure 2.3).

Term ... (teaching ...)	Example Literature
English as an International Language	Grundy (2004), Hassall (1996), Holliday (2005), Jenkins (1998, 2000), Llurda (2004), McKay (2002, 2004), Modiano (2001), Schnitzer (1995), Sharifian (2009), Sifakis (2004), Sifakis and Sougari (2005), Strevens (1992).
English as a Global Language	Crystal (1997), Gnutzmann (1999), Graddol (1997, 2006).
English as a Lingua Franca	Baker (2011), Cenoz and Jessner (2000), Firth (1996), Jenkins (2004, 2007b), Kuo (2006), Conrad and Mauranen (2003), Rajagopalan (1999), Seidlhofer (2001, 2004, 2005), Sifakis (2007, 2009), Sifakis and Fay (2011), and Widdowson (1998).
English for Intercultural Communication	Alptekin (2002), Baxter (1983), Corbett (2003), Levine and Adelman (1987), and Sifakis (2004).
World Englishes	Bamgbose (1998), Brown (1995), Brutt-Griffler (2002), Jenkins (2003), Kirkpatrick (2007), Kubota (2001), Melchers and Shaw (2003), Smith (1987), and Smith and Foreman (1997).

Figure 2.1 Some terms in the debate

If we now focus on the intercultural (and not just international) communication in English, then we can usefully extend this classification of patterns. In our earlier work, we tried to do this in a number of discrete ways including viewing intercultural communication through English as a subset of English for specific purposes (ESP) (e.g. Fay, 1997) and disentangling international from intercultural use of English (Sifakis, 2004). In our more recent work, we have considered English learning and use in Greece (and by/for Greeks) in terms of the intranational and international dimensions (e.g. Fay *et al.*, 2010; Sifakis & Fay, 2011). It is now time to bring these separate discussions together in our articulation of the intercultural dimensions of ELF.

Issue	Example Literature
deciding what *cultural content* is appropriate for what teaching context and paradigm.	Adaskou *et al.* (1990), Alptekin (1993), Alptekin and Alptekin (1994), Cortazzi and Jin (1996, 1999), Heiman (1994), Hyde (1994), Kramsch *et al.* (1996), Lessard-Clouston (1996), Merkestein (1998), Prodromou (1988, 1992), and Stapleton (2000).
considering the relationship between *globalisation and TESOL / FLE*	Block and Cameron (2002), Gnutzmann and Intemann (2005), Pakir (1999), and Sifakis and Sougari (2003).
determining the value of *nativeness and non-nativeness* in teaching norms and in teacher identity	Alvarez (2007), Braine (1999), Brutt-Griffler and Samimy (2001), Cook (1999), Davies (2003), Jenkins (2007a, 2007b), Llurda (2004), Medgyes (1992, 1994), Phillipson (1992a), Rampton (1990), Timmis (2002), and Widdowson (1994).
considering the *political nature* of teaching English to speakers of other languages	Canagarajah (1999), Edge (2006), Pennycook (1994), and Phillipson (1994b)
recognising the beliefs that teachers and learners bring to the English language classroom	Jenkins (2007b), Sifakis and Sougari (2005), Sifakis (2014), Sifakis and Bayyurt (in press)

Figure 2.2 Some areas of the debate

To do so, we need a working definition of English-medium 'intercultural communication' which, for us, is: interaction (including technology-mediated communication) predominantly in English involving individuals between whom there is some difference (as well as some potential similarity) in cultural backgrounds, identities and experiences. This understanding of

Types of EIL interaction		Examples
a	L2 ←→ L1	a Greek speaker of English communicating with a native of e.g. standard British English
b	L2 ←→ L2 (international)	a Greek communicating in English with e.g. a Japanese
c	L1 ←→ L1 (international)	a native of British English interacting with a native of e.g. Australian English

Figure 2.3 Classifications of EIL interactions (adapted from Smith, 1978: 10)

intercultural communication can be used with Kachru's (1985) map of the worlds of Englishes comprising an Inner Circle (a space primarily for native-speaker English usage, e.g. the UK), an Outer Circle (a space primarily for English as a second language, e.g. India), and an Expanding Circle (a space primarily for English as a foreign language, e.g. Greece). Putting all this together: whereas Smith makes use of the binary distinction between L1/L2 English users (see Figure 2.3), for our purposes a broader spectrum of English user possibilities can be exemplified (see Figure 2.4).

We should immediately clarify that such possibilities represent a somewhat crude heuristic; for example, many individuals (depending on their language learning trajectories, interactional histories, and above on the identities with which they use languages, and English in particular, to represent themselves variously to others in changing contexts of interaction) might be placed across the possibilities delineated in this broad spectrum. Thus, the possibilities in Figure 2.4 should not be seen as a menu of fixed and essentially separate options but rather as an illustrative expansion of the previously-delineated possibilities within the English-language user spectrum. An interesting case in point is the tension felt by many non-native English-speaking teachers between their identity (for many in the local context) as users, teachers, and guardians of standard English and their ELF-user identity, a tension which may reduce their appreciation of ELF's pedagogical consequences (Sifakis, 2009).

	Broadening the Types of English User in the Intercultural Era
L1a	International – e.g. using English American-ly, British-ly, etc
L1b	Intranational – e.g. internal variation in how English is used American-ly
L2a	Intranational - i.e. English as an Additional Language, but we should be mindful of the variation within EAL user communities, e.g. using EAL Pakistan-ly, Polish-ly, etc typically in Inner Circle contexts
L2b	Intranational and international - i.e. English as a Second Language/World Englishes, but we should be mindful of the variation within as well as between different varieties, e.g. using ESL Nigerian-ly, Jamaican-ly etc in Outer Circle contexts
L2c	International - i.e. English as a Foreign Language, but we should be mindful of the variation between as well as within varieties, e.g. using English Greek-ly, Japanese-ly etc in Expanding Circle contexts, and also mindful that a Greek living in France for example might use English-ly French-ly as well as / instead of Greek-ly.
ELF	International and beyond - i.e. English as a Lingua Franca in the International Forum, as used potentially by any type of English user anywhere in our transnational world of cultural flows of people, products, and ideas as mediated through English

Figure 2.4 More English-user possibilities for our complex era

The specification, in Figure 2.4 of L1a/b and L2a–c possibilities, goes some way towards addressing the tendency to oversimplify the types of English-medium interaction occurring within and across contexts. It does not, however, fully accommodate the prominence of technology-mediated English-based communication, nor the important roles of Englishes in our era of transnational/global flows and local cultural complexities (Risager, 2006). Therefore, in Figure 2.4 we have added the ELF classification as an addition to Kachru's framework. In doing so, we follow Goethals (undated), who proposed extending Kachru's circles to include the International Forum in which ELF predominates, i.e. the space where English-mediated communication takes place anywhere in our transnational world of cultural flows of people, products, and ideas.

To go further, English-medium interactions between any of these types of user (in Figure 2.4) could have an intercultural dimension. For example, we do not restrict English-medium interculturality to users who might be linked to differing possibilities but would also include, for example, L1b ⇔ L1b interaction as intercultural in many ways. In this sense, what we are proposing is a conceptualisation of the interculturalities of Englishes (rather than a conceptualisation of the complexities of EFL for example). This proposal is anchored in the above ELF possibilities (with all their intercultural potential) rather than in native-English-speaking norms. As we do so, we are not only problematising the use of the native/non-native distinction (and with it the issue of native culture) but also embracing the complexities within the world of English language users. Greece represents the site where we have been exploring the pedagogical implications of such thinking for a post-TEFL era in English language education. These explorations need, however, to be set in broader educational context.

The Greek Context for Interculturalism and Multiculturalism

From the 1970s onwards, Greece has seen the arrival of repatriated Greeks from Europe, the US, Canada and Australia as well as immigrants from different countries of origin. The resulting increase of linguistic, cultural, ethnic and religious diversity in Greek society created new opportunities and challenges for schools. In response, in 1996, the Greek Ministry of Education introduced διαπολιτισμική εκπαίδευση (or 'intercultural education') into Greek state education as part of a law defining the educational provision for 'young people with special educational, social and cultural needs' (Law 2413/17-6-96. Article 34). The same initiative established διαπολιτισμικά σχολεία ('intercultural schools') which would follow 'the national curriculum, adapting it to the special needs of their diverse pupil population' (Article 35). This provision sought to engage all pupils and teachers, regardless of their cultural backgrounds and identities, in intercultural dialogue and the development of intercultural competence (Androussou, 1996).

Although the intercultural education initiative radically reconceptualised the assumed homogeneity of Greek society (and with it the ubiquitous notion of 'one teacher, one textbook, one curriculum' in Greek schools, instead, foregrounding diversity in terms of pupils' and teachers' language, gender, religion, culture and socioeconomic backgrounds), in practice, this new educational discourse developed in parallel with the dominant monolingualising ideology of Greek education which emphasises Greek language learning to the detriment of minority and immigrant languages and cultures (Gogonas, 2010; Lytra, 2007). Today, intercultural schools remain by and large a marginal phenomenon in Greek education and the broadly conceived redesign of intercultural education seems to be confined almost exclusively to specific pupil populations that are perceived as chronically underachieving: children of Roma heritage, of repatriated Greeks and of other immigrant groups. Many majority-Greek parents shy away from enrolling their children in schools with a high percentage of 'foreign' pupils. This not only leads to further ghettoisation and marginalisation of these pupils in state education, it also exemplifies the dissonance between intercultural education rhetoric and actual educational practice.

Parallel to the emergence of the new intercultural discourse in Greek education, the late 1990s saw the beginning of the development of a discourse of πολυπολιτισμικότητα (multiculturalism) in Greek society which sought to destabilise the dominant discourse of cultural homogeneity by endorsing cultural diversity within the nation-state, thereby providing discursive spaces for alternative definitions of 'Greekness' (Agelopoulos, 2000). However, the resulting promotion of diversity can easily slip into exoticisation and folkorisation of the 'Other' and his/her cultural practices and the production of new essentialist constructions (Yiakoumaki, 2007: 146). These processes may lead to what Fish (1997: 378–379, reported in Yiakoumaki, 2007: 156) calls 'boutique multiculturalism ... the multiculturalism of ethnic restaurants, weekend festivals, and high-profile flirtations with the other ... characterized by its superficial or cosmetic relationship to the objects of its affection'.

Both interculturalism in Greek education and multiculturalism in Greek society emerged as responses to managing difference within the nation state; however, they coexist awkwardly with dominant national(ist) discourses. It is against these Greek discourses of interculturalism and multiculturalism that our thinking about the interculturality of ELF is set. One issue looms large. Although these discourses represent a response to increasing diversity within the Greek state, the stance they maintain towards the relationships between a language and a culture is out of step with the thinking in the earlier discussions of EIL. Despite some positive indicators in recent curriculum changes, all attempts to reconceptualise post-TEFL English language education in Greece runs counter to this issue. Nonetheless, we have been seeking to accomplish such a reconceptualisation in some of our recent work (Fay et al., 2010; Sifakis & Fay, 2011; Sifakis et al., 2010, 2012).

Post-TEFL possibilities for English language education in Greece

Traditionally, a linguistically and culturally homogeneous narrative has been used to characterise Greek society. This has proved to be a storyline of enduring power despite the fact that, until the recent economic crisis complicated things further, Greece was transforming from a migrant-sending to a migrant-receiving country with significant numbers of newly arrived immigrant children as well as Greek-born children of immigrant parents attending mainstream schools. In terms of English language education, Greece has typically been positioned in the Expanding Circle, in which English has been viewed mainly as a foreign language to be examined (in order to maximise further educational end employment possibilities) as much as to be used for communication.

The most recent school curriculum positions English alongside other foreign languages, as one of the main set of languages through which plurilingualism (i.e. an aspiration, in line with EU thinking, for competence in two or more foreign languages) is sought. No special lingua franca status or function is acknowledged for English. However, some wriggle-room does seem to be available in ancillary documentation in which one very open-ended aim (which could include the myriad interactions between the different kinds of English users identified in Figure 2.4) is that 'the curriculum prepares citizens who can operate efficiently in diverse social and communicative contexts and situations'. Another aim is that pupils become 'citizens who can act as an intercultural and inter-lingual mediator for the facilitation of communication between people from different social and cultural groups' although the way 'mediation' is conceptualised elsewhere suggests that the emphasis is on communication between users between countries rather than within the same country (i.e. Greece). More helpfully for an ELF perspective, users employ the language for their own interests and to take part in the 'activities of the international community'. In a similar way, we can identify a number of phrases which, read in an post-TEFL ELF challenge to the homogeneous narrative, could provide curricular support for a repositioning of English language teaching.

There are also some more explicit pointers for such a repositioning. For example, in the teachers' handbook accompanying the new curriculum, under the subheading 'Differences in the "nature" of language', the authors refer to 'multiple Englishes' and then continue:

> English is lingua mundi (international language) and lingua franca (common language for communication in commerce, politics, the media). There are many national variants of English as well as functional Englishes – technical, professional, hobbyist etc). The teaching of a single mutually accepted standard English language is no longer the case.

We recognise that we are exploiting this 'Englishes' possibility which the curriculum has made available, and we accept that to move on this possibility we need to downplay the less promising wider discourses referred to above. However, in recent years we have been proposing the repositioning of English language education away from the TEFL paradigm towards something more in tune with the interculturalities of Englishes. Such a proposal builds on the abovementioned ELF-leaning curricular statements but also recognises that, in order for a new approach to be adopted, teachers need to become more aware of the possibilities and be willing to explore them (see our most recent work on teacher awareness vis-à-vis ELF: Sifakis, 2014; Sifakis & Bayyurt, in press).

In concrete terms: We have, in fact, identified two related repositionings – one international and one intranationally oriented. The balance between them would need to be determined by context. We understand both of these options to be constituents of a more broadly understood pedagogic framing of ELF, one which embraces the intercultural communication aspects rather than privileging the linguistics ones.

First, the teaching of EIL is a pedagogic response – both international and intercultural in character – to the increasingly complex global English language phenomenon. In practical terms, TEIL might involve: (a) acceptance that English is a major language of intercultural communication between members of different societies (i.e. the International Forum) and not just between English users from Inner Circle contexts and their foreign English-learning counterparts; (b) a focus on the functions and emerging characteristics of ELF rather than on the norms of any specific native variety of English; (c) the development of learners' language awareness towards the multiplicity of Englishes available; (d) a focus on developing learners' generic cultural awareness rather than focusing specifically on cultural details associated with a particular native-speaker Inner Circle context; and (e) the acceptance that such generic culture-work might involve intercultural skills-developing activities more than activities structured around the exploration of cultural topics.

Second, the development of multicultural awareness through English (MATE) is a pedagogic response, intranational and multicultural in character, to the increasing diversity evident within Greece and more particularly within many schools. In practical terms, MATE might involve: (a) the recognition that English may be a significant language of communication between members of diverse societies such as Greece's (i.e. not just in Outer Circles contexts but also in some Expanding Contexts); (b) the recognition that such intranational English-medium communication (e.g. in the classroom, on the playground) would be primarily between non-native speakers of English; (c) the acceptance that the facilitation of English-medium interactions between learners from diverse backgrounds would be an appropriate curriculum objective; (d) the embrace of locally emerging characteristics of ELF and the development of learners' language awareness towards this locally enriched variety of English; (e) the building of a more generic cultural awareness on which learners might develop specific cultural awareness relating to the multiple cultural resources available to them locally; and (f) the acceptance that such 'culture work' might involve multicultural awareness of particular topics as well as general intercultural skills development.

Concluding Thoughts

In this chapter, mindful of the current intensity and distribution of current debates about ELF, and especially of the need for more discussion of the pedagogical, cultural and intercultural aspects of ELF, we have returned to the seeds sown in much earlier debates – ones in which the native/non-native distinction was problematised vis-à-vis the teaching, learning and use of English as a language of international and intercultural communication. In those earlier ESP debates, whilst the cultural was often absent, the intercultural was explicitly present. Those discussions are a useful starting point today but we need, and in this chapter have provided, a working map of the spectrum of intercultural possibilities through and in Englishes.

Greece represents an interesting case study for two main reasons: on the one hand, it is a TESOL context traditionally seen as belonging to the Expanding Circle, where native-modeled TEFL has dominated and still does; and, on the other, it is a societal context where both intranational and international communication increasingly require intercultural communication skills. For both of these reasons, Greek TESOL represents a rich site for exploring what teaching and learning paradigms might be appropriate in a post-TEFL, ELF-inflected intercultural age and, importantly, how such repositioning debates might be stimulated (e.g. through the teacher awareness projects mentioned above, i.e. Sifakis, 2014; Sifakis & Bayyurt, in press) by building upon the affordances of, but also recognising the obstacles provided by, the educational discourses and curricular documents in this Greek context. Our main contribution is the proposal for an interculturally inflected pedagogic response to ELF consisting of both intranational (i.e. MATE) and international (i.e. TEIL) dimensions. We see these two complementary paradigms as being interculturally driven and ELF-informed pedagogic responses to the post-TEFL moment in English language education in Greece, and offer them here in the hope that they may also have relevance beyond the particularities of Greece and its TESOL context.

Acknowledgements

We are grateful to Richard West, an ESP specialist formerly of the University of Manchester, for drawing our attention to Close's (1959) discussions of ESP.

References

Adaskou, K., Britten, D. and Fahsi, B. (1990) Design decisions on the cultural content of a secondary English course for Morocco. *English Language Teaching Journal* 44 (1), 3–10.
Agelopoulos, G. (2000) Political practices and multiculturalism: the case of Salonica. In J. Cowan (ed.) *Macedonia: The Politics of Identity and Difference* (pp. 140–155). London: Pluto Press.
Alptekin, C. (1993) Target culture in EFL materials. *English Language Teaching Journal* 47 (2), 136–143.
Alptekin, C. (2002) Towards intercultural communicative competence in ELT. *English Language Teaching Journal* 56 (1), 57–64.
Alptekin, C. and Alptekin, M. (1984) The question of culture: EFL teaching in non-English-speaking countries. *English Language Teaching Journal* 38 (2), 14–20.
Alvarez, I. (2007) Foreign language education at the crossroads: Whose model of competence? *Language, Culture and Curriculum* 20 (2), 126–139.
Androussou, A. (1996) An intercultural dimension in educational practice. In A. Vafea (coordinator) *The Multicultural School: An Experience of Intercultural Education through Art* (pp. 11–23). Athens: Nisos.
Baker, W. (2011) Intercultural awareness: Modelling an understanding of cultures in intercultural communication through English as a lingua franca. *Language and Intercultural Communication* 11 (3), 197–214.
Bamgbose, A. (1998) Torn between the norms: Innovations in World Englishes. *World Englishes* 17 (1), 1–13.

Baxter, J. (1983) English for intercultural competence: An approach to intercultural communication training. In D. Landis and R.W. Brislin (eds) *Handbook of Intercultural Training* (vol. 1, pp. 290–324). Oxford: Pergamon Press.
Block, D. and Cameron, D. (eds) (2002) *Globalization and Language Teaching*. London: Routledge.
Braine, G. (ed.) (1999) *Nonnative Educators in English Language Teaching*. Mahwah, NJ: Lawrence Erlbaum Associates.
British Council (1978) *English as an International Language* (ELT Docs). London: British Council.
Brown, K. (1995) World Englishes: To teach or not to teach? *World Englishes* 14 (2), 233–246.
Brutt-Griffler, J. (2002) *World English: A Study of Its Development*. Clevedon: Multilingual Matters.
Brutt-Griffler, J. and Samimy, K.K. (2001) Transcending the nativeness paradigm. *World Englishes* 20 (1), 99–106.
Canagarajah, A.S. (1999) *Resisting Linguistic Imperialism in English Teaching*. Oxford: Oxford University Press.
Cenoz, J. and Jessner, U. (eds) (2000) *English in Europe: The Acquisition of a Third Language*. Clevedon: Multilingual Matters.
Close, R.A. (1959) English as World English. *The Linguist's Review* 1 (6), 116–117.
Close, R.A. (1965) *The English We Use for Science*. London: Longman.
Close, R.A. (1981) *English as a Foreign Language: Its Constant Grammatical Problems*. London: HarperCollins.
Conrad, S. and Mauranen, A. (2003) The corpus of English as a lingua franca in academic settings. *TESOL Quarterly* 37 (3), 513–527.
Cook, V. (1999) Going beyond the native speaker in language teaching. *TESOL Quarterly* 33 (2), 185–209.
Corbett, J. (2003) *An Intercultural Approach to English Language Teaching*. Clevedon: Multilingual Matters.
Cortazzi, M. and Jin, L. (1996) Cultures of learning: Language classrooms in China. In H. Coleman (ed.) *Society and the Language Classroom* (pp. 169–205). Cambridge: Cambridge University Press.
Cortazzi, M. and Jin, L. (1999) Cultural mirrors: Materials and methods in the EFL classroom. In E. Hinkel (ed.) *Culture in Second Language Teaching and Learning* (pp. 196–219). Cambridge: Cambridge University Press.
Crystal, D. (1997) *English as a Global Language*. Cambridge: Cambridge University Press.
Davies, A. (2003) *The Native Speaker: Myth or Reality*. Clevedon: Multilingual Matters.
Edge, J. (ed.) (2006) *(Re)Locating TESOL in an Age of Empire*. Basingstoke: Palgrave Macmillan.
Fay, R. (1996) Boundaries, thresholds and participant perceptions: Intercultural awareness in an ELT context. In S. Sebbage and T. Sebbage (eds) *Paper given at the Fifth International NELLE Conference (19–22 September 1996, Zaragoza, Spain, Languages through Culture; Culture through Languages) and published in the proceedings*, (pp. 54–59). Bielefeld: NELLE.
Fay, R. (1997) Intercultural communication as a specific purpose. Paper given at the VII Congreso Luso-Hispano de Lenguas Aplicadas a Las Ciencias y La Technologia (28–31 May 1997, Jarandilla, Spain); subsequently published in R. Marín Chamorro and A. Romero Navarrete (eds) *Lenguas Aplicadas a Las Ciencias y La Technología: Aproximaciones* (pp. 319–326). Caceres, Spain: University of Extremadura.

Fay, R. and Hyde, M. (1999) Language norms and intercultural competence: Target norms and effective negotiation. Paper given at the SIETAR Europa Congress 1999, Trieste, Italy; published in A. Cuk and F. Del Campo (eds) *One Community and Many Languages: On the Crossroads of a New Europe (SIETAR Europa Proceedings 1999)* (pp. 266–275). Trieste: Batello Stampatore.

Fay, R., Lytra, V. and Ntavaliagkou, M. (2010) Multicultural awareness through English: A potential contribution of TESOL in Greek schools. *Intercultural Education* 21 (6), 579–593.

Firth, A. (1996) The discursive accomplishment of normality. On 'Lingua franca' English and conversation analysis. *Journal of Pragmatics* 26 (2), 237–259.

Gnutzmann, C. (ed.) (1999) *Teaching and Learning English as a Global Language*. Tubingen: Staffenburg.

Gnutzmann, C. and Intemann, F. (eds) (2005) *The Globalisation of English and the English Language Classroom*. Tubingen: Gunter Narr Verlag.

Goethals, M. (undated) The use of English as an International Language (EIL) and/or Lingua Franca (ELF) in transnational programmes of learning and in on-line in-service teacher training. Paper delivered at a conference in Shenyang, China, in 2007. See https://sites.google.com/site/englishconvers10/information/michael-s-teaching-principles (accessed 30 May 2013).

Gogonas, N. (2010) *Bilingualism and Multilingualism in Greek Education: Investigating Ethnic Language Maintenance Among Pupils of Albanian and Egyptian Origin in Athens*. Newcastle upon Tyne: Cambridge Scholars Publishing.

Graddol, D. (1997) *The Future of English? A Guide to Forecasting the Popularity of the English Language in the 21st Century*. London: British Council. http://www.britishcouncil.org/learning-research-futureofenglish.htm

Graddol, D. (2006) *English Next. Why Global English May Mean the End of 'English as a Foreign Language'*. London: British Council. http://www.britishcouncil.org/learning-research-englishnext.htm

Grundy, P. (2004) Methodology and the pragmatics of English as an international language. *Journal of Asia TEFL* 1 (1), 23–46.

Hassall, P.J. (1996) 'Where do we go from here?' TEIL: A methodology, *World Englishes* 15 (3), 419–425.

Heiman, J.D. (1994) Western culture in EFL language instruction. *TESOL Journal* 3 (3), 4–7.

Holliday, A. (2005) *The Struggle to Teach English as an International Language*. Oxford: Oxford University Press.

Holmes, P. and Derwin, F. (2011) The cultural and intercultural dimensions of English as a lingua franca (book proposal). (mimeo)

Jenkins, J. (1998) Which pronunciation norms and models for English as an International Language? *English Language Teaching Journal* 52 (2), 119–126.

Jenkins, J. (2000) *The Phonology of English as an International Language: New Models, New Norms, New Goals*. Oxford: Oxford University Press.

Jenkins, J. (2003) *World Englishes: A Resource Book for Students*. London: Routledge.

Jenkins, J. (2004) The ABC of ELT ... 'ELF': In this issue, Jennifer Jenkins looks at English as a lingua franca. *IATEFL Issues* 182, 9.

Jenkins, J. (2007a) ELF: English as a lingua franca - Coffee with Jennifer Jenkins. *IATEFL Issues* 103, 8–10.

Jenkins, J. (2007b) *English as a Lingua Franca: Attitude and Identity*. Oxford: Oxford University Press.

Kachru, B.B. (1985) Standards, codification and sociolinguistic realism: The English Language in the Outer Circle. In R. Quirk and H.G. Widdowson (eds) *English in the World* (pp. 11–34). Cambridge: Cambridge University Press.

Kirkpatrick, A. (2007) *World Englishes. Implications for International Communication and English Language Teaching.* Cambridge: Cambridge University Press.

Kramsch, C., Cain, A. and Murphy-Lejeune, E. (1996) Why should language teachers teach culture? *Language, Culture and Curriculum* 9 (1), 99–107.

Kubota, R. (2001) Teaching World Englishes to native-speakers of English in the USA. *World Englishes* 20 (1), 47–64.

Kuo, I-Chun (2006) Addressing the issue of teaching English as a lingua franca. *English Language Teaching Journal* 60 (3), 213–221.

Lessard-Clouston, M. (1996) Chinese teachers' views of culture in their EFL learning and teaching. *Language Culture and Curriculum* 9 (3), 197–224.

Lester, M. (1978) International English and language variation. In British Council (1978) *English as an International Language* (ELT Docs) (pp. 6–14) London: British Council.

Levine, D. and Adelman, M. (1982) *Beyond Language: Intercultural Communication for English as a Second Language.* Englewood Cliffs, NJ: Prentice Hall.

Llurda, E. (2004) Non-native-speaker teachers and English as an International Language. *International Journal of Applied Linguistics* 14 (3), 314–323.

Lytra, V. (2007) *Play Frames and Social Identities: Contact Encounters in a Greek Primary School.* Amsterdam and Philadelphia: John Benjamins.

McKay, S.L. (2002) *Teaching English as an International Language: Rethinking Goals and Objectives.* Oxford: Oxford University Press.

McKay, S.L. (2004) Teaching English as an international language: The role of culture in Asian contexts. *Journal of Asia TEFL* 1 (1), 1–22.

Medgyes, P. (1992) Native or non-native: Who's worth more? *English Language Teaching Journal* 46 (4), 340–349.

Medgyes, P. (1994) *The Non-Native Teacher.* London: Macmillan.

Melchers, G. and Shaw, P. (2003) *World Englishes.* London: Arnold.

Merkestein, A. (1998) Deculturalising Englishes: The Botswana context. *World Englishes* 17 (2), 171–185.

Modiano, M. (2001) Linguistic imperialism, cultural integrity, and EIL. *English Language Teaching Journal* 55 (4), 339–346.

Pakir, A. (1999) Connecting with English in the context of internationalisation. *TESOL Quarterly* 33 (1), 103–114.

Pennycook, A. (1994) *The Cultural Politics of English as an International Language.* London: Longman.

Phillipson, R. (1992a) ELT: The native-speaker's burden? *English Language Teaching Journal* 46 (1), 12–18.

Phillipson, R. (1992b) *Linguistic Imperialism.* Oxford: Oxford University Press.

Prodromou, L. (1988) English as cultural action. *English Language Teaching Journal* 42 (2), 73–83.

Prodromou, L. (1992) What culture? Which culture? Cross-cultural factors in language learning. *English Language Teaching Journal* 46 (1), 39–50.

Rajagopalan, K. (1999) Of ELF teachers, conscience and cowardice. *English Language Teaching Journal* 53 (3), 200–260.

Rampton, M.B.H. (1990) Displacing the 'native speaker': Expertise, affiliation and inheritance. *English Language Teaching Journal* 44 (2), 97–101.

Risager, K. (2006) *Language and Culture: Global Flows and Local Complexity*. Clevedon: Multilingual Matters.

Schnitzer, E. (1995) English as an International Language: Implications for interculturalists and language educators. *International Journal of Intercultural Relations* 19 (2), 227–236.

Seidlhofer, B. (2001) Closing a conceptual gap: The case for a description of English as a lingua franca. *International Journal of Applied Linguistics* 11 (2), 133–158.

Seidlhofer, B. (2004) Research perspectives on teaching English as a lingua franca. *Annual Review of Applied Linguistics* 24, 209–239.

Seidlhofer, B. (2005) English as a lingua franca (key concepts in ELT). *English Language Teaching Journal* 59 (4), 339–341.

Sharifian, F. (ed.) (2009) *English as an International Language: Perspectives and Pedagogical Issues*. Bristol: Multilingual Matters.

Sifakis, N. (2004) Teaching EIL – Teaching international or intercultural English? What teachers should know. *System* 32 (2), 237–250.

Sifakis, N. (2007) The education of teachers of English as a lingua franca: A transformative perspective. *International Journal of Applied Linguistics* 17 (3), 355–375.

Sifakis, N. (2009) Challenges in teaching ELF in the periphery: The Greek context. *English Language Teaching Journal* 63 (3), 230–237.

Sifakis, N. (2014) ELF awareness as an opportunity for change: A transformative perspective for ESOL teacher education. *Journal of English as a Lingua Franca* 3 (2), 317 – 335.

Sifakis, N. and Bayyurt, Y. (in press) Educating the ELF-aware teacher: Insights from a teacher training project. *World Englishes*.

Sifakis, N. and Fay, R. (2011) Integrating an ELF pedagogy in a changing world: The case of Greek state schooling. In A. Archibald, A. Cogo and J. Jenkins (eds) *Latest Trends in ELF Research* (pp. 285–289). Newcastle upon Tyne: Cambridge Scholars Press.

Sifakis, N. and Sougari. A.-M. (2003) Facing the globalisation challenge in the realm of English language teaching. *Language and Education* 17 (1), 59–71.

Sifakis, N. and Sougari. A.-M. (2005) Pronunciation issues and EIL pedagogy in the periphery: A survey of Greek state school teachers' beliefs. *TESOL Quarterly* 39 (3), 467–488.

Sifakis, N., Lytra, V. and Fay, R. (2010) English as a lingua franca in an increasingly post-EFL era: The case of English in the Greek state education curriculum. Paper presented at the Third International Conference on English as a Lingua Franca, 22–25 May 2010, the University of Vienna, Austria.

Sifakis, N., Lytra, V. and Fay, R. (2012) Curricular discourses and ELF in the Greek state school context. Paper presented at the Fifth International Conference on English as a Lingua Franca, 24–26 May 2012, Boðaziçi University, Faculty of Education, Department of Foreign Language Education, Istanbul, Turkey.

Smith, L.E. (1976) English as an international auxiliary language. *RELC Journal* 7 (2), 38–42.

Smith, L.E. (1978) Some distinctive features of EIIL vs. ESOL in English language education. *Cultural Learning Institute Report* 5 (3).

Smith, L.E. (ed.) (1981) *English for Cross-Cultural Communication*. London: Macmillan.

Smith, L.E. (ed.) (1983) *Readings in English as an International Language*. Oxford: Pergamon.

Smith, L.E. (ed.) (1987) *Discourse Across Cultures: Strategies in World Englishes*. London: Prentice Hall.

Smith, L.E. and Foreman, M.L. (eds) (1997) *World Englishes 2000*. Honolulu: College of Languages, Linguistics, and Literature, University of Hawai'i Press.

Smith, L.E. and Rafiqzad, K. (1979) English for cross-cultural communication: The question of intelligibility. *TESOL Quarterly* 13 (3), 371-380.
Stapleton, P. (2000) Culture's role in TEFL: An attitude survey in Japan. *Language, Culture and Curriculum* 13 (3), 291-305.
Strevens, P. (1992) English as an international language: Directions in the 1990s. In B.B. Kachru (ed.) *The Other Tongue: English Across Cultures* (2nd edn, pp. 27-47). Urbana: University of Illinois Press.
Timmis, I. (2002) Native-speaker norms and international English: A classroom view. *English Language Teaching Journal* 56 (3), 240-249.
Widdowson, H.G. (1994) The ownership of English. *TESOL Quarterly* 28 (2), 377-381.
Widdowson, H.G. (1997) EIL, ESL, EFL: Global issues and local interests. *World Englishes* 16 (1), 135-46.
Widdowson, H.G. (1998) EIL: Squaring the circles. A reply. *World Englishes* 17 (3), 397-401.
Yiakoumaki, V. (2007) Ethnic Turks and 'Muslims', and the performance of multiculturalism: The case of the Drómeno of Thrace. In D. Theodossopoulos (ed.) *What Greeks Think About Turks: The View From Anthropology* (pp. 145-161). London: Routledge.
Νόμος 2413/17-6-96. ΦΕΚ 124Α. Η Ελληνική Παιδεία στο Εξωτερικό, η Διαπολισμική Εκπαίδευση και άλλες Διατάξεις [Law 2413/17-6-96. FEK 124A. Greek Education Abroad, Intercultural Education and other Articles]. See http://isocrates.minedu.gov.gr/content_by_cat.asp?contentid=355&catid=38&how=&keywords=(accessed 30 May 2013).
Υπουργείο Παιδείας, Δια Βίου Μάθησης και Θρησκευμάτων. Ειδική Γραμματεία Παιδείας Ομογενών και Διαπολιτισμικής Εκπαίδευσης. [Ministry of Education, Continuing Education and Religious Education. Special Secretariat for the Education of Greeks Abroad and Intercultural Education]. See http://isocrates.minedu.gov.gr/content_by_cat.asp?catid=165 (accessed 30 May 2013).

3 Culture and Language in Intercultural Communication, English as a Lingua Franca and English Language Teaching: Points of Convergence and Conflict

Will Baker

Introduction

English as a lingua franca (ELF) studies, intercultural communication research and English language teaching (ELT) have all been concerned with ideas of 'successful' communication and the competencies needed to achieve this. While all three fields have recognised the importance of language and culture in understanding communication, little agreement has been reached on how to characterise the relationship between language and culture or how this relates to 'competent' communication. This chapter will therefore investigate the convergences and conflicts among the fields of ELF studies, applied linguistics research in intercultural communication and ELT in terms of their perspectives on language and culture. These issues are explored first through a discussion of how culture has been conceived of in ELT and a critique of the often essentialist manner in which this has been done, followed by an examination of intercultural communication studies as related to language teaching. A distinction is drawn between essentialist approaches and more recent dynamic characterisation of intercultural communication. How culture and intercultural communication have been conceptualised in ELF is then presented, highlighting features of the intercultural communication literature which have been drawn on and also a number of points of difference.

I argue herein that ELF studies add to the growing body of postmodernist thinking and research in applied linguistics that can inform intercultural communication research through underscoring the dynamic and fluid manner in which form, function and context are constructed in intercultural communication through English as a lingua franca. At the same time, intercultural communication research can be of use to ELF studies through the extensive body of work exploring conceptions of intercultural communicative competence (ICC). Crucially, it is this focus on ICC and communicative competence that ELT, intercultural communication studies and ELF share. However, ELF research emphasises the importance of a conceptualisation of ICC in which language and culture are seen as emergent resources in intercultural communication which need to be approached critically. To this end, the notion of intercultural awareness is proposed as a dynamic framework for intercultural competence. Such critical perspectives in understanding intercultural communication through ELF and associated notions of competencies have fundamental implications for ELT which have yet to be adequately taken up in theory or practice.

Examining Culture and Language in ELT, Intercultural Communication and ELF

Culture and language in ELT: Essentialism and neglect

Within applied linguistics and language teaching there has generally been a consensus that language and culture are closely linked often to the extent of seeing them as inseparably intertwined. Such a perspective has drawn on ethnographic and sociolinguistic understandings which see language as the primary semiotic resource which both enacts and creates much of our cultural context (Geertz, 1973; Halliday, 1979) as well as sociocultural theories of learning that view language learning as a socially situated activity (Lantolf & Thorne, 2006). This 'marriage of language and culture' (Risager, 2007: 73), has given rise to a number of influential approaches in language teaching since the 1990s that have attempted to bring culture into the classroom in a more overt and systematic manner and, in so doing taking, a more intercultural stance to language education (see for example Byram, 1997, 2008; Kramsch, 1993, 1998, 2009).

Many of the earlier approaches (for example Valdes, 1986) often took a simplistic, or essentialist, notion of culture and language in which they were seen as 'inexorably' linked as in the strongest interpretation of linguistic relativity (Whorf, 1939). Such approaches proposed that particular languages contained and constructed particular cultures in unique ways that meant that the two were inseparable. Thus, Valdes writes that 'language, culture, and thought... the current consensus is that the three aspects are three parts of a whole' (1986: 1) and that 'a native culture is as much of an *interference* for second language learners as is native language' (1986: 2, my italics).

Despite advances in the field, such attitudes persist. For example, in the influential *ELT Journal* Sybing claims that 'native-speaker culture cannot simply be separated from a language that has already left its cultural imprint on non-English-speaking cultures' (2011: 467). The suggestion is that 'English' culture is inexorably linked to both the linguistic forms and communicative practices of the language. The influence of this perspective can still be seen in language teaching approaches and materials which associate a particular language with a nationally defined culture.

Thus, in much ELT, English is typically associated with the US or UK or other 'traditional' Anglophone countries. This association is reflected in the continued influence of reified models of native English speakers (NES) from these Anglophone 'cultures' and remains the most common approach to culture in textbooks and teaching materials (Cortazzi & Jin, 1999; Vettorel, 2010). Furthermore, despite the extensive discussion of culture and language teaching in the research and theoretical literature, in practice, culture and the intercultural have remained relatively low in teachers' priorities (Sercu, 2005; Young & Sachdev, 2011). Both this neglect of the intercultural dimension to language teaching and the essentialist, nationalist correlations between languages and cultures are problematic for ELT when we consider that English is predominantly used for intercultural communication as a lingua franca and in ways which are frequently not related to predefined national cultures.

Culture and language in intercultural communication and language teaching: Alternatives, expansions and limitations

An overview of the different approaches to intercultural communication research is not within the scope of this chapter[1]; however, it is worth noting an important dichotomy identified by Scollon and Scollon (2001) between earlier 'cross-cultural studies' and 'intercultural studies'. The distinction is of course something of an essentialisation in itself and more nuanced cross-cultural research is possible (as discussed by Spencer-Oatey & Franklin

(2009); see also the special issue of *Language and Intercultural Communication* (2012, 12/4)). Nonetheless, in cross-cultural studies cultures have been viewed as relatively homogenous and bounded entities at the national level which could be compared as distinct 'units' (*cf.* Hall, 1979; Hofstede, 1991). Scollon and Scollon (2001) contrast this with intercultural approaches which study intercultural interaction (as opposed to comparing 'cultures') and adopt a more dynamic characterisation of cultures in which the boundaries between one culture and the next are blurred and where national cultures are one of many communities that individuals orientate towards (Scollon & Scollon, 2001). Furthermore, cultures are viewed as heterogeneous with individuals differing in the extent to which they may identify with national cultures and also contesting different interpretations of cultures. Following this, Scollon *et al.* (2012) advocate a 'discourse' approach to culture in which participants in intercultural communication are seen as drawing on a multitude of discourse systems such as gender, profession and generation.

In relation to intercultural communication and language teaching, the main focus of this chapter, this discourse approach has been developed most influentially by Kramsch (1993, 1998). Kramsch's oft-quoted definition of culture is '(1) membership in a discourse community that shares a common social space and history, and a common system of standards for perceiving, believing, evaluating, and acting. (2) The discourse community itself. (3) The system of standards itself' (1998: 127). She further suggests that intercultural communication should be viewed as taking place on a 'cultural faultline' (1993: 205) in which linguistic and cultural practices and products occupy a 'third space' (1993: 233) that is neither part of the language users' first language and culture (L1/C1) or the target language and culture (L2/C2). However, although these characterisations of using an L2 highlight the fluidity of such communication and emphasise the need to move away from L1/C1 and L2/C2 norms, they still retain the notion of established 'target' communities with which particular languages are associated. This is problematic in that for intercultural communication through ELF it is not clear what particular target communities and language norms the communication is 'in between'.

Last, the notion of global flows has been drawn on in both intercultural communication and language education literature. Canagarajah (2005), in an examination of global uses of English and English teaching, views cultures as hybrid, diffuse and deterritorialised with constant movement between different local and global communities. Pennycook discusses 'the ways in which cultural forms move, change and are reused to fashion new identities in diverse contexts' (2007: 6). Similarly, Risager (2007) discusses transnational flows of linguistic and cultural practices that involve a divergent approach to understanding their relationships and offers 'a theoretically justified alternative to the national paradigm' (2007: 195) in language teaching. Both Canagarajah and Pennycook also underline the tensions that alternative contextualisations of culture and language contain, for Canagarajah in relation to local and global settings and for Pennycook as 'caught between fluidity and fixity, then, cultural and linguistic forms are always in a state of flux, always changing, always part of a process of the refashioning of identity' (Pennycook, 2007: 8).

All three authors offer perspectives of relevance to intercultural communication through ELF; however, the extent to which their positions are fully commensurable with ELF studies is debatable. Risager, despite advocating a transnational approach, still believes that native speaking communities provide the most appropriate models of language use and rejects ELF approaches stating that 'the ultimate aim (the decisive model) for language learning must be a variety (or several) used by native speakers or near native speakers' (2007: 197). In contrast to Risager's wish to take a more normative approach than ELF would suggest, Pennycook (2010) and Canagarajah (2013) claim that ELF studies are too normative in attempting to account for homogenous features of what are heterogeneous interactions and reifying distinctions between different linguistic and cultural groups such as native, non-native speakers and monolingual, multilingual communication. However, while such concerns are valid, these views are based on a misinterpretation of the majority of current ELF research, as will be explained below.

Culture and language in ELF

ELF[2] research has, unsurprisingly, given the multifarious contexts in which English is used, eschewed essentialist correlations between national conceptions of language and culture as regards English. The key notions of variability, fluidity and emergence[3] in ELF, in which any descriptions of 'features' of ELF are viewed as snapshots of an ongoing process (Jenkins et al., 2011; Seidlhofer, 2011), are likely to be equally applicable to understanding the relationship between culture and language in ELF. However, researchers in ELF studies have proposed that ELF might in some way be a culturally neutral means of communication (House, 2014) or at least capable of existing on a continuum between neutrality and being used to construct identity and cultures (Kirkpatrick, 2007; Meierkord, 2002). This position, while avoiding essentialist associations of language and culture at the nation level, nonetheless takes an equally untenable stance in proposing that 'neutral' language and communication is possible. As with all communication, languages in intercultural communication 'are never just neutral' (Phipps & Guilherme, 2004: 1); communication always involves participants, contexts, histories, purposes and linguistic choices, none of which are neutral.

Although the concept of culture has received comparatively little attention in ELF research, the related notion of identity has begun to be dealt with quite extensively (e.g. Baker, 2011b; Canagarajah, 2007; Jenkins, 2007; Phan, 2008). These studies illustrate how ELF, as with any language use, is utilised to construct identity, but, in common with much postmodern research in linguistics and outside it (cf. Bauman, 2004; Kramsch, 2009; Sarup, 1996), the types of identifications constructed are often fluid, emergent and multiple with participants identifying with a range of different communities. Dewey (2007), Ehrenreich (2009) and Seidlhofer (2007, 2011) all adopt the notion of communities of practice (Wenger, 1998) to explain the types of dynamic and temporary communities that ELF users may form and identify with. However, they add the caveat that communities of practice need to be treated as more fluid than originally envisaged and that they are perhaps better seen as 'constellations of interconnected practice' (Wenger, 1998, cited in Ehrenreich, 2009: 134). Nevertheless, with the exception of Ehrenreich (2009), little empirical data is presented to support these claims.

Baker's research on uses of ELF in Thailand (2009, 2011a, 2011b, 2012b) provides one of the few examples of studies that draw on empirical data to explicitly deal with conceptualisations of culture in ELF. Making use of the intercultural communication literature discussed earlier related to notions of global flows, third places and communities of practice, Baker suggests that ELF is used to refer to communities and cultures that are salient to the communication at hand and also to create new cultural practices and products (2009: 577–579). Baker's data show ELF users drawing on multiple cultural frames of reference in the same conversation and moving between and across local, national and global contexts in dynamic ways. Crucially, the data highlight new cultural products, practices and interpretations emerging from ELF communication. This is demonstrated in the extract below (Baker, 2009: 581–582) taken from a recording of a conversation in a café in Bangkok. The two speakers, Nami (Thai L1 speaker) and Philippe (Belgian French L1 speaker), are discussing the game of petanque.

Extract 1

1 **PHILIPPE**: no Marseilles is really nice really nice city south of France close you have
2 Nice Cannes it's really cool the food is amazing and they drink err Ricard
3 **NAMI**: Ricard
4 **PHILIPPE**: they play err petanque

5   **NAMI**: err
6   **PHILIPPE**: petanque
7   **NAMI**: petanque ahh petanque
8   **PHILIPPE**: yeah (¿)
9   **NAMI**: there's some there's some people from my school that
10 **PHILIPPE**: you know that the French embassy they organise err a
11 championship every year in Thailand
12 **NAMI**: yeah
13 **PHILIPPE**: I've been there a few times
14 **NAMI**: do you play
15 **PHILIPPE**: ah
16 **NAMI**: do you play
17 **PHILIPPE**: no. I'm shit
18 **NAMI**: [laughs] you're really young [laughs]
19 **PHILIPPE**: I know you have to be really old to play that game
20 **NAMI**: NO [laughs]
21 **PHILIPPE**: maybe I'm not old enough
22 **NAMI**: no at school a lot of young students play petanque
23 **PHILIPPE**: maybe they think it's cool …uhu

Their discussion of petanque moves from national and regional associations (Southern France), to more global contexts (the French Embassy in Bangkok), to other local associations (school students in Thailand). Importantly, the discussion also leads to alternative perceptions of the game beginning with Philippe's assertion that you have to be old to play the game (Line 19), to Nami's claim that it is also a game for the young in her experience (Line 22) and to Philippe's acceptance that other interpretations of the game are possible (Line 23), with no one interpretation appearing dominant.

Thus, contrary to what has been claimed (Canagarajah, 2013; Pennycook, 2010), ELF interpretations of culture and the links with language, as presented here, have generally eschewed binary distinctions between particular languages and cultures characteristic of earlier intercultural communication research. In contrast, ELF research has adopted postmodernist approaches to the relationship between culture and language entailing fluid, dynamic and multiple viewpoints. This is not to deny that more normative influences often associated with national languages and cultures may exist; and indeed, the tension between normativity and creativity, fixity and fluidity has been a major part of the discussion of ELF communication in general (Seidlhofer, 2011) and in relation to identity and culture (Baker, 2009, 2011a, 2011b; Jenkins, 2007).

Therefore, alongside recognition of these more established local, national or global language and cultural links, we need conceptions of culture and language where the relationship is viewed as contingent and emergent and not 'between' any particular communities. Furthermore, the relevance of any cultural category, whether fixed or fluid, is similarly emergent and cannot be assumed *a priori*; we should always question how and why such categories are used. This is not to suggest that this is unique to ELF, indeed Björkman (2013) details a number of reasons for not regarding ELF communication as *sui generis*. Nonetheless, ELF researchers in viewing culture and language in this manner contribute to a necessary critique of how we understand and what we regard as necessary for successful intercultural communication and the associated concept of intercultural competence.

Rethinking Communicative and Intercultural Competence

Communicative competence

Understanding effective communication, however that might be defined, has been a central driving force in all three fields under discussion here. However, the characterisations of language and culture in ELF research present a number of challenges to current conceptions. Within ELT and intercultural communication this interest in 'effective communication' has also been combined with approaches to teaching and training that aim to develop the appropriate knowledge, skills and attitudes in learners to accomplish successful communication. The core of understanding successful communication in ELT has been communicative competence. There is general agreement in language teaching that communicative competence has proved to be a fruitful concept and an appropriate pedagogic goal; however, there is also considerable debate as to what this competence entails. Although there are many aspects of this debate, the issues that are of relevance to the discussion here are the models of communicator, community and communication that are envisaged in this competence. Both Chomsky's (1965) and Hymes' (1972) original formulations, although different in many ways, were focused on communication between native speakers of a language in a defined community. This has been carried through to ELT in Canale and Swain's (1980) seminal paper, which, with the exception of strategic competence, focused on the sort of language and communication we might expect between an idealised homogenous community of speakers and such assumptions are still pervasive in much ELT literature (for critiques see Jenkins, 2007; Seidlhofer, 2011; Widdowson, 2012).

In fact, the realities of intercultural and lingua franca communication, particularly through ELF, have challenged many of these original assumptions. The appropriateness of measuring competence against an ill-defined and imaginary native English speaker (NES) baseline is questionable in relation to the types of communication many language learners and users of English engage in. For communication through ELF in the majority of instances NES are not present and when they are they need to adapt their communicative practices to their interlocutors in the same way as other participants. Equally important is the challenge intercultural communication and ELF raises for understanding community and, as detailed above, we need more dynamic accounts of community and any associated communicative conventions. Thus, the notion of a homogenous community of native speakers, as imagined in much ELT,[4] to which learners of the language are moving toward, is of little relevance, despite its prevalence. As has already been suggested, what is needed is an understanding of communication from a multilingual and multicultural perspective with an accompanying range of knowledge, skills and attitudes related to successful communication in this sphere. The challenge of detailing these knowledge, skills and attitudes has been taken up extensively in intercultural communication studies, particularly related to intercultural education and language teaching, and more recently in ELF research as well (Baker, 2011; Cogo & Dewey, 2012; Jenkins *et al.*, 2011).

Intercultural communicative competence

Within intercultural communication studies the notion of intercultural competence has been as central as communicative competence has been in ELT. As with the discussion of communicative competence, there is not space here for a comprehensive overview of the field. Instead the focus will be on one of the most influential approaches in applied linguistics and language pedagogy, intercultural communicative competence (ICC) as developed by Byram (1997). ICC was not proposed as a rejection of communicative competence but as an extension of it that took greater account of the intercultural dimension to using a foreign language, while retaining many of the original elements of communicative competence (Byram, 1997: 73). This extension involves a range of knowledge, skills and attitudes related to interacting with those from other cultures. These include an awareness of our own and others' cultures, the ability to compare between cultures, an awareness of the relative nature of cultural norms and the ability to mediate between different cultures. Importantly, the inappropriate native speaker model was replaced with an alternative model of the 'intercultural speaker' (1997: 31). Although this approach recognised the multi-voiced nature of cultural characterisations, it still retained the association between cultures and particular countries and binary distinctions between 'Our' and 'Other' cultures, as illustrated in the definition of a crucial component of ICC, critical cultural awareness, 'an ability to evaluate critically and on the basis of explicit criteria perspectives, practices and products in *one's own* and *other cultures and countries*' (1997: 53, my italics). Furthermore, initial formulations of ICC rooted in nationalist characterisations of culture contained little on the role of language and culture on a more global scale.

Byram's conception of ICC has been further developed by a number of scholars such as Guilherme (2002), who take a more critical approach to culture and deal with the tensions between multi-voiced, heterogeneous accounts of cultures and the more homogeneous, national characterisations of cultures often used in foreign language education. Risager (2007) in particular explicitly addresses the global nature of languages and language learning. In her conception of the intercultural competence of the world citizen she attempts to transcend the national paradigm, associated with earlier concepts of ICC, with a transnational paradigm (2007: 222). Byram has also further developed ICC through the related idea of intercultural citizenship (2008), with language users viewed from a more global perspective in which they may relate to other proficient intercultural communicators and less clearly defined national cultural groupings.

Nevertheless, even these critical heterogeneous understandings of culture still centred on differences and/or similarities within national cultural boundaries rather than those which transcended them. Crucially, the dichotomy between 'Our' culture and language and a foreign 'Other' culture and language is retained (Baker, 2011a; Holliday, 2011). Although Risager's transnational paradigm goes some way towards moving beyond seeing cultures solely in national terms, she retains the notion of native speakers as the model (as discussed above) and languages and cultures as belonging to identifiable target communities, even if they are now a diaspora: 'The *target-language community* is not confined to a nationally defined language area but exists in a linguistic network with a potentially global range, mainly as a result of transnational migration and communication' (2007: 236, my italics). Thus, the notion of intercultural competence here still involves competencies associated with pre-defined communities and native speakers, both of which are of questionable relevance to ELF communication.

Symbolic competence

An alternative to ICC is offered by Kramsch's notion of symbolic competence (2009, 2011). Symbolic competence, as with ICC, does not reject communicative competence, but instead seeks to incorporate a more reflexive perspective that addresses the ideological, historic and aesthetic aspects of intercultural communication and language teaching (2010: 354). As previously noted, Kramsch's use of 'third cultures' can be criticised as reifying distinctions between learners' cultures/languages and other 'target' cultures/languages. Kramsch herself has been very aware of this and symbolic competence has come about as a response in which 'the notion of third culture must be seen less as a place than as a symbolic process of meaning-making that sees beyond the dualities of national languages (L1-L2) and national cultures (C1-C2)' (2010: 354). Thus, symbolic competence is described as a 'dynamic, flexible and locally contingent competence' (2009: 200).

This realisation moves us beyond a competence associated with knowledge of the cultural and communicative practices of particular groups and into more emergent terrain, in which competence involves a reflexive stance to the communication at hand, 'embracing multiple, changing and conflicting discourse worlds' (Kramsch, 2011: 356) and a critical awareness of the symbolic systems being used to construct any representation of culture. Such an approach to intercultural competence would seem well suited to ELF communication in which evaluations of successful communication are likely to be equally 'dynamic, flexible and locally contingent', and will be returned to later in this regard; however, Kramsch remains silent on the issue of languages as a lingua franca.

Alternative approaches: Intercultural awareness

Within ELF studies there has also been a concern with successful communication. One of the earliest features noted was that despite the expected difficulties, ELF communication was on the whole surprisingly successful (Firth, 1996). Much of this success has been attributed to the communication strategies observed in communication through ELF. Seidlhofer and Widdowson go so far to suggest that 'it may turn out that what is distinctive about ELF lies in the communicative strategies that its speakers use' (2009: 37). Although, as suggested above, the extent to which ELF is 'distinctive' to other forms of intercultural communication is debatable, the quotation underscores the recognition in ELF research of the central role of communicative strategies.

In contrast to communicative competence, these communication strategies are those associated with multilingual and multicultural communication (Canagarajah, 2007; Jenkins, 2007; Seidlhofer, 2011). There have been various suggestions as to what these might be, but all seem to include pragmatic strategies such as accommodation, code-switching, preempting misunderstanding and letting unimportant misunderstandings pass, linguistic awareness, cultural awareness and the ability to adapt linguistic forms to the communicative needs at hand. Detailed attempts to account for all these features are beginning to emerge (for an overview, see Jenkins *et al.*, 2011) as are discussions on how to translate this into teaching practice (Dewey, 2012; Seidlhofer, 2011). At present, however, the literature is considerably less extensive than that associated with intercultural competence and ICC.

One approach which draws on this work on intercultural competence and pedagogy in intercultural communication research from an ELF perspective is intercultural awareness (ICA) (Baker, 2009b, 2011a, 2012a). Like ICC, ICA offers an expanded characterisation of communicative competence that focuses on the intercultural dimension. However, crucially, ICA also recognises that for English used as a lingua franca we cannot make *a priori* assumptions about predefined target communities or cultures which interlocutors may make use of or refer to in communication. Instead the emergent, complex and dynamic nature of culture and communication in ELF is highlighted and ICA is thus defined as 'a conscious understanding of the role culturally based forms, practices and frames of reference can have in intercultural communication, and an ability to put these conceptions into practice in a flexible and context specific manner in communication' (adapted from Baker, 2011a: 202).

Although there is not space here to discuss ICA in detail (for a fuller explanation, see Baker, 2011a), there are a number of important distinctions between ICA and previous conceptions of intercultural competence. ICA emphasises, like ICC, the need to mediate between different communicative practices which may be perceived as culturally based, but also that in ELF communication there is a need to negotiate between more emergent and complex cultural associations 'moving between the local and the global in dynamic ways that often result in novel, emergent practices and forms' (Baker, 2011a: 205). The short extracts below from Baker (2011a), in which the participants discussed their experiences of intercultural communication through English, illustrate a number of these themes.

Extract 2

YIM: ... when there is a way to help Thai people with the English language and if there
is a possibility to do that I will want to do that because like I like I told you earlier that
about like the teaching writing ... there is some spaces between the foreign teachers and
the students and yeah and I think as I have had some experience with those problems
and I should be able to you know to delete the gaps between yeah and solve the problem

Extract 3

POR: because I get used to American culture and I can't see the difference because I've
been there and I came back and I just can't figure it out which one is real American
which one is real Thai like like the culture is mixed

In Extract 2, Yim takes on the role of mediator and attempts to 'delete the gaps' she sees between different perceptions of writing. She places herself in 'spaces between' that are part of neither one set of perceptions nor the other. In Extract 3, Por explicitly adopts a fluid and contingent approach to cultures and claims that there is no 'real' Thai or American culture and rejects the distinction in favour of seeing them as 'mixed'. Of course it must be recognised that these fluid understandings of culture and language, as expressed by these participants, exist alongside other more 'traditional' bounded notions of cultures and language, which the participants also make use of (see Baker, 2009). However, the extracts show an awareness of alternative characterisations and an ability on the part of the participants to position themselves in spaces that do not conform to national conceptions of culture and language.

This realisation brings us back to Kramsch's notion of symbolic competence, whereby 'effective communication has increasingly come to mean not only "getting things done in the real world", but "redefining the symbolic reality of the real world"' (2011: 359). Therefore, users and learners of ELF can be seen as drawing on the existing symbolic resources that construct and represent language and culture, but they are also able to challenge, reinterpret and redefine them in ways that suit the communicative situations in which they find themselves. Kramsch makes no reference to ELF. However, her ideas can be seen as commensurable with ICA – which offers a framework for applying many of the knowledge, skills and attitudes documented in intercultural communicative competence in a more critical way that recognises not only the context-specific nature of our communicative practices but also that they are temporal and negotiable. It may thus be more appropriate to think of a set of resources or repertoires of communicative and cultural practices (Blommaert, 2010; Pennycook, 2010; Seidlhofer, 2011), rather than specific languages and cultures, that we can draw on and apply in flexible and contextually appropriate ways as outlined in ICA.

By approaching the relationship between culture and communication in such a fluid manner, ICA moves beyond the binary distinctions of Our culture/Their culture and first language/culture vs. target language/culture that have been premises in much previous intercultural communication literature (Dervin, 2011; Holliday, 2011). This is not to deny the role of nationally conceived of cultures and languages or the influence of knowledge of specific cultures and subsequent generalisations in intercultural communication; however, it does underscore the necessity of critically engaging with such characterisations and of taking take a more situated and emergent approach in intercultural communication through ELF. Of course such an emergent understanding of culture, language and communication may be characteristic of much communication, not only ELF and intercultural communication.

It should also be stressed that ICA is not presented as a prescriptive formula for any one particular set of 'good' or 'efficient' communicative practices in terms of specific language use or knowledge of cultures. Neither is it suggested that all instances of communication through ELF involve participants approaching culture in the manner characterised by ICA. The kind of critical and sophisticated characterisation of culture and language in ICA is one that is likely to only come about from extensive experience of intercultural communication and/or appropriate educational experiences (see Baker, 2011a). Nonetheless, ICA attempts to focus attention on an awareness of how the cultural background of participants and cultural contexts can influence communication in complex and multifarious ways, as highlighted in ELF research, and how this can be translated into our understanding of intercultural communication and teaching practice in locally relevant ways.

Conclusion

At the beginning of this chapter, I suggested that the reconceptualisation of language and culture in intercultural communication that has resulted from studies of multilingual intercultural communication, including ELF, has yet to be recognised in ELT. To conclude, I shall sketch out some of the implications for ELT; however, it should be stressed that at present research on ELF and language pedagogy is still in the early stages, particularly in terms of classroom practice, and as such any recommendations must necessarily be tentative. Nonetheless, it is apparent that if ELT is focused on enabling learners to communicate in English, then the realities of its global spread mean that it is not adequate to focus on the features of lexis, syntax and phonology of a single idealised form of the language. Learners need to be able to manage the inherent variability in not only in both the form and function of English but also in the multitude of contexts and interlocutors that they will encounter. The skills, knowledge and attitudes related to comparisons of and negotiations between differing communicative practices highlighted in intercultural competence are clearly of relevance here. Likewise, so are many of the pragmatic strategies associated with multilingual communication such as accommodation, code-switching, and repair.

Crucial to this expanded set of competencies is the need to employ them in a flexible and contextually appropriate manner as suggested in ICA. This means that it is not possible to specify in advance the linguistic forms and communicative norms that will best enable learners to successfully engage in all the communicative situations they may encounter. Instead, it is better to approach teaching as providing learners with communicative repertoires which can then be made use of as appropriate. This approach will involve a critical dimension since there are always alternative communicative practices that could be employed and an associated range of identifications and cultural groups which may or may not be drawn on. Furthermore, whereas communicative practices are always to an extent emergent and contingent, the fluid nature of much intercultural communication, including ELF, means that learners must be prepared for a high degree of 'flux' with temporal and emergent communicative practices and cultural associations a common part of interactions.

Translating such an understanding of communication into classroom practice is clearly challenging. However, there is a growing recognition in pedagogic research that what many learners of English are likely to engage in is communication using ELF. The extent of this increased awareness is reflected in the number of research papers (often in mainstream journals), research collections and monographs with pedagogic orientations that refer to ELF. A small sample of current research includes teachers' and students' attitudes (Jenkins, 2007), teacher training (Dewey, 2012), materials (Baker, 2012a, 2012b), motivation (Csizér & Kontra, 2012), writing (Horner, 2011), English for specific purposes (Mauranen & Hynninen, 2010), English medium instruction in higher education (Jenkins, 2014), phonology (Walker, 2010) and online communication (Guth & Helm, 2012).

Overall, pedagogically focused ELF research has generally demonstrated awareness on the part of learners and teachers of the use of English as a global lingua franca no longer tied to the Anglophone world. However, the research has also produced mixed findings as regards the influence this awareness has had on language ideology and teaching practices. Many learners and teachers display ambivalence in their approach to language and communication, recognising both the fluidity of communicating in English but also being drawn towards a more normative approach in teaching (cf. Jenkins, 2007).

Given the pervasiveness of normative and idealised NES-based approaches in ELT, it is hardly surprising that both teachers and learners hold such conflicting views. It is also tempting to speculate on the extent to which these more normative views would be held if awareness of the varieties and variation in Englishes, and other languages, were a more prominent part of language learning and teacher education. Awareness of ELF and its implications for ELT does appear to be growing though, as the research quoted above shows, and as Seidlhofer (2011) and Dewey (2012) suggest, it will be with teachers and teaching training that ELT practices change. Approaches to language, culture and intercultural communication that emphasise the complexity and fluidity of the relationships do not offer teachers easy answers to what they should teach or to the aims of language education.

However, in highlighting the inherent variety of communicative practices and cultural characterisations, these approaches offer a validation to alternative and diverse approaches to ELT that draw on teachers informed experiences and are more suited to the needs of different learners and settings. Equally, such approaches give greater status to the variety of experiences and knowledge that teachers may bring to the language classroom. In so doing, while it would be naïve to suggest that conflicts between research and practice in intercultural communication, ELF and ELT will disappear, through greater alignment it may be possible to develop ELT practices that allow teachers and learners to challenge existing models and to approach the subject in a manner that better reflects the realities of their communicative and educational needs and aspirations.

Notes

(1) See Lavanchy *et al.* (2011) for a discussion of the differing interpretations of the term 'intercultural', including in intercultural communication research and intercultural education.
(2) ELF is defined here, following Seidlhofer's functional definition, as 'any use of English among speakers of different first languages for whom English is the communicative

medium of choice, and often the only option' (2011: 7). This includes native speakers of English using ELF for intercultural communication.

(3) Although it should be noted that the extent to which ELF is seen as truly emergent in Hopper's (1998) sense of the term is debatable, Seidlhofer (2011: 111–112) takes the view that ELF users are still drawing on an 'underlying abstract set of rules', which would suggest a different interpretation of language to that detailed by emergentist positions. The focus on identifying 'innovative features' of ELF communication through corpus studies (e.g. Cogo & Dewey, 2012) would also suggest a degree of tension between variationist descriptions of language as a bounded entity and more postmodern, dynamic views of language and communication.

(4) See for example the extensive reference to native speakers in the Common European Framework of Reference for Language (Council of Europe, 2001), which has been used in English language teaching worldwide.

References

Baker, W. (2009) The cultures of English as a lingua franca. *TESOL Quarterly* 43 (4), 567–592.

Baker, W. (2011a) Intercultural awareness: Modelling an understanding of cultures in intercultural communication through English as a lingua franca. *Language and Intercultural Communication* 11 (3), 197–214.

Baker, W. (2011b) Culture and identity through ELF in Asia: Fact of fiction? In A. Cogo, A. Archibald and J. Jenkins (eds) *Latest Trends in ELF Research* (pp. 35–52). Newcastle upon Tyne: Cambridge Scholars.

Baker, W. (2012a) From cultural awareness to intercultural awareness: Culture in ELT. *ELT Journal* 66 (1), 62–70.

Baker, W. (2012b) Using online learning objects to develop intercultural awareness in ELT: A critical examination in a Thai higher education setting. *British Council Teacher Development Research Papers*. See http://www.teachingenglish.org.uk/publications

Bauman, Z. (2004) *Identity*. Cambridge: Polity.

Bjorkman, B. (2013) *English as an Academic Lingua Franca*. Berlin: De Gruyter Mouton.

Blommaert, J. (2010) *The Sociolinguistics of Globalization*. Cambridge: Cambridge University Press.

Byram, M. (1997) *Teaching and Assessing Intercultural Communicative Competence*. Clevedon: Multilingual Matters.

Byram, M. (2008) *From Foreign Language Education to Education for Intercultural Citizenship: Essays and Reflections*. Clevedon: Multilingual Matters.

Canagarajah, A.S. (ed.) (2005) *Reclaiming the Local in Language Policy and Practice*. Mahwah, NJ and London: L. Erlbaum Associates.

Canagarajah, A.S. (2007) Lingua franca English, multilingual communities, and language acquisition. *The Modern Language Journal* 91 (5), 923–939.

Canagarajah, A.S. (2013) *Translingual Practice: Global Englishes and Cosmopolitan Relations*. London: Routledge.

Canale, M. and Swain, M. (1980) Theoretical bases of communicative approaches to second language teaching and testing. *Applied Linguistics* 1 (1), 1–47.

Chomsky, N. (1965) *Aspects of the Theory of Syntax*. Cambridge, MA: MIT Press.

Cogo, A. and Dewey, M. (2012) *Analysing English as a Lingua Franca*. London: Continuum.

Cortazzi, M. and Jin, L. (1999) Cultural mirrors: Materials and methods in the EFL classroom. In E. Hinkel (ed.) *Culture in Second Language Teaching and Learning* (pp. 196-219). Cambridge: Cambridge University Press.
Council of Europe (2001) *Common European Framework of Reference for Languages: Learning, Teaching, Assessment*. Cambridge: Cambridge University Press.
Csizér, K. and Kontra, E.H. (2012) ELF, ESP, ENL and their effect on students' aims and beliefs: A structural equation model. *System* 40 (1), 1-10.
Dervin, F. (2011) A plea for change in research on intercultural discourses: A 'liquid' approach to the study of the acculturation of Chinese students. *Journal of Multicultural Discourses* 6 (1), 37-52.
Dewey, M. (2007) English as a lingua franca and globalization: An interconnected perspective. *International Journal of Applied Linguistics* 17 (3), 332-354.
Dewey, M. (2012) Towards a post-normative approach: Learning the pedagogy of ELF. *Journal of English as a Lingua Franca* 1 (1), 141-170.
Ehrenreich, S. (2009) English as a lingua franca in multinational corporations: Exploring business communities of practice. In A. Mauranen and E. Ranta (eds) *English as a Lingua Franca: Studies and Findings* (pp. 126-151). Newcastle upon Tyne: Cambridge Scholars.
Firth, A. (1996) The discursive accomplishment of normality: On 'lingua franca' English and conversational analysis. *Journal of Pragmatics* 26, 237-259.
Geertz, C. (1973) *The Interpretation of Cultures*. New York: Basic Books.
Guilherme, M. (2002) *Critical Citiizens for an Intercultural World*. Clevedon: Multilingual Matters.
Guth, S. and Helm, F. (2012) Developing multiliteracies in ELT through telecolloaboration. *ELT Journal* 66 (1), 42-51.
Hall, E.T. (1979) *The Silent Language*. New York: Doubleday Anchor.
Halliday, M. (1979) *Language as Social Semiotic*. Victoria: Edward Arnold.
Hofstede, G.H. (1991) *Cultures and Organizations: Software of the Mind*. London: McGraw-Hill.
Holliday, A. (2011) *Intercultural Communication and Ideology*. London: Sage.
Hopper, P. (1998) Emergent Grammar. In M. Tomasello (ed.) *The New Psychology of Language* (pp. 155-175). London: Lawrence Erlbaum.
Horner, B. (2011) Writing English as a Lingua Franca. In A. Archibald and A. Cogo (eds) *Latest Trends in ELF Research* (pp. 299-311). Newcastle upon Tyne: Cambridge Scholars.
House, J. (2014) English as a global lingua franca: A threat to multilingual communication and translation? *Language Teaching* 47 (3), 363-376.
Hymes, D. (1972) On communicative competence. In J. Pride and J. Holmes (eds) *Sociolinguistics* (pp. 269-293). Harmondsworth: Penguin.
Jenkins, J. (2007) *English as a Lingua Franca: Attitude and Identity*. Oxford: Oxford University Press.
Jenkins, J. (2014) *English as a Lingua Franca in the International University: The Politics of Academic English Language Policy*. London: Routledge.
Jenkins, J., Cogo, A. and Dewey, M. (2011) Review of developments in research into English as a Lingua Franca. *Language Teaching* 44 (3), 281-315.
Kirkpatrick, A. (2007) *World Englishes: Implications for International Communication and English Language Teaching*. Cambridge: Cambridge University Press.
Kramsch, C. (1993) *Context and Culture in Language Teaching*. Oxford: Oxford University Press.
Kramsch, C. (1998) *Language and Culture*. Oxford: Oxford University Press.

Kramsch, C. (2009) *The Multilingual Subject*. Oxford: Oxford University Press.
Kramsch, C. (2011) The symbolic dimensions of the intercultural. *Language Teaching*, 1–44 (3), 354–367.
Lantolf, J. and Thorne, S. (2006) *Sociocultural Theory and Genesis of Second Language Development*. Oxford: Oxford University Press.
Lavanchy, A., Gajardo, A. and Dervin, F. (2011) Interculturality at Stake. In F. Dervin, A. Gajardo and A. Lavanchy (eds) *Politics of Interculturality* (pp. 1–24). Newcastle upon Tyne: Cambridge Scholars.
Mauranen, A. and Hynninen, N. (2010) English as a lingua franca: introduction. *Helsinki English Studies* 6, 1–5.
Meierkord, C. (2002) 'Language stripped bare' or 'linguistic masala'? Culture in lingua franca communication. In K. Knapp and C. Meierkord (eds) *Lingua Franca Communication* (pp. 109–134). Frankfurt am Main: Peter Lang.
Pennycook, A. (2007) *Global Englishes and Transcultural Flows*. London: Routledge.
Pennycook, A. (2010) *Language as a Local Practice*. London: Routledge.
Phan, L.H. (2008) *Teaching English as an International Language: Identity, Resistance and Negotiation*. Clevedon: Multilingual Matters.
Phipps, A.M. and Guilherme, M. (2004) *Critical Pedagogy: Political Approaches to Language and Intercultural Communication*. Clevedon: Multilingual Matters.
Risager, K. (2007) *Language and Culture Pedagogy*. Clevedon: Multilingual Matters.
Sarup, M. (1996) *Identity, Culture and the Postmodern World*. Edinburgh: Edinburgh University Press.
Scollon, R., and Scollon, S.W. (2001) Discourse and intercultural communication. In D. Schiffrin, D. Tannen and H. Hamilton (eds) *The Handbook of Discourse Analysis* (pp. 538–547). Oxford: Blackwell.
Scollon, R., Scollon, S.W. and Jones, R. (2012) *Intercultural Communication* (3rd edn). Oxford: Blackwell.
Seidlhofer, B. (2007) English as a lingua franca and communities of practice. In S. Volk-Birke and J. Lippert (eds) *Anglistentag 2006 Halle Proceedings* (pp. 307–318). Trier: Wissenschaftlicher Verlag.
Seidlhofer, B. (2011) *Understanding English as a Lingua Franca*. Oxford: Oxford University Press.
Seidlhofer, B. and Widdowson, H.G. (2009) Accommodation and the idiom principle in English as a lingua franca. In K. Murata and J. Jenkins (eds) *Global Englishes in Asian Contexts: Current and Future Debates* (pp. 26–39). Basingstoke: Palgrave Macmillan.
Sercu, L. (2005) *Foreign Language Teachers and Intercultural Competence: An International Investigation*. Clevedon: Multilingual Matters.
Sybing, R. (2011) Assessing perspectives on culture in EFL education. *ELT Journal* 65 (4), 467–469.
Valdes, J.M. (1986) *Culture Bound: Bridging the Cultural Gap in Language Teaching*. Cambridge: Cambridge University Press.
Vettorel, P. (2010) EIL/ELF and representation of culture in textbooks: Only food, fairs, folklore and facts? In C. Gagliardi and A. Maley (eds) *EIL, ELF, Global English: Teaching and Learning Issues*. Bern: Peter Lang.
Walker, R. (2010) *Teaching the Pronunciation of English as a Lingua Franca*. Oxford: Oxford University Press.
Wenger, E. (1998) *Communities of Practice: Learning, Meaning, and Identity*. Cambridge: Cambridge University Press.

Whorf, B.L. (1939) The relation of habitual thought and behavior to language. In J. Carroll (ed.) *Language, Thought and Reality – Selected Writings of Benjamin Lee Whorf.* Cambridge, MA: MIT Press.
Widdowson, H.G. (2012) ELF and the inconvenience of established concepts. *Journal of English as a Lingua Franca* 1 (1), 5–26.
Young, T.J. and Sachdev, I. (2011) Intercultural communicative competence: Exploring English language teachers' beliefs and practices. *Language Awareness* 20 (2), 81–98.

Part 2
Grounding Conceptual Understandings of Interculturality in ELF Communication

4 Talking Cultural Identities into Being in ELF Interactions: An Investigation of International Postgraduate Students in the United Kingdom

Chris Jenks

Introduction

In the UK, universities have increased efforts to recruit international students. Given the current economic climate, these students provide an important revenue stream for universities. The push to recruit international students from different regions of the world is also underpinned by the taken for granted assumption that cultural diversity and exchange are important to the academic environment of universities, and this is reflected in how institutions of higher education are ranked internationally. For some areas of study (e.g. Applied Linguistics, English Literature, English Language Teaching), UK universities represent a place where international students can immerse themselves in a language and culture that are highly regarded in their home country. Despite these ostensible benefits, however, cultural diversity and exchange do not simply happen – they are highly complex phenomena that require a great deal of social, institutional and interactional work.

The move to promote cultural diversity and exchange in universities has been a topic of great interest in the humanities and social sciences (e.g. Jones, 2010; Kinginger, 2013; Knight, 2004). Although numerous studies have investigated the internationalisation of higher education (e.g. Deardorff et al., 2012; Guo & Chase, 2011), less work has been done on how international students discursively achieve interculturality in university contexts (cf. Dervin, 2013; Mori, 2003).

Interculturality is defined here as the discursive process in which interactants treat cultural artifacts – for example, the food ingredients that go into Korean dishes – as resources for social actions and practices. Using conversation analysis (CA) and membership categorisation analysis (MCA), this study narrows the aforementioned empirical gap by examining international students discussing academic and personal issues in a university kitchen space. This space provides a unique opportunity to examine international students discussing their identities in an informal, naturally occurring setting, as the bulk of interaction-oriented research done in universities is carried out in formal, educational contexts. The kitchen represents an important place of socialisation, where students come together to discuss, among other things, academic achievements, the challenges of being a student, plans for the weekend, and personal problems. The kitchen space is one of a few locations on campus where students can discuss amongst themselves their experiences of studying abroad.

The aim of this study is to show how national identities are used as resources to manage lingua franca interactions and kitchen-based activities, a focus that has not been given a great deal of attention in the intercultural communication literature (see, however, Behrent, 2007). The findings reveal that national identities are used as interactional resources to (1) manage talk related to being an international postgraduate student in the UK; (2) mitigate escalating disagreements; and (3) negotiate participatory roles during kitchen-based activities. These findings contribute to the intercultural and lingua franca literature by uncovering the complexities involved in constructing identities in a study abroad setting. The study builds on a growing body of research that shows how national identities and culture are used as interactional resources in lingua franca interactions.

National Identity as Resource

Nationality is membership to a geographic region that is granted as a result of some political process and/or acquired in and through shared beliefs and histories. A national identity is a collection of values and traditions that, in various semiotic and discursive ways, are created and reproduced by a region's members. A national identity is not fixed, and can possess different meanings for different people. National identities often imbue deep feelings of social and political affiliation and disaffiliation. Thus, for many people, membership to a nation or region is an important part of their identity.

Indeed, a growing body of research has shown that national identities are used as interactional resources to perform a number of different social activities. Such studies adopt what can be broadly defined as a social-interaction approach to national identities – related methodologies include, but are not limited to, conversation analysis (CA) and discursive psychology (for methodological overviews, see, respectively, Hutchby & Wooffitt, 2008; Edwards & Potter, 1992). Social interaction approaches are concerned primarily with the methods people apply in interactions. That is, social interaction approaches seek to understand how interactants sequentially display an understanding of each other and their immediate communicative context (more is said on this issue in the methodology section).

Studies that investigate national identities from a social-interaction perspective have demonstrated that a person's membership to a nation or region is in a constant state of negotiation, and that interculturality is achieved in, and through, this dialogic process (e.g. Fukuda, 2006). A key principle in a social-interaction perspective is the idea that national identities are sequentially embedded in talk-based activities (Day, 1998; see also Moerman, 1988).

For example, Nishizaka's (1995) investigation of conversations between a Japanese talk radio host and callers studying Japanese in Japan shows that students' status as non-Japanese nationals is not established *a priori*, but is made interactionally relevant through topic selection, turn design, repair, and turn taking. Similarly, Mori's (2003) investigation of Japanese and American students studying in a US university reveals that question-answer sequences provide the interactional framework for co-constructing an understanding of national identities. Specifically, Mori (2003) demonstrates that national identities are made relevant in, and through, questions and answers that treat interactants as experts of their country of origin. Brandt and Jenks (2011) demonstrate that stereotypical beliefs emerge from the work that is involved in ascribing and contesting cultural assumptions that are associated with certain regions. Similarly, in the present study, interactants from different countries use various interactional resources, including lighthearted banter, to co-construct an understanding of cultural food-eating practices. What we see here is Self and Other emerging out of interactions (cf. Brandt & Jenks, 2011).

Although different empirical foci have been investigated in the social-interaction literature, all of the studies discussed above establish that national identities are used as interactional resources. In Nishizaka (1995), talk radio participants used their status as nationals or non-nationals of Japan to negotiate notions of language ownership. In Mori (2003), students used their country of origin to manage getting-to-know-you exchanges. In Brandt and Jenks (2011), Korean and Chinese food-eating practices are used to joke and ridicule. The notion that national identities are used as discursive resources is important to the intercultural communication (IC) and English as a lingua franca (ELF) literature in that it highlights the highly complex, collaborative interactional work that is involved in the co-construction of Self and Other.

While these studies have contributed much to the idea that national identities are not fixed, the contexts and settings investigated with social-interaction approaches have been, by and large, limited to situations where communication takes place between two groups of interactants from different nation states (e.g. American and Japanese students; cf. Mori, 2003). That is, social interaction studies of national identities are based largely on contexts or settings where interactants share a common language (e.g. English). In these situations, there is often one 'home' group (e.g. American students studying in a US university) and one 'visitor' group (e.g. Japanese international students studying in a US university).

It should be no surprise that such situations lead to the co-construction of national identities. It is not uncommon for interactants from two nation states to make relevant their cultural similarities and differences when communicating in situations where binary categories, like home and visitor, are important institutionally and interactionally (cf. Fukuda, 2006). Often in such situations national identities manifest themselves in the management of interaction and social activities. For example, Japanese international students studying in the US may not possess the same level of knowledge of North American culture as their American counterparts; this disparity or asymmetry in understanding may present itself as an important interactional resource when talking to unacquainted interactants (i.e. it is a means by which to generate talk with strangers).

However, the banality of investigating national identities in these so-called binary settings should not be seen as a limitation of previous research. Although intercultural communication (IC) research is not limited to investigating the type of encounters identified in the previous paragraph, significant contributions have been made from investigating such binary settings (e.g. Ware & Kramsch, 2005). These studies contribute to the IC literature by uncovering the complexities involved in constructing identities in intercultural interactions. However, IC often occurs with interactants from three or more different nations or regions, as in the case of many ELF encounters (e.g. Jenks, 2012). In order to advance current understandings of IC and ELF, research must begin examining how interactants from three or more nations or regions, with varying degrees of cultural and linguistic similarities and differences, use national identities as resources to manage talk and talk-based activities. Such an investigation can provide insights into several IC issues that have not received a great deal of attention in the literature. For instance, are national identities less likely to be made relevant when all of the interactants are international students?

This study answers this question by examining the co-construction of national identities in ELF interaction. Before proceeding with the presentation and analysis of data, the literature on the co-construction of identities in ELF encounters is explored.

Identity Construction in ELF

A lingua franca is most commonly defined as a contact language spoken by interactants that do not share a common L1 (Jenkins, 2006). Accordingly, an ELF encounter is when English is spoken by interactants that possess different first languages (e.g. a first language Japanese speaker interacting in English with a first language Greek speaker or a first language English speaker conversing in English with a first-language Korean speaker). The word 'contact' in the aforementioned definition is germane to a discussion of identity construction in ELF encounters. In the literature, ELF is often understood and examined as a means to an end (e.g. Baumgarten & House, 2010; Firth, 1996). That is, ELF is seen as a tool for transactional purposes rather than a vehicle for the transmission of identity (cf. House, 2003). One prevailing thought in the literature is that interactants who come into 'contact' with each other are using English primarily to close a business deal, arrange a meeting, or deliver a conference presentation (e.g. Pullin, 2010).

However, a small, but growing body of research demonstrates that identities are relevant to, and constructed by speakers of, ELF encounters. For instance, Baker's (2009a) work on Thai students shows that speaking English does not simply entail conforming to, and identifying with, American or British cultural and linguistics norms and conventions. This study reveals that identities in relation to being an English speaker are not fixed, but are constantly changing according to context and setting (see also Baker, 2009b). Similarly, but in a European context, Virkkula and Nikula (2010) report that study abroad students' identities in relation to being an English speaker change over time. Doubt and uncertainty in relation to what it means to be a user of English changes as students come into contact with other speakers in ELF encounters (cf. Dervin, 2013). Specifically, features of 'Inner Circle' English are less likely to be regarded as ideal models of language use if students are exposed to a variety of Englishes (Virkkula & Nikula, 2010).

Similarly, Dervin (2013) reports that speaking in ELF encounters requires a level of cultural and linguistic accommodation that, over time, shapes identities in relation to being an English speaker in Europe. For instance, international students in Finland reported sounding Finnish in order to fit in with local norms. Despite the hybridity reported in his study, if students exhibited local varieties of English (i.e. did not conform to American or British English conventions), then they identified themselves as deficient speakers.

Perhaps most influentially, Jenkins (2007) shows that there are perceptual tensions between the values placed on native-like English accents and local varieties. In her interview study, Jenkins (2007) argues that identities in relation to English are not stable. On the one hand, 'native-like' accents are regarded as ideal linguistic models despite, and perhaps irrespective to, the importance placed on regional varieties in so-called 'native' countries (e.g. the UK). On the other hand, speakers of English as an additional language have a strong desire to maintain their national identity and the cultural and linguistic influences local varieties of English have on language use.

While it is clear that identities are relevant to, and constructed by speakers of, ELF encounters, the studies cited above by and large rely on interview data. Accordingly, much of what is known about identity construction in ELF encounters is related to perceptions of cultural identities in relation to English rather than the use of cultural identities as interactional resources. (NB. It could be argued that these interactants use cultural identities as resources to participate in research interviews, though this is not the same as participating in naturally-occurring ELF interactions).

Few studies have in fact investigated how cultural identities are used as interactional resources in ELF encounters. In an early study, Pölzl (2003) shows that code-switching and lexical borrowing are used to affiliate with cultural groups. For instance, using a first language (e.g. Arabic) during an ELF encounter allows interactants to make relevant their 'home' cultural identity while maintaining their membership to the English-speaking community. Pölzl (2003) argues that using a first language is not a sign of linguistic deficiency, but rather demonstrates that participants of ELF encounters possess multiple linguistic identities (see also Meierkord, 2002).

In a more recent study, Jenks (2013a) examines how giving and responding to language proficiency compliments provides opportunities for interactants to make relevant their English language identities. Although interactants may possess multiple identities in relation to English (e.g. second language speaker, Korean speaker of English, expert user, lingua franca speaker of English; see Jenks, 2013b), the participants of this study responded to language proficiency compliments by making relevant their status as language learners. In other words, providing and responding to language proficiency compliments reveals the complex interactional work involved in constructing identities in ELF encounters.

It should be evident from the discussion in this section that there is still much to be investigated with regard to what identities are constructed in ELF encounters, and even more social-interaction work is needed to show how this is done. Furthermore, much of what is known about identity construction in ELF encounters has been derived from interview data. Therefore, the literature is in need of studies that examine how identities are used as interactional resources in naturally occurring ELF interactions. This study makes a small, but important, contribution to this endeavor by uncovering how interactants from three or more nations or regions, with varying degrees of cultural and linguistic similarities and differences, use national identities as resources to manage talk-based activities in ELF encounters.

The Study

The study is based on the analysis of over nine hours of video data gathered during a four-month period of interactions that took place in a kitchen. One camera was placed in one corner of the room. Although the presence of the camera could have had an impact on what was discussed, it is nearly impossible to know whether this is the case. Kitchen participants rarely mentioned the presence of the camera, and if they did, this was done very briefly and in reference to the study that was being conducted.

The kitchen was located in a dormitory that housed international postgraduate students. The kitchen was used primarily for cooking and eating, but the space also represented a meeting point for talk. While the kitchen space was shared, students lived in separate studio apartments in the same building.

This space was recorded because it represents an important place of socialisation for international students. The kitchen was used to discuss the joys and difficulties of studying abroad, forge friendships with other students, seek academic advice, and plan social activities. The naturally occurring interactions that took place in the kitchen provide a unique opportunity to understand how international students co-construct identities in a setting that has not received a great deal of attention in the IC and ELF literature.

Six students, who were allocated the same kitchen and had been using the space for several months, agreed to have their interactions recorded. All participants were international postgraduate students in the UK. Countries of origin are China, India, Japan, Greece, Nigeria and Taiwan. Informed consent was given prior to data collection, and all names that appear in the transcripts below are pseudonyms. Data were collected by one of the kitchen participants who used some of the recordings for her MA thesis on intercultural interactions – this was the only kitchen participant who knew the researcher of this study. The MA student gave consent for the use of her data several months after she completed her thesis when she no longer had any use for it.

Data were examined using CA and membership categorisation analysis (MCA). Both approaches are concerned with showing how identities are relevant and procedurally consequential for the interactants under investigation (Hutchby & Wooffitt, 2008). What this means for the present study is that analytic descriptions of national identities must be situated in the sequential environment of talk and interaction (Antaki & Widdicombe, 1998; Benwell & Stokoe, 2006). So, for example, the social category 'Chinese' is not interactionally relevant for a Chinese student until she and her fellow interactants have made being Chinese relevant and procedurally consequential in the talk, and to the talk-based activities at hand. Interactants can make relevant social categories by, for example, asking and answering questions that pertain to knowledge and/or membership of certain cultures (cf. Mori, 2003).

This rather strict understanding of identities can be traced back to ethnomethodology (Garfinkel, 1967). An ethnomethodological understanding of identities is informed by the idea that observations of social categories must be 'grounded in data' while at the same time revealing that 'the people we are talking about are actually oriented to that category with respect to their own talk and action' (Francis & Hester, 2004: 39). Put differently, researchers using CA and MCA take the view that an interactant belongs to a number of different social categories (e.g. Asian, Taiwanese, student, foreigner), and that it is the job of the researcher to show how any given category is used as a resource to organise social interaction (Sacks, 1992; see also Kasper, 2009).

Using CA and MCA, the analysis below examines how national identities are used to organise talk-based activities in the kitchen. The examples analysed in this chapter emerged from a larger concern for how identities are constructed in ELF encounters. The analysis uncovers how national identities are used as interactional resources to (1) manage talk related to being an international postgraduate student in the UK; (2) mitigate a debate regarding food spices, and (3) negotiate participatory roles in a food preparation activity.

These three foci were selected because they represent a large part of what occurs in the kitchen space. For instance, the topic of academic life as an international student is discussed almost daily. Students defined their social welfare according to their academic experiences and progress. The first analytic section, 'The supervisor', shows how national identities are used to discuss supervisor-supervisee relations. The kitchen was also a place where students would talk about food-eating practices. These discussions often led to invocations and ascriptions of national identities. The second analytic section, 'Food spices', is concerned with how students use national identities to manage a disagreement about food-eating practices. As a space used primarily for cooking and eating, food preparation and consumption were the main activities that took place in the kitchen. Thus, the third analytic section, 'Food preparation', demonstrates how national identities are used to negotiate participatory roles in a food preparation activity.

Following CA and MCA principles, the analyses below focus on how national identities are procedurally consequential for the interactants and interactions under investigation. Therefore, it is necessary for the analysis of data extracts to provide a descriptive, turn-by-turn account of how interactants manage their interactions in the kitchen. This descriptive account is necessary for the detailed analysis of how national identities are sequentially embedded in, and made use of, for the management of talk and interaction.

Furthermore, CA and MCA studies do not aim to generalise from one setting to another. The core analytic aim of such studies is to provide a detailed account of how interactional practices are organised and how social actions are accomplished. Therefore, it is not uncommon for CA and MCA studies to draw on a small number of analytic examples, sometimes even relying on one extended data extract, to achieve this aim. In the following sections, three examples are used to demonstrate the collaborative work involved in constructing identities in lingua franca interactions. These examples are presented in no particular order, and have been selected for this study because they provide vivid examples of students talking national identities into being.

The supervisor

In the following extract (see Appendix 1 for transcription conventions), Anne, Pete and Philip are all discussing their experiences of postgraduate studies in the UK. Pete has just informed his co-interactants that his supervisor is very angry with him. In previous recordings, it was revealed that Pete was not forthcoming with the mistakes he made in his supervised research project. Pete's supervisor was later informed of these mistakes from a third party, which led to the current situation and topic of discussion. The extract begins after a short discussion concerning the academic role of Pete's supervisor. Pete is washing dishes at the sink, Philip is using the microwave oven, and Anne is sitting at the dinner table.

Extract 1

39	Pete:	<because< I've never seen him so angry
40		(0.3)
41	Philip:	°really°
42	Anne:	[how angry]
43	Pete:	[really] really really got angry I mean he was like (0.7) shouting
44	Anne:	°oh::°
45		(1.1)
46	Pete:	you are no business to do this
47		((Pete imitates his supervisor))
48	Anne:	you are what↑
49	Pete:	no business to do this (1.7) you had no right to:: [tell me
50	Philip:	[to (right)
51		(0.7)
52	Philip:	yeah
53		(0.5)
54	Anne:	to what↑
55	Philip:	but (0.2.) in any case you- the answer I can give you you know it was
56		your [mistake
57	Pete:	[hh
58	Philip:	it wasn't my mistake =
59	Pete:	=hh
60	Philip:	hh
61	Anne:	h:hhhh
62	Philip:	so (1.5) no matter how: loud (.) she: shout (0.7) it was still her mistake
63	Pete:	yeah but I mean like (0.2) I'm for me coming from Indian where (0.2)
64		you never ever correct your professors (0.2) you never do that
65	Philip:	in [Greece you]
66	Anne:	[yeah yeah]

67	**Philip:**	you ask [for]
68	**Pete:**	[hh]
69	**Philip:**	a permission to talk=
70	**Pete:**	=hh exactly <u>EXA</u>ctly
71	**Philip:**	but not not not to a young one (0.3) not even here it's different (0.6)
72		the (0.5) the supervisors (1.6) that:: thirty-five forty years old we'll talk
73		to them with the first name (0.9) the [other] the olders (.) with the::

The extract begins with Pete explaining the emotional state of his supervisor during a previous academic meeting. Philip responds by mimicking Pete's voice and providing responses that should have been given in the previous meeting. Philip's turn provides an implicit assessment of the situation (i.e. the blame should be placed on the supervisor), which is made more explicit in Line 62, when he informs Pete that despite the yelling and anger, the supervisor is at fault. Pete then uses his country of origin to explain why he did not follow Philip's suggestion ('I'm for me coming from Indian where you never ever correct your professors...you never do that'). In other words, Pete uses his national identity to justify his actions in a previous meeting. With regard to identity construction, Pete uses the social category of being an Indian as a resource to define himself as a postgraduate student (i.e. Pete is not just a postgraduate student, but an Indian postgraduate student). What is particularly interesting in this exchange is that although Pete could respond to his supervisor according to local UK norms and conventions, he chooses to 'transport' his national identity into his host country and academic institution.

Anne later acknowledges Pete's invocation of national identity ('yeah yeah'), while Philip identifies a similar cultural practice in Greece ('in Greece you...you ask for a permission to talk'). In so doing, all three interactants do being postgraduate students by comparing and contrasting their experiences and understanding of academic practices (cf. 'third space'; Bhabha, 1994), thereby creating a discursive space where cultural meaning and representations are constructed and reconstructed (Block, 2007; Hall, 1996). The discussion of academic practices occurs again in Lines 71–73, when Philip qualifies his previous statement regarding what is the norm in Greece ('but not not not a young one'), and compares this with the UK ('not even here it's different...').

Extract 1 shows how national identities are used to create a space for discussing issues related to being an international postgraduate student. In this extract, Philip and Pete compared the academic practices of their home countries with managing supervisory relationships in the UK. In so doing,

Philip and Pete transported their home national identities into UK academic life. The interactants' status as postgraduate students was made relevant through a discursive orientation to cultural similarities and differences, as well as talk based on how these similarities and differences fit within the host academic institution. These observations demonstrate that national identities are used as interactional resources, and are thus contingent upon the context in which interactants communicate (Jenks, 2012).

The idea that national identities are interactional resources is of particular importance to researchers working in university contexts. Although the kitchen is an informal learning environment, the space is used to co-construct an understanding of what it means to be a student living and studying in the UK. In this sense, the kitchen space can act as an important pedagogical setting, where students are given opportunities to negotiate appropriate forms of interaction. More importantly, this example illustrates how the kitchen provides a space where students can strategically use their national identities to manage social relations, as is done in the next example when discussing food-eating practices.

Food spices

A great deal of intercultural interaction in the kitchen involved the discussion of food-eating practices. Students often drew on their cultural backgrounds to participate in discussions and activities related to cooking and eating. In many instances of talk in the data set, cultural identities are used to engage and disengage in kitchen-based discussions and activities. In arguments, for example, cultural identities are sometimes used to mitigate escalating disagreements, as in the following example.

The interactants in Extract 2 are preparing to have lunch together. Wendy is cooking, while Philip, Pete and Anne are all sitting at the dining table.

Extract 2

67	**Wendy:**	no but spices are good for me [so:: it stimulates you
68	**Philip:**	[eh:: they use the
69	**Wendy:**	it's good =
70	**Philip:**	= it's NOT good (0.3) a[nyway we've] been talking about this
71	**Wendy:**	[°why is it not good°]
72	**Philip:**	because [they increase] they increase the stomach problems of
73	**Wendy:**	[°tell me why ↑ °]

74	**Philip:**	stomach and er:: oral [cancer]
75	**Wendy:**	[and] oral ↑ =
76	**Philip:**	= of course [mainly
77	**Wendy:**	[oral.
78	**Philip:**	oral cancer =
79	**Wendy:**	= and that's when you- when- when- you go extremely hot
80		(0.9)
81	**Philip:**	aheh? I've(h) tried your food hehehehe
82	**Wendy:**	IS that extremely ↑HOT
83	**Anne:**	hahahaha
84	**Philip:**	yeah but I tell you [because
85	**Wendy:**	[that means you can't eat in Nigeria my
86		mi:ld I don't even use the red you know the sort of red pepper at all
87		(1.6) I use just half of a bit if somebody is cooking a typical
88		Nigerian will use two in his food I- I can't even eat it
89	**Pete:**	same thing in in where I come from in India the thing is =
90	**Wendy:**	= HOT
91	**Pete:**	very hot
92	**Wendy:**	I can't even eat it I don't like very hot food

The extract begins with Wendy and Philip discussing the benefits of food spices. Wendy states that she believes spices are good for her ('no but spices are good for me'), and Philip provides a medical explanation as to why she is wrong ('because they increase... the stomach problems of stomach and... oral cancer'). In Lines 67–74, Wendy and Philip are in disagreement, and both provide different explanations as to why their positions are correct.

In Line 75, Wendy acknowledges the medical explanation by repeating 'oral', which Philip later reiterates ('of course mainly oral cancer'). Wendy subsequently builds on the medical explanation by linking oral cancer with the consumption of hot spices ('and that's when you- when- when- you go extremely hot'). Although Philip could continue arguing the medical consequences of consuming spices, he uses Wendy's previous turn to transition into a discussion of food-eating practices ('I've tried your food'). In so doing,

Philip downgrades the discussion from an argument about spices to a discussion of food. The attempt to move into less confrontational talk is further demonstrated by his laughter tokens in Line 81.

Although there is not enough information in Philip's turn to determine whether 'your food' refers to Wendy's individual or national food-eating practices, Wendy treats this turn as an opportunity to make relevant her country of origin ('that means you can't eat in Nigeria'). In so doing, Wendy's national identity is used as an interactional resource to mitigate the argument with Philip. In the same vein, Pete in lines 89 and 91 uses his national identity as an interactional resource to participate in the ongoing discussion of food-eating practices ('same thing in in where I come from in India').

In this extract, national identities are used to mitigate an escalating argument and manage talk based on food-eating practices. Specifically, Philip was able to move a discussion away from an argument by lightheartedly referencing Wendy's food-eating practices, which she treated as an opportunity to make relevant her country of origin. This is noteworthy, as it shows that national identities are not omnipresent social structures that perpetually shape the communicative behaviours of these interactants, but are rather used selectively and strategically.

The analyses also showed that national identities are not simply talked into being. When participating in kitchen activities, interactants engage in a series of practices that interactionally build on previous invocations of national identity. For instance, Philip refers to a food-eating practice (i.e. using hot spices), and thus creates an opportunity for Wendy to make relevant her national identity. However, Philip's turn in itself does not make relevant any specific social category. The social category of being Nigerian is talked into being when Wendy, in the next turn, discusses the food-eating practices of her home country. That is to say, national identities are co-constructed in, and through, talk and interaction.

Food preparation

International postgraduate students also use their national identities to negotiate participatory roles during food preparation activities. Take, for example, Nigerian food. In preparing Nigerian food, interactants can position themselves according to how knowledgeable they are of the ingredients that make up the food of that country. Interactants can cross-reference Nigerian foods with their own culinary knowledge and practices, or distance themselves if they do not want or cannot add to the discussion and activity.

In Extract 3, Wendy is preparing a Nigerian soup for dinner. Shine is assisting with the preparation, and Pete is listening to their discussion about preparing the soup. The extract begins when Shine asks Wendy how to cut the tomatoes for the soup. Shine is at the sink, preparing the tomatoes, Wendy is using the oven, and Pete is standing near Wendy.

Extract 3

1	Shine:	tomato↑
2	Wendy:	m:: just cut it into half and then just drop it there
3		(3.5)
4	Shine:	can I use all ↑
		((looks at Wendy))
5		(1.0)
6	Wendy:	too much.
7	Shine:	half
8		(0.6)
9	Pete:	yeah. [only half
10	Wendy:	[mmm only half
11		(0.5)
12	Pete:	yeah.
13	Shine:	hehe DO YOU KNOW THAT you seem like you cook you know (0.3)
14		but can't cook (0.4) but Wendy cook=
		((points to Pete))
15	Pete:	=because I have [eh::]
16	Wendy:	[did you] come he I am sure you have an idea what I
17		am doing
18		(0.6)
19	Shine:	hhh
20	Pete:	yeah I think so(h)
21	Shine:	hHH
22		(0.4)
23	Pete:	hh m:
24	Shine:	hhh
25	Wendy:	we have similar::

26   (0.9)
27 **Pete:**   similar vegetables yeah [yeah]
                ((looks at Wendy))
28 **Wendy:**   [mixtures]
29 **Pete:**   mm:
                ((nods heavily))
30 **Wendy:** and tastes
31 **Pete:**   mm:
                ((nods heavily))
32 **Wendy:** °hmhm°
33   (2.5)
34 **Pete:**   can actually put the:: pepper separately in
35   (1.0)
36 **Wendy:** no I have pepper
                ((Pete approaches Wendy))
37 **Pete:**   no I mean that's what I am saying (0.3) a(h)fter you(h)
38   fi(h)nish making
                ((Wendy nods))
39 **Wendy:** °for those°
40 **Pete:**   yeah:

The extract begins with Shine seeking help regarding the preparation of the soup and Wendy telling Shine what to do with the tomatoes. By preparing the tomatoes for the dish (lines 1–3), positioning her body and establishing eye contact with Wendy (Line 4), and requesting for directions and clarification (lines 4 and 7), Shine treats Wendy as the knowledgeable preparer of the dish.

Despite Shine's attempt to seek clarification from Wendy in Line 7, no answer is immediately given. Pete then provides an answer ('yeah only half'). In overlap, but after an acknowledgement token ('yeah'), Wendy also states that only half is needed ('mmm only half'). Peter subsequently confirms Wendy's directions ('yeah'). In answering Shine's request for clarification and confirming Wendy's directions, Pete positions himself as a knowledgeable co-participant who can assist in the food preparation activity.

However, in lines 13 and 14, Shine does not treat Pete as a legitimate contributor to the ongoing talk and activity. This is demonstrated in Shine's response to Pete's directions: the turn is constructed with an initial outburst of laughter ('hehe'), an explicit assessment of Pete's ability to cook ('DO YOU

KNOW THAT you seem like you cook you know...but can't cook'), and a reorientation to Wendy as expert of the food preparation activity ('but Wendy cook').

In lines 16 and 17, Wendy 'authenticates' Pete's contribution by treating him as a knowledgeable participant (see Shenk, 2007; Thornborrow, 2001). Despite Wendy's attempt to incorporate Pete into the discussion (which Pete accepts in Line 20), Shine can be heard laughing throughout the exchange. These laughter tokens continue to treat Pete as an illegitimate co-participant. In Line 23, Pete lowers his head and produces a minimal laughter token, possibly to display embarrassment and/or acknowledge Shine's laughter.

Although Pete's verbal contributions are challenged by Shine, his knowledge of cooking and expertise in the kitchen is further authenticated in Line 25. Here Wendy incorporates Pete into the discussion more explicitly by referring to their shared understanding of the dish, as evidenced in the pronoun 'we' ('we have similar'). Although 'we' could refer to a number of different things (e.g. we as members of similar national food-eating cultures or we as members of similar individual food-cooking practices), it is likely, given the frequent invocations of national identity during food-related activities in this setting, that the pronoun 'we' represents the collective food cultures of Wendy and Pete. While Pete does not explicitly refer to his Indian national identity or food-cooking practices, he treats 'we' to mean the two interactants' collective food-cooking cultures. This is demonstrated when Pete completes Wendy's turn by referencing the fact that they have similar vegetables ('similar vegetables yeah yeah'). In so doing, Wendy and Pete use their national identities to shape the ongoing organisation of the food preparation activity. This is further evidenced in Wendy's response to Pete, where she adds that the two interactants also share similar 'mixtures' (Line 28) and 'tastes' (Line 30).

Mixtures and tastes are often more distinct than vegetables. Thus, Wendy's references to mixtures and tastes further validate Pete's contribution to the food-preparation activity. These references also allow Pete to take a more active role in the task at hand. At the same time, Shine disengages in the discussion and positions herself back to the task of washing and cutting vegetables near the sink. In lines 34–40, Pete embodies the role of active participant by positioning himself closer to Wendy and providing suggestions about how to season the soup.

In Extract 3, the interactants use their national identities as resources to negotiate participatory roles in the kitchen. Pete positions himself as a participant who is capable of contributing to the food-preparation activity. While Shine dismisses Pete's initial attempt to play an active role in the activity, Wendy treats Pete as a legitimate contributor. As national and regional food-eating practices are identified and discussed, Pete's contribution and participation to the activity changes and evolves. Pete moves from an illegitimate co-interactant to a legitimate contributor. At the same time, Shine, who was verbally and interactionally active in the beginning of the food preparation activity, disengaged from the discussion when Wendy and Pete made relevant their shared national food-eating practices.

Discussion and Conclusion

The observations made in this study contribute to the IC and ELF literature by showing how international postgraduate students use their national identities for specific social-interaction purposes (cf. Gumperz, 1982), and revealing how talk of culture is sequentially embedded in kitchen activities. Similarities and differences in cultural practices are used by the interactants of this study as resources to organise lingua franca interactions. Specifically, regional values and conventions are used to manage talk, social relations, and kitchen activities.

The observations also demonstrate that national identities are fundamental to the ways in which these international postgraduate students organise their understanding of, and participation in, university life. The kitchen provided a space where international postgraduate students could freely explore and discuss their national identities. Although the students developed their own kitchen norms and conventions (e.g. food sharing and inviting guests), and were all members of a larger international student community, the organisation of talk and activities in this space were often shaped by the cultural practices of individuals.

The three examples analysed herein demonstrate that ELF interactions are not culturally neutral (cf. House, 2003). That is, ELF interactions are not simply used for transactional purposes (e.g. to exchange information). ELF encounters are potentially intercultural encounters because interactants may use their national identities to co-construct an understanding of each other and carry out interactional practices and actions.

Furthermore, in the entire corpus of kitchen data, interactants rarely see themselves as 'global' citizens or members of a lingua franca community, though they would occasionally talk about differences in English varieties. Put differently, when identities are brought into being in the kitchen space, national identities are more often than not the social category used to engage in intercultural interactions. This observation has also been made of ELF interactions in second language chat rooms (cf. Jenks, 2013b).

While only three extracts were examined, the analysis contributes to the literature by showing how identities are constructed in ELF interactions. This contribution is noteworthy, as a focus on the 'how' stands in contrast to the majority of previous ELF studies that examine identity construction by conducting interviews and/or administering questionnaires. With regard to the setting investigated in this study, more attention must be paid to kitchens and other types of informal university spaces where intercultural communication occurs, as researchers and educators can glean important insights into how students make sense of each other and others in their host academic country and institution. The kitchen is an important site of socialisation and identity construction for international postgraduate students, and a deeper understanding of what goes on – interactionally and socially – in these spaces is needed in order to advance the IC and ELF literature.

This study builds on a growing body of literature that examines how identities are used as interactional resources in naturally occurring communicative settings between interactants that come from different regions of the world, though further studies are clearly needed to expand the empirical database on ELF interactions. This study has made a small, but important, contribution to this endeavor by revealing how national identities are talked into being in an informal academic setting.

References

Antaki, C. and Widdicombe, S. (1998) *Identities in Talk*. London: Sage.
Atkinson, J.M. and Heritage, J. (1984) *Structures of Social Action: Studies in Conversation Analysis*. Cambridge: Cambridge University Press.
Baker, W. (2009a) Language, culture and identity through English as a lingua franca in Asia: Notes from the field. *The Linguistics Journal* 8 (35). See http://www.linguistics-journal.com/September-2009.pdf
Baker, W. (2009b) The cultures of English as a lingua franca. *TESOL Quarterly* 43 (4), 567–592.
Baumgarten, N. and House, J. (2010) I think and I don't know in English as lingua franca and native English discourse. *Journal of Pragmatics* 42, 1184–1200.
Behrent, S. (2007) *La Communication Alloglotte*. Paris: L'Harmattan.
Benwell, B. and Stokoe, E. (2006) *Discourse and Identity*. Edinburgh: Edinburgh University Press.
Bhabha, H. (1994) *The Location of Culture*. London: Routledge.
Block, D. (2007) The rise of identity in SLA research, post Firth and Wagner (1997). *The Modern Language Journal* 91, 863–876.
Brandt, A. and Jenks, C.J. (2011) 'Is it okay to eat a dog in Korea...like China?' Assumptions of national food-eating practices in intercultural interaction. *Language & Intercultural Communication* 11 (1), 41–58.
Day, D. (1998) Being ascribed, and resisting, membership of an ethnic group In C. Antaki and S. Widdicombe (eds) *Identities in Talk* (pp. 151–170). London: Sage.
Deardorff, D.K., de Wit, H., Heyl, J. and Adams, T. (eds) (2012) *The Sage Handbook of International Higher Education*. London: Sage.

Dervin, F. (2013) Politics of identification in the use of lingua francas in student mobility to Finland and France. In C. Kinginger (ed.) *Social and Cultural Aspects of Language Learning in Study Abroad* (pp. 101–125). Amsterdam: John Benjamins.

Edwards, D. and Potter, J. (1992) *Discursive Psychology*. London: Sage.

Firth, A. (1996) The discursive accomplishment of normality: On 'lingua franca' English and conversation analysis. *Journal of Pragmatics* 26, 237–259.

Francis, D. and Hester, S. (2004) *An Invitation to Ethnomethodology: Language, Society and Interaction*. London: Sage.

Fukuda, C. (2006) Resistance against being formulated as cultural other: The case of a Chinese student in Japan. *Pragmatics* 16 (4), 429–456.

Garfinkel, H. (1967) *Studies in Ethnomethodology*. Cornwall: Polity.

Gumperz, J. (1982) *Discourse Strategies*. Cambridge: Cambridge University Press.

Guo, S. and Chase, M. (2011) Internationalisation of higher education: Integrating international students into Canadian academic environment. *Teaching in Higher Education* 16 (3), 305–318.

Hall, S. (1996) Introduction: Who needs 'identity'? In S. Hall and P. du Gay (eds) *Questions of Cultural Identity* (pp. 1–17). London: Lawrence and Wishart.

House, J. (2003) English as a lingua franca: A threat to multilingualism? *Journal of Sociolinguistics* 7 (4), 556–78.

Hutchby, I. and Wooffitt, R. (2008) *Conversation Analysis*. London: Polity.

Jenkins, J. (2006) Current perspectives on teaching world Englishes and English as a lingua franca. *TESOL Quarterly* 40 (1), 157–181.

Jenkins, J. (2007) *English as a Lingua Franca: Attitude and Identity*. Oxford: Oxford University Press.

Jenks, C.J. (2012) Doing being reprehensive: Some interactional features of English as a lingua franca in a chat room. *Applied Linguistics* 33 (4), 386–405.

Jenks, C.J. (2013a) 'Your pronunciation and your accent is very excellent': Orientations of identity during compliment sequences in English as a lingua franca encounters. *Language & Intercultural Communication* 13 (2), 165–181.

Jenks, C.J. (2013b) Are you an ELF? The relevance of ELF as an equitable social category in online intercultural communication. *Language and Intercultural Communication* 13 (1), 95–108.

Jones, E. (2010) *Internationalisation and the Student Voice: Higher Education Perspectives*. New York: Routledge.

Kasper, G. (2009) Categories, context, and comparison in Conversation Analysis. In H. Nguyen and G. Kasper (eds) *Talk-in-Interaction: Multilingual Perspectives* (pp. 1–28). Honolulu: University of Hawaii, National Foreign Language Resource Center.

Kinginger, C. (2013) *Social and Cultural Aspects of Language Learning in Study Abroad*. Amsterdam: John Benjamins.

Knight, J. (2004) Internationalization remodeled: Definition, approaches, and rationales. *Journal of Studies in International Education* 8 (1), 5–31.

Meierkord, C. (2002) 'Language stripped bare' or 'linguistic masala'? Culture in lingua franca communication. In K. Knapp and C. Meierkord (eds) *Lingua Franca Communication* (pp. 109–134). Frankfurt am Main: Peter Lang.

Moerman, M. (1988) *Talking Culture: Ethnography and Conversation Analysis*. Philadelphia: University of Pennsylvania Press.

Mori, J. (2003) The construction of interculturality: A study of initial encounters between Japanese and American students. *Research on Language and Social Interaction* 36 (2), 143–184.

Nishizaka, A. (1995) The interactive constitution of interculturality: How to be a Japanese with words. *Human Studies* 18, 301–326.
Pölzl, U. (2003) Signalling cultural identity: The use of L1/Ln in ELF. *Views* 12 (2), 3–24.
Pullin, P. (2010) Small talk, rapport, and international communicative competence: Lessons to learn from BELF. *Journal of Business Communication* 47 (4), 455–476.
Sacks, H. (1992) *Lectures on Conversation*. Oxford: Blackwell.
Shenk, P.S. (2007) 'I'm Mexican, remember?' Constructing ethnic identities via authenticating discourse. *Journal of Sociolinguistics* 11 (2), 194–220.
Thornborrow, J. (2001) Authenticating talk: Building public identities in audience participation broadcasting. *Discourse Studies* 3 (4), 459–479.
Virkkula, T. and Nikula, T. (2010) Identity construction in ELF contexts: A case study of Finnish engineering students working in Germany. *International Journal of Applied Linguistics* 20 (2), 251–273.
Ware, P.D. and Kramsch, C. (2005) Toward an intercultural stance: Teaching German and English through telecollaboration. *The Modern Language Journal* 89 (2), 190–205.

Appendix 1

Transcription Conventions (modified from Atkinson & Heritage, 1984)

[[ ]]	Simultaneous utterances – (beginning [[ ) and (ending]])
[ ]	Overlapping utterances – (beginning [ ) and (ending])
=	Contiguous utterances
(0.4)	Represents the tenths of a second between utterances
(.)	Represents a micro-pause (1 tenth of a second or less)
:	Sound extension of a word (more colons demonstrate longer stretches)
.	Fall in tone (not necessarily the end of a sentence)
,	Continuing intonation (not necessarily between clauses)
-	An abrupt stop in articulation
¿	Rising inflection (not necessarily a question)
!	Words ending with emphasis
	Underline letters or words indicate emphasis
↑ ↓	Rising or falling intonation
° °	Surrounds talk that is quieter
hhh	Audible aspirations
·hhh	Inhalations
.hh.	Laughter within a word
> >	Surrounds talk that is spoken faster
< <	Surrounds talk that is spoken slower
(( ))	Analyst's notes
( )	Approximations of what is heard
$ $	Surrounds 'smile' voice

5 Conflict Talk and ELF Communities of Practice

Anne Kari Bjørge

Introduction

In the field of ELF research, relatively little attention has been paid to the expression of conflict (Bjørge, 2009; Bjørge, 2012; Ehrenreich, 2009; Knapp, 2002). However, as ELF is used in all kinds of contexts it is also of interest to look into situations where interlocutors challenge each other's opinions. Previous research has established the concept of conflict talk (Grimshaw, 1990), which may be employed to discuss situation-specific discourse where participants express different views on one or more issues, without being restricted to a single speech act or turn sequence (Leung, 2010).

Expressions of disagreement may take both mitigated or unmitigated forms, but corpus-based research has established that the mitigated forms predominate (Bjørge, 2012; Locher, 2004; Stalpers, 1995). This is a practice that is encouraged by textbooks aimed at the non-native speaker of English, some of which may even contain warnings against using expressions like 'no' and 'you can't' in the interest of politeness (Bjørge, 2012). However, such advice ignores the fact that these kinds of expression may be preferred for reasons of clarity (Stalpers, 1995), and because of their simplicity, they may also be used by those who would otherwise remain silent due to limited proficiency.

The issue of mitigation in an ELF context may be linked to the traditional distinction between low and high context communication, which is associated with directness versus indirectness in discourse (Gudykunst, 2003; Gudykunst *et al.*, 1996; Hall, 1976). Directness is generally associated with a communicative style that emphasises clarity, conciseness and avoidance of ambiguity, and has positive connotations of sincerity, honesty and openness. Indirectness, by contrast, is associated with developing a context for the message, and is positively associated with relationship building, politeness and face-saving. From the direct communicator's point of view, indirect messages may be perceived as ambiguous, difficult to understand, a waste of time, and perhaps even lacking in straightforwardness. The indirect communicator, however, may find directness off-putting, brusque and lacking in sophistication.

Textbooks on intercultural communication link this distinction to specific national or regional cultures, creating expectations when it comes to the communicative styles of different nationalities (e.g. Beamer & Varner, 2008; Utley, 2004; Victor, 1992). According to Beamer and Varner (2008: 177), 'Saying no is more difficult for high-context cultures. As when they communicate about problems, they would rather not actually have to put a refusal into words'. This is supported by studies such as that of Dunkerley and Robinson (2002), who found that UK managers were perceived as less direct than their US counterparts, and that of Søderberg and Worm (2011) with respect to communication between Chinese and expatriate managers. However, the link between Hall's (1976) contexting dichotomy and national stylistic preferences has been found to be based on 'little or no empirical validation' (Cardon, 2008: 424). Thus, proposing 'a straightforward language-culture-nation correlation must be seen as a gross oversimplification' (Baker, 2009: 567).

When ELF speakers meet in a negotiation situation, a number of factors come into play, including previous international experience, individual aspects such as age and gender, notions of politeness, and previous exposure to textbook advice on nation-based cultural preferences. These are among the contributing factors to 'the underlying processes that motivate the use of one or another form at any given moment in an interaction' (Jenkins et al., 2011: 296). Thus, essentialist positions concerning issues like directness need to be modified to take this meta-level into account. The following description of Japanese-Norwegian interaction may serve to illustrate this point:

> Norwegians think that one cannot speak so directly to the Japanese, so therefore they try to speak as indirectly as possible. Then, what happens next, is that the Japanese who hears it, thinks that the Norwegian does not have a very firm opinion about the matter since he puts it that indirectly. (Rygg, 2012: 278)

Discourse strategies employed by ELF speakers may thus reflect the cultural hybridity (Canagarajah, 2006) or transcultural flows (Pennycook,

2007) inherent in ELF discourse. Adopting an essentialist notion of cultural differences when analysing ELF disagreement may miss aspects of the interactional process that may be revealed through a constructionist approach (Piller, 2011).

The interaction referred to above may be related to the potential input into ELF discourse strategies represented by textbook advice. An analysis of the recommended expressions used to express disagreement in a set of business English textbooks revealed that they generally recommended using a mitigation strategy, presumably in the interests of rapport management (Bjørge, 2012). It would thus appear that indirectness is generally regarded as the safest approach. The impact of directness has received less attention, and should be looked into to see whether it does have a negative impact on rapport management in ELF interaction.

The participants in the corpus employed for this study are discussed in terms of a community of practice (Bjørge, 2012; Ehrenreich, 2009; House, 2003; Jenkins, 2007; Seidlhofer, 2007; Wenger, 1998). This is a construct that refers to mutual engagement, joint enterprise and shared repertoire (Ehrenreich, 2009: 131–34). As for mutual engagement, the participants are all international master's-level business students in the same age bracket, which means that status is not a central issue. Group sizes are limited; participants have the opportunity to interact and network in class discussions and in breaks; and the negotiation scenarios represent another such arena for interaction. With respect to joint enterprise, they all follow a study programme that prepares them for working in international business.

However, as pointed out by Ehrenreich (2009: 133), it is the criterion of shared repertoire that is of main interest to ELF research, in this case, the students' communicative competence within the field of economics and business studies. Business English constitutes an identifiable field in terms of genres and vocabulary issues, as witnessed by the term 'BELF' (business English lingua franca; Charles, 2008; Louhiala-Salminen et al., 2005). The ability to handle conflict talk while taking into account rapport management may be discussed as one aspect of this shared field of competence. Expressing conflict is a culturally sensitive issue, as negotiation participants may have different preferences when it comes to using direct disagreement. Thus, if the use of unmitigated disagreement may lead to negotiation breakdown, there will be sound reasons to warn against its usage and advise ELF speakers to avoid using this form.

In the following, I shall look into how expressions of unmitigated disagreement impact on the ELF negotiations process, including a discussion of directness in ELF communication.

Unmitigated expressions of disagreement

In order to discuss unmitigated disagreement the concept should be delimited from expressions of mitigation (Locher, 2004; Stalpers, 1995). The analysis of Stalpers (1995: 278) is based on three categories of features that may be used to mitigate a disagreement act. These are features that delay the disagreement act, for example by a pause, a discourse marker or token agreement; features that support the disagreement act, for example by providing an explanation; and features that modulate or make the disagreement more indirect. Stalpers (1995: 280) also refers to disagreement acts that do not exhibit mitigation strategies, but provides no examples. Locher (2004: 143) discusses 'non-mitigating disagreement strategies', including 'unmitigated disagreement' ('straightforward disagreement, which was not accompanied by any additional boosting'); '*but* without mitigation', 'repetition/own: emphasis'; 'repetition/previous: criticism', and the inclusion of the boosters 'I think', 'just' and 'of course'. While straightforward disagreement and the use of 'but' are central to the analysis of unmitigated disagreement, Locher's categories do not focus explicitly on the use of negative markers and the use of 'no', which are common in my corpus. I have therefore adopted a corpus-driven approach (Tognini-Bonelli, 2001: 84) to reflect the variety in my material.

Herein, the term 'unmitigated disagreement acts' will be used to subsume statements that do not exhibit any of the mitigating features referred to by Stalpers (1995: 278). In addition to their immediate context, all expressions should be interpreted in the wider context of the entire negotiations discourse (Leung, 2010). Thus, in Extract 1, BF1's counterargument relates to a different issue than the one put forward by AM1, viz. who is to pay the transaction costs. (For abbreviations, see Appendix 1; for information on individual negotiators, see Appendix 2. Unmitigated disagreement acts are set out in italics.)

Extract 1

AM1:   I mean admin fee] admin fee is just [(paper) work
BF3:   (xx)]
AM1:   which you pay yours your people to do anyway [(xx)
BF1:   *but you know] we have transaction costs* (INB9)

It should also be noted that '*no*' must be interpreted in context, as it can also be used to express agreement with a negative statement from a team member, which is what BM1 does in Extract 2.

Extract 2

BM2: but that is not the issue here that's not what I'm asking about
BM1: *no* (INB6)

The categories used to analyse unmitigated disagreement are set out in the Methods section. The subcategories have been established on the basis of a linguistic analysis and demonstrate the variety identified in the usage of this ELF community of practice.

Corpus and Method

Corpus

The corpus consists of 28 simulated negotiations involving 118 master's-level students. Thirteen took place in an oral exam situation (CEMS) and 15 as part of coursework (INB). The CEMS students were filmed with two examiners present in the room, in a pass/fail situation. The INB students were also filmed but were not monitored and graded. As all the students use English as their working language, it can be claimed that their usage meets the ELF description of 'an emerging English that exists in its own right' (Jenkins, 2007: 2).

The 118 speakers came from 28 different nationalities (cf. Appendix 2) and, with one exception (CEMS11), all negotiations included participants from more than one national background. In the CEMS set, the students were given an assignment in the form of an individual role brief and negotiated in groups of three or four. The INB set negotiated as opposite teams of two or three members each (A and B). Thus, they are not professional negotiators, which should be borne in mind when evaluating the data (Planken, 2005). While there are disadvantages in using this kind of material, there is also the advantage of being able to analyse sets of recorded negotiations based on scenarios that provide comparable data. As the scenarios were designed to make participants bargain over specific issues, they were also suitable for generating expressions of disagreement as an aspect of conflict talk. This kind of discourse is difficult to handle; textbooks recommend using mitigating or indirect strategies. As indicated above, expressing conflict is also a culturally sensitive issue, as interactants may have different preferences when it comes to using direct disagreement. As the aim is to reach consensus, a lack of mitigation may carry a risk of negotiation breakdown due to insufficient attention to rapport management.

Conflict Talk and ELF Communities of Practice   119

Method

The scenarios used for the team negotiations (the INB set) related to international sales negotiations, and involved 30 minutes preparation and an upper limit of 30 minutes of negotiation time, while the scenarios used for the individual role negotiations (the CEMS set) concerned issues like establishing joint ventures, Sunday trading, marketing strategies, and private use of the internet at work. This set had one hour to prepare, and a strict 15-minute limit to reach an agreement.

Each negotiation was read through with a view to identifying examples of unmitigated disagreement. This process required analysis of longer sequences of interaction, so a discourse analytical approach was adopted. Each instance was identified according to how it expressed disagreement with the preceding statement(s), and whether this was done without including mitigating elements. Further, to analyse the impact of unmitigated disagreement on the progress of the negotiation an analysis was made of how it was followed up by the next speaker(s), and how it related to issues raised at an earlier stage in the negotiation (Leung, 2010). In addition, the roles assigned to each speaker needed to be taken into account to decide whose position they supported in the negotiation (see e.g. F2 in (16) below).

In general, the negotiation process adopted was linear, proceeding via initiation, problem-solving and resolution phases (Holmes, 1992), but also had features of circularity, as different issues were revisited to make a package in the problem-solving phase. The two sets of negotiations were recorded under different circumstances. The CEMS set negotiated in an exam situation where rapport management is important to avoid a negotiation breakdown and exam failure, while the INB set did not have the pass/fail requirement. It is thus of interest to look into whether these different circumstances impacted on the students' choice of strategy. If directness represents a potential threat to rapport management and completing the negotiation task, it would be expected that CEMS students had a lower incidence of this type. For this reason the two sets are compared where relevant.

In Table 5.1, unmitigated disagreements acts (in italics) are presented under the category headings of (i) Blunt contradictions; (ii) Blunt contradictions introduced by *but*; (iii) Blunt contradictions introduced by *no*; (iv) *No*; (v) Blunt contradiction introduced by *not*; and (vi) Questions.

The forms of unmitigated disagreement described in (i) – (vi) above represent the kind of expressions that may be regarded as paying little regard to rapport management. In the following, I discuss how directness, in the form of unmitigated expressions of disagreement, impact on the ELF negotiation progress.

Table 5.1 Categories of unmitigated disagreement

Category/definition	Examples (expression of disagreement in italics)
(i) Blunt contradiction (not introduced by marker of negation (*no*, *not*), or *but*)	(3) **BM2**: so the rest you you don't want to pay anything at all basically **AM2**: yeah not really **AF1**: *we don't see that why we should* (INB18) (4) **AM1**: [(xx) sorry **AM2**: ok but we] are in a negotiation I mean you need to [(better be) flexible so **AM1**: yeah yeah we need] to be [we need to come **BF2**: *(we are) flexible*] (INB9)
(ii) Blunt contradiction introduced by *but*	(5) **BM2**: eh well ehm eh maybe we should run the cd back just a little bit eh a fifty per cent reduction in the cost is eh is a little bit too much **AM3**: *but it seems like both of your partners think fifty-fifty is a good thing* (INB17) (6) **F1**: ...and for instance if we sponsored a rugby cup eh we would attract a television audience we would really reach a lot of people and that's important **F3**: *but in a way we would only attract people interested in rugby* (CEMS11) (7) **BF2**: and I'm showing you that I'm willing to give you what you want and I'm showing you that I'm willing to give you free service **AM2**: *but* **BF2**: and we're going down way way I mean we're talking about a halving of the price (INB12)
(iii) Blunt contradictions introduced by *no*	(8) **BM3**: so have we [agreed on two per cent discount **AF2**: *no two per cent discount that is less* (INB7) (9) **AF2**: would that be okay if we such as you drop the price by ten per cent and **BM2**: [*no that's not possible* (INB3)
(iv) *No*	(10) **BF2**: ... the educational background of the maintaining engineering for for Latin Americans local company is just high school **AF1**: [*no* **AM2**: *no*] our partners are mainly Americans (INB1) (11) **BM2**: ...you want eight percent and you want also the other **AF1**: [*no, no* **AF2**: *no no* **BM2**: because if] we okay for us like otherwise we can talk about two per cent of discount... (INB3)

Table 5.1 (Continued)

Category/definition	Examples (expression of disagreement in italics)
(v) Blunt contradictions introduced by *not*	(12) **AF2**: would that be okay if we such as you drop the price by ten per cent [and] **BM2**: *no that's not possible* **AF1**: we will stand **BM2**: *not negotiable*] (INB3)
(vi) Questions	(13) **AM3**: ...and to to put an an administration fee that's that's the worst thing when it comes to we don't mean the money we mean like put an administration fee that's **BM2**: *you don't have an administrations fees in your bureau bureaucratic country of China* (INB6)

Results and Discussion

As indicated above, the preference for mitigation may be due to issues relating to rapport management, notions of politeness and also, perhaps, influence from textbooks. Although unmitigated expressions are not preferred, they do occur; in the following I discuss how the use of unmitigated disagreement impacts on the progress of the negotiation, whether a link can be found between unmitigated disagreement and whether an agreement was reached.

As shown in Table 5.2, the 118 participants in the present study produced 216 instances of unmitigated disagreement.

The preference was clearly for mitigated expressions, but we may note that the INB set had a higher proportion of unmitigated instances than the CEMS set did. This difference may be due to a greater concern for rapport management in the CEMS situation, as the students had to reach an agreement to pass the exam. There is also the fact that the INB students negotiated as teams, which creates a clearer opposition than the more individualised roles of the CEMS set in addition to the fact that the students were not being monitored in an exam situation. In comparison, it may be noted that Locher (2004: 143) identified lack of mitigation in 26% of her disagreement strategies.

Table 5.2 Total results of mitigated vs unmitigated disagreement

	MITIGATED	UNMITIGATED	TOTAL
INB (15 neg.)	378 (69.4%)	167 (30.6%)	545 (100%)
CEMS (13 neg.)	203 (80.6%)	49 (19.4%)	252 (100%)
INB + CEMS	581 (72.9%)	216 (27.1%)	797 (100%)

From a discourse analytical perspective it is clear that the unmitigated disagreement acts occurred in the problem-solving and resolution phases of the negotiations and not in the initial stages when the focus was on establishing the issues at stake (Holmes, 1992: 87–89).

In Table 5.1 I identify six different formal realisations of unmitigated expressions of disagreement. The disagreement acts subsumed under (i)–(iv) accounted for 95.3% of the total, as set out in Table 5.3. Repeated instances of *no* by the same speaker were counted as one occurrence, as in (11) above.

Whereas the INB set preferred using blunt contradiction (i), the CEMS set preferred introducing blunt statements by *but* or *no* (ii, iii). The INB set also made more use of *no*, either on its own or repeated. The difference in the use of *no* could be related to an increased attention to rapport management in the CEMS exam situation, as *no* – either on its own or repeated – is very direct. One may also speculate whether the higher incidence of blunt contradictions for the INB set relates to the same issue. Perhaps 'but' serves to signal a counterargument as part of a negotiation process, which a blunt contradiction may not do to the same extent. 'But' may also be used as an attempt to get the floor (Locher, 2004: 16). In some cases the bid for the floor was unsuccessful, and the speaker's turn consisted of *but* only. However, as the speaker clearly wished to express an objection in these cases, these examples have been included. As for (vi) Questions, we may note that BM2's question cited in Example 13 (Table 5.1) has polemical overtones, which may not be conducive to a positive rapport.

As lack of mitigation may pose a threat to rapport management, it is of interest to see how the speakers followed up these statements by looking at

Table 5.3 Results of categories of unmitigated disagreement

Unmitigated disagreement	CEMS	INB	CEMS + INB
(i) Blunt contradictions (BC)	18.4%	40.1%	35.2%
(ii) BC introduced by *but* (includes 11 ex. of *but* only)	53.1%	27.5%	33.3%
(iii) BC introduced by *no*	22.4%	15.6%	17.1%
(iv) No	4.1%	11.4%	9.7%
(v) BC introduced by *not* (includes 1 ex. of *not* only)	0%	4.2%	3.3%
(vi) Questions	2.0%	1.2%	1.4%
TOTAL	49 (100%)	167 (100%)	216 (100%)

the following turn(s). A case in point is the following exchange between AF2, AF1 and BM2. Turns following an unmitigated disagreement act (in italics) are set out in bold.

(14) **AF2:** would that be okay if we such as you drop the price by ten per cent and
  BM2: *[no that's not possible*
  AF1: **we will stand**
  BM2: *not negotiable]*
  AF2: **but we will stand for all the delivery costs you pay no you pay no delivery costs at all you will have one-year warranty given to us as well** (INB3)

In (14) above, BM2's first statement is followed by AF1 initiating an offer, but she is immediately interrupted by BM2. AF2 then comes in to complete the offer initiated by team member AF1. AF1's contribution could also be interpreted as a counterargument, as it objects to BM2's ultimatum that the issue is *not negotiable*. In Table 5.4, however, this type will be classified as an offer, as it does include a definite offer respecting one of the issues that are subject to negotiation.

In analysing the first turn following an unmitigated disagreement act, the following categories may be distinguished: (i) Counterarguments; (ii) Elucidation/completion of own argument; (iii) Agreement or concession; (iv) Offers; (v) Questions; (vi) Unintelligible speech and Other. Their relative distribution in the material is set out in Table 5.4.

Table 5.4 Follow-up of unmitigated disagreement acts

Follow-up of unmitigated disagreement act	INB	CEMS
(i) Counterargument	38.3%	42.9%
(ii) Elucidation/completion of own argument	26.9%	18.4%
(iii) Agreement or concession	12.6%	22.4%
(iv) Offers	5.4%	0%
(v) Questions	4.2%	2.0%
(vi) Unintelligible speech	4.2%	2.0%
Other (e.g. laughter/joke, repeating other side's position, personal comment)	8.4%	12.3%
Total	167 (100%)	49 (100%)

Each of these categories is illustrated by examples below.

(i) *Counterarguments*
These are statements made in response or retaliation to an argument. Thus, in (15), BM2's blunt disagreement is followed by AM3's counterargument, which BM2 tries to interrupt without success.

(15) **AM3**: but] I think you can always sign contracts but you will always come to situations which are not covered by the contract
BM2: *but this part is covered by the contract I mean that is I mean you have no reason [to say that*
AM3: **this part is] covered [but**
BM2: *this is]*
AM3: **even if you have a 1000 pages you can come to situations which you have have to build a trust** (INB6)

In (16), M1's blunt disagreement to the preceding argumentation is overlapped by F1's counterargument, which also includes F2's support for M1's position on bonuses:

(16) **M1**: *but the bonus] should should eh based on the individual effort [of each eh*
F1: **eh I think it should be**
F2: **yes]**
F1: **be based on on group eh achievements also** (CEMS14)

It is interesting to note that counterarguments represent the most common response to an unmitigated disagreement. Thus, the exchange of opinions carries on even if one or more of the participants express their views without mitigation.

(ii) *Elucidation or completion of own argument*
In (17), BF2 follows up AM2's unmitigated disagreement by elucidating her own position:

(17) **BF2**: because I mean for our engineers to come to a totally different country and
AM2: *but you've been here before to install the drilling piece*

BF2: oh well it's not always the same we keep re-education re-educating them so that they would be able to have the latest knowledge (INB12)

Another example is (18), where F1 sets out her position on retailing and is interrupted by F2, who unsuccessfully tries to get the floor, which allows F1 to complete her argument:

(18) F1: it might be costly] but on the other hand we're opening up a new market new possibilities and looking at the market [as
F2: *but*
F1: **it] is today it's eh there are possibilities** (CEMS 8)

This is a behaviour that is hardly helpful as it gives insufficient attention to what the other party has to say.

(iii) *Agreement or concession*
In (19), an exchange of blunt contradictions between teams A and B leads to a concession by Team B:

(19) BM1: well you say if you put the money over six months and we we delivery on 60 on 90 days
AM1: *you said it was possible for [60 days*
AF2: *60 days is really*
BM2: *no I think it's impossible*
AF2: *you just said it]*
BM3: **yes okay maybe we supply you in 60 days and we give you**
BM2: **payment on delivery** (INB7)

In (20), M1 and M2 debate whether it is feasible to restrict employees' access to internet at work, and M1 concedes that M2 has a point:

(20) M1: but then on the other hand it would perhaps ruin your learning experience if you were hindered from going there so how do you want to [solve that

M2:   *but] as internet user you know that some pages just pop up*
M1:   **I do** (CEMS17)

It may be surprising that unmitigated statements should lead to concession or agreement, but this behaviour is in fact relatively common (cf. Table 5.4).

(iv) *Offers*
In some cases, the follow-up may be a specific offer relating to one or more of the issues at stake, which is what BM3 does in (21):

(21) **AF2**:   *but that's discount [(five year)*
   BM3:   **we give you five year warranty] to prove our quality just to prove our quality** (INB7)

(v) *Questions*
In (22), M1 tries to work out F2's position on which subjects should be taught in a business school. Following F2's blunt *no* F3, who chairs the session, asks F2 to make her position explicit:

(22) **M1**:   is that what you're talking about as well you [(those) kind of subjects or you're talking about
   F2:   *no*
   F3:   **you focus on the student level]** (CEMS2)

(vi) *Unintelligible speech*
In (23), F2's statement concerning marketing strategy initiates an exchange of unmitigated statements with F3. This leads to unintelligible and overlapping speech, and F4 joins in to get the discussion back on track:

(23) **F2**:   but we can't say to the retailer you have to put our product in that corner or you have to decorate it like this
   F3:   *yeah we can do it*
   F2:   *no we can't*
   F3:   *@yes we can@*
   F2:   **[(xx)**

F3: (xx)
F4: yeah there are (some incentives and] solutions of course but (xx) (CEMS9)

In negotiations contexts, Fells (2010: 114) distinguishes between helpful and unhelpful behaviours, stating that 'interrupting, criticising and generally being in a hurry are counterproductive. They tend to close the discussion down'. In the corpus of this study, unmitigated disagreement frequently involves interruptions and overlapping speech. This is a kind of behaviour that may be due to a wish to express a counterargument, but the competition for the floor is so strong that the speakers cannot rely on sequential turn-taking to give them an opportunity to express their opinion. Another thing to note is that unmitigated disagreement is occasionally followed by unintelligible speech, which may occur for the same reason. However, negotiations continued even after the negotiators displayed Fells' (2010: 98, 114) 'unhelpful behaviour'.

Of the negotiations examined for this chapter, only three did not reach an agreement, and they failed for different reasons. In INB1, one of the teams tried to change the premises for the scenario, which derailed the negotiation as the opposite side did not want to pursue this option. The negotiators in INB3, which had the highest incidence of unmitigated disagreement, were unable to negotiate on packages, which turned much of the bargaining into exchanges on individual issues. They also included accusations, e.g. 'you are being too not flexible' (INB3). This latter feature was also present in INB7, where one of the negotiators applied time pressure on the opposite team to force through an agreement. This negotiator also used ultimatums, and expressed suspicion of the other side's motives, which may be related to Fells' (2010) 'unhelpful behaviours'. We may also note that many of the unmitigated disagreement acts were interruptions, and that the opposite team frequently continued by elucidating their own argument rather than paying attention to the opposite side's attempt to get the floor.

The participants in the corpus material came from 28 different national backgrounds. Their performance, however, did not give grounds for establishing an overall link between their national identities and a preference for using unmitigated disagreement. Nor was there any metadiscourse relating to how conflict talk was handled to show that the negotiators reflected on this issue. These results indicate that any nation-based cultural traditions are not automatically transferable to an ELF context, and that a certain cultural hybridity may take place. This also supports our community of practice analysis, as the participants may be said to have developed a shared approach when it comes to handling disagreement when using ELF. As indicated above, the use of unmitigated disagreement tended to be strategically motivated, and used to promote clarity and directness.

Handling conflict talk also involves rapport management, which is the major argument given in favour of mitigated forms. On the whole, however, rapport was maintained, even when unmitigated disagreement was used.

Conclusions

This chapter recounts an investigation of how expressions of unmitigated disagreement impacted on the ELF negotiations process, and the role of directness in ELF communication. From a textbook standpoint ELF speakers are encouraged to use mitigated expressions of disagreement. This implies that unmitigated disagreement may be negative for rapport management, and may thus carry a risk of negotiations breaking down. In analysing the discourse that followed such statements, however, it became clear that the negotiators were able to carry on negotiating following unmitigated disagreement acts, even when these led to unmitigated exchanges and overlapping speech. The most common follow-ups were counterarguments and agreement/concession, in addition to speakers elaborating on their own argument. While the two former are conducive to moving forward, the latter is less so, as it indicates insufficient attention to the other party's contribution. In general, negotiators seemed to take unmitigated disagreement in their stride and carry on.

As for a link between a high incidence of unmitigated disagreement acts and not reaching agreement, no firm conclusions may be drawn on the basis of this study. Only three of the negotiations did not end in agreement. This could not be directly linked to unmitigated disagreement, but concerned whether the scenario was to be followed, insistence on bargaining over individual issues rather than packages, the application of time pressure, and also using accusations, which is high on the list of unhelpful behaviour in negotiations. Thus, the results of this limited study indicate that there is no demonstrable link between the use of unmitigated disagreement and negotiations breakdown. Whether such a link can be established in real-life negotiations including professional negotiators, or by using a bigger corpus, is of course a different issue, and beyond the scope of the present investigation.

Thirteen of the negotiations took place as part of an exam, which requires an agreement for a pass grade. This set had a lower incidence of unmitigated disagreement, and less use of 'no' and blunt contradictions, which may be due to increased attention paid to rapport management by being less direct. In essentialist theory preferences for a direct versus an indirect communicative style are linked to national cultural differences. The present investigation revealed little systematic interference from any such interactional norms, indicating that any nation-based cultural traditions may not be automatically transferable to an ELF context, where cultural hybridity may come into play. The community of practice approach also pinpoints aspects of the participants in this study that may be relevant in ELF interaction, as they all have international experience, and belong to the same age bracket. While the overall preference was for using mitigation, the use of unmitigated disagreement did not prevent negotiators from reaching an agreement as long as the negotiators adhered to the negotiation scenario and paid attention to the other party's arguments. Thus, it would appear that the issue of mitigation in ELF conflict talk should be related to overall strategy, and take both the need for clarity and for rapport management into account.

Acknowledgments

I would like to thank Prue Holmes and Fred Dervin for their extensive comments and suggestions concerning earlier versions of this chapter. Any mistakes and misunderstandings are, of course, my own.

References

Baker, W. (2009) The cultures of English as a Lingua Franca. *TESOL Quarterly* 43 (4), 567–592.
Beamer, L. and Varner, I. (2008) *Intercultural Communication in the Global Workplace*. Boston: McGraw-Hill.
Bjørge, A.K. (2009) Conflict or cooperation: The use of backchannelling in ELF negotiations. *English for Specific Purposes* 29, 191–203.
Bjørge, A.K. (2012) Expressing disagreement in ELF business negotiations: Theory and practice. *Applied Linguistics* 33 (4), 406–427.
Canagarajah, A.S. (2006) Negotiating the local in English as a lingua franca. *Annual Review of Applied Linguistics* 26, 197–218.
Cardon, P.W. (2008) A critique of Hall's contexting model. *Journal of Business and Technical Communication* 22 (4), 399–428.
Charles, M. (2008) English as a lingua franca in global business. Presentation at ELF Forum March 6–8, 2008, University of Helsinki, Helsinki, Finland.
Dunkerley, K.J. and Robinson, W.P. (2002) Similarities and differences in perceptions and evaluations of the communication styles of American and British managers. *Journal of Language and Social Psychology* 21 (4), 393-409.

Ehrenreich, S. (2009) English as a lingua franca in multinational corporations: Exploring business communities of practice. In A. Mauranen and E. Ranta (eds) *English as a Lingua Franca: Studies and Findings* (pp. 126–151). Newcastle upon Tyne: Cambridge Scholars Publishing.
Fells, R. (2010) *Effective Negotiation*. Cambridge: Cambridge University Press.
Grimshaw, A.D. (ed.) (1990) *Conflict Talk*. Cambridge: Cambridge University Press.
Gudykunst, W.B. (ed.) (2003) *Cross-cultural and Intercultural Communication*. Thousand Oaks, CA: Sage.
Gudykunst, W.B., Ting-Toomey, S. and Nishida, T. (eds) (1996) *Communication in Personal Relationships across Cultures*. Thousand Oaks, CA: Sage.
Hall, E.T. (1976) *Beyond Culture*. Garden City, NY: Anchor Press.
Holmes, M.E. (1992) Phase Structures in Negotiation. In L.L. Putnam and M.E. Roloff (eds) *Communication and Negotiation* (pp. 83–105). Sage Annual Reviews of Communication Research 20. Newbury Park, CA: Sage.
House, J. (2003) English as a lingua franca: A threat to multilingualism? *Journal of Sociolinguistics* 7 (4), 556–578.
Jenkins, J. (2007) *English as a Lingua Franca: Attitude and Identity*. Oxford: Oxford University Press.
Jenkins, J., Cogo, A. and Dewey, M. (2011) State-of-the-Art Article: Review of developments in research into English as a lingua franca. *Language Teaching* 22 (3), 281–315.
Knapp, K. (2002) The fading-out of the non-native speaker. In K. Knapp and C. Meierkord (eds) *Lingua Franca Communication* (pp. 217–244). Frankfurt am Main: Peter Lang.
Leung, S. (2010) Conflict talk: A discourse analytical perspective. *Columbia University Working Papers in TESOL & Applied Linguistics*.
Locher, M.A. (2004) *Power and Politeness in Action*. Berlin: Mouton de Gruyter.
Louhiala-Salminen, L., Charles, M. and Kankaanranta, A. (2005) English as a lingua franca in Nordic corporate mergers. *English for Specific Purposes* 24 (4), 401–421.
Pennycook, A. (2007) *Global Englishes and Transcultural Flows*. London: Routledge.
Piller, I. (2011) *Intercultural Communication. A Critical Introduction*. Edinburgh: Edinburgh University Press.
Planken, B. (2005) Managing rapport in lingua franca sales negotiations: A comparison of professional and aspiring negotiators. *English for Specific Purposes* 24 (4), 381–400.
Rygg, K. (2012) Direct and indirect communicative styles. PhD dissertation, University of Bergen, Norway. See http://www.nb.no/idtjeneste/URN:NBN:no-bibsys_brage_30114
Seidlhofer, B. (2007) English as a lingua franca and communities of practice. In S. Volk-Birke and J. Lippert (eds) *Anglistentag 2006 Halle. Proceedings* (pp. 307–318). Trier: Wissenschaftlicher Verlag Trier.
Søderberg, A.-M. and Worm, V.D. (2011) Communication and collaboration in subsidiaries in China: Chinese and expatriate accounts. *European J. Cross-Cultural Competence and Management* 2 (1), 54–76.
Stalpers, J. (1995) The expression of disagreement. In J.F. Wagner and K. Ehlich (eds) *The discourse of business negotiation. Studies in Anthropological Linguistics* 8, 275–290.
Tognini-Bonelli, E. (2001) *Corpus Linguistics at Work*. Studies in Corpus Linguistics 6 series. Amsterdam: Benjamins.
Utley, D. (2004) *Intercultural Resource Pack*. Cambridge: Cambridge University Press.

Victor, D.A. (1992) *International Business Communication.* New York: HarperCollins.
Wenger, E. (1998) *Communities of Practice: Learning, Meaning, and Identity.* Cambridge: Cambridge University Press.

Appendix 1

Abbreviations/Acronyms

CEMS = Negotiation carried out as exam activity.
INB = Negotiation carried out as part of coursework.

Transcription conventions (extracts)

Based on ELFA (*English as a Lingua Franca in Academic Settings*). TranscriptionGuide 7/2004. Accessed 22 December 2008 from http://www.uta.fi/laitokset/kielet/engf/research/elfa/

Speakers

F	female participant (e.g. F1) (CEMS)
M	male participant (e.g. M2) (CEMS)
AF	team A, female member (e.g. AF1) (INB)
AM	team A, male member (e.g. AM1) (INB)
BF	team B, female member (e.g. BF1) (INB)
BM	team B, male member (e.g. BM1) (INB)
Utterances	speaker reference + space + utterance
Uncertain transcription	(text)
Unintelligible speech	(xx)
Laughter	@@
spoken laughing	@text@
Overlapping speech (word level)	[text] [A1 text, B1 text]
Capital letters	only in acronyms: EU

For ease of reading, the personal pronoun I, nationality nouns, and nationality adjectives have also been capitalised.

132 Part 2: Grounding Conceptual Understandings of Interculturality

The negotiations are numbered as INB1–INB18 and CEMS1–CEMS19; episode numbers are given in parentheses. Negotiations INB8, 10, 11 and CEMS1, 3, 5, 7, 10 and 13 were not included for this chapter, as they had no instances of unmitigated disagreement.

Appendix 2 Additional information on INB and CEMS negotiations

National backgrounds of participants cited, by group and negotiation number:

INB1 (AF1 Dutch, AM2 German, BF2 Chinese); INB3 (AF1 Spanish, AF2 Russian, BM2 Italian); INB6 (AM3, BM1, BM2 Swedish); INB7 (AM1 US

Setting	INB (course activity)	CEMS (exam activity)
Number of negotiations	15	13
Participants	69	49
Register	Formal	Formal
Total negotiation time (rounded)	5:24:00 (324 minutes)	3:10:00 (190 minutes)
Median negotiation time	23:30 min	13 min
Timespan	13–26 min	10–20 min
Participants (each neg.)	4–6	3–4
Preparation time	30 min	30 min
Grading	No grading	Pass/fail
Age (most candidates)	20–25	20–25
Gender	38 F, 31 M	26 F, 23 M
Time span	2006–2009	1995–2006
Nations represented	28: Australia, Austria, Belgium (French Belgian), Brazil, China, Colombia, Czech Republic, Finland, France, Germany, Ghana, Hungary, Italy, Latvia, Netherlands, Norway, Peru, Philippines, Poland, Russia, Spain, Sweden, Switzerland (Swiss German), Tunisia, Turkey, UK, US	10: Austria, Czech Republic, France, Germany, Hungary, Italy, Netherlands, Norway, Spain, Switzerland (Swiss German)

American, AF2 Dutch, BM1 Peruvian, BM2 Chinese, BM3 Ghanaian); INB9 (AM1 English, AM2 Turkish, BF1 Hungarian, BF2 Russian, BF3 Tunisian); INB12 (AM2 US American/Brazilian, BF2 Norwegian); INB17 (AM3 Norwegian, BM2 Colombian); INB18 (AF1 Polish, AM2 Chinese, BM2 German).

CEMS2 (M1 Norwegian, F2 Spanish, F3 Norwegian); CEMS8 (F1 Norwegian, F2 Italian); CEMS9 (F2 German, F3 French, F4 Italian); CEMS11 (F1, F3 Norwegian); CEMS14 (F1 Norwegian, F2 Russian, M1 Austrian); CEMS17 (M1 Norwegian, M2 Spanish).

CEMS11 had only Norwegian participants; in all the other negotiations (INB and CEMS) there were representatives from two or more nationalities.

6 Intercultural Misunderstanding Revisited: Cultural Difference as a (non) Source of Misunderstanding in ELF Communication

Jagdish Kaur

Introduction

The various approaches to intercultural communication have traditionally been based on the 'principle of difference' (Casmir & Asuncion-Lande, 1988: 284; see also Sarangi, 1994: 413). Differences across cultures presuppose that miscommunication and misunderstandings will occur in intercultural interaction. The greater the differences, the more complex and difficult the communication is predicted to be. This positive incremental association stems from the assumption that the absence of shared norms, values, beliefs, ways of thinking and usage of language between participants of different cultural backgrounds is likely to give rise to severe problems in communication. As Scollon and Scollon explain:

> When we are communicating with people who are very different from us, it is very difficult to know how to draw inferences about what they mean, and so it is impossible to depend on shared knowledge and background for confidence in our interpretations. (1995: 22)

This lack of common experiences and assumptions is said to contribute to the greater incidence of misunderstanding and miscommunication in intercultural communication. Samovar and Porter make this point when they say that 'the chief problem associated with intercultural communication is error in social perception brought about by cultural diversity that affects the perceptual process' and later add that 'unintended errors in meaning may arise because people with entirely different backgrounds are unable to understand one another accurately' (1991: 21).

More recent work in intercultural communication has attempted to move away from a preoccupation with misunderstanding and the supposed causal role of cultural difference. The edited volume *Beyond Misunderstanding* (Buhrig & ten Thije, 2006), for instance, showcases research that attempts to shift the analytical focus from concern with misunderstanding to the accomplishment of understanding. Further, the volume underscores the need to consider other variables that may contribute to misunderstanding in international encounters, in particular the institutional context of the interaction. Elsewhere, Piller shows how 'some misunderstandings that are considered "cultural" are in fact linguistic misunderstandings' whereas others 'are based on inequality' (2007: 215), thereby further emphasising the need to refrain from making *a priori* assumptions about cultural group membership. Scollon and Scollon (2001), working within a discourse approach, also assert that cultural background can only be considered a relevant category in communication when the participants themselves orient to it as such. After all, participants are also at any given time members of various other groups (e.g. gender-related, generational and professional, etc.) and these memberships can equally impact their communication. Similarly, Koole and ten Thije (2001) warn against solely focusing on cultural differences when analysing intercultural data as this could result in other significant features of the communication being overlooked. The methodological approach they adopt, i.e. a reconstruction method, seeks to uncover how participants in international interaction establish common ground in pursuit of their communicative goals; in this way they depart from the traditional focus on cultural differences and communicative failure. These studies are representative of some of the alternative approaches to intercultural communication that are based on an understanding of language and culture as dynamic and inherently heterogenous, rather than static and homogenous.

English is today acknowledged as a 'global lingua franca' (Seidlhofer, 2011: 2) that facilitates communication between speakers of varied first-language backgrounds and cultures in a wide range of domains. To date, much of the work on ELF has focused on the nature of English when used as a lingua franca, on how this linguistic resource is exploited in lingua franca settings to fulfil the communicative goals of its users, and the changes it undergoes at all linguistic and pragmatic levels as it is used to serve a variety of functions in an increasing number of domains by diverse groups of people. ELF researchers investigate a range of phenomena, including the variability of ELF, the practices and strategies used in successful ELF communication and the creative use of English in lingua franca settings. Moreover, they address issues that have to do with the reconceptualisation of English, the ownership of English and the implications of ELF to second language pedagogy (Seidlhofer, 2011; Jenkins *et al.*, 2011). Because the research focus has primarily been on English, certain aspects have been somewhat neglected; for example, the influence on ELF of various contextual factors such as its cultural and intercultural dimension as a global phenomenon. Thus a research gap has been created that both ELF and IC researchers should address in order to provide a more complete and comprehensive picture of ELF.

One aspect of ELF pragmatics that has received much research attention concerns miscommunication. Researchers not only investigate the causes of misunderstanding and non-understanding but also examine how such problems are pre-empted and resolved when they occur. Contrary to findings from mainstream intercultural communication research, studies on the use of ELF reveal that the occurrences of misunderstanding and miscommunication are not as widespread as initially thought and the misunderstandings that do occur cannot in fact be attributed to differences in the participants' cultural background (House, 1999; Mauranen, 2006). These findings suggest that the lingua franca context exerts some influence on interactions between participants of different cultural groups. In this chapter[1] I set out to investigate further the apparent acceptance of cultural difference in the ELF context of interaction and consider the relevance of notions like 'third culture' and 'third space' in explaining the phenomenon. Findings from research into ELF also provide further evidence to support an alternative approach to intercultural communication, one which accepts understanding as the default rather than misunderstanding.

Research on Misunderstanding in English as a Lingua Franca

For communication to be successful, shared understanding between the interacting parties is essential. However, the reality is that mutual understanding is not always achieved in the first instance and sometimes, not at all. Partial understanding, non-understanding and even misunderstanding can result as participants attempt to get meaning across. In this regard, communication in English as a lingua franca is perceived as being particularly problematic given that the speakers are not only of different cultural backgrounds but are also non-native speakers of the language in question (Mauranen, 2006, 2007). Although English functions as a medium of communication in interactions between its native speakers and other non-native speakers and ELF research itself 'does not exclude native speakers of English' (Jenkins et al., 2011: 283) from its study, many researchers to date have tended to focus their investigations on interactions in which English is not the native language of the participants. Participants in an ELF interaction thus not only have to contend with lack of shared knowledge and assumptions but also with different varieties of English, including those of native speakers, and levels of competence, all of which can heighten the risk of misunderstanding.

Notwithstanding the aforementioned challenges, findings from studies on ELF suggest that the problem of misunderstanding is far from critical. House, who examined a 30-minute interaction between four university students (i.e. a German, a Korean, a Chinese and an Indonesian) using English as a lingua franca, noted the 'paucity of misunderstandings' (2002: 251) in her data; while speech perturbations, poorly managed turn-taking and 'non-aligned, "parallel talk"' (House, 1999: 80) were common, open or overt misunderstandings could not be detected. Meierkord similarly commented on the lack of misunderstanding in her dinner-table ELF talk, recorded at a hall of residence for international students in the UK, and concluded that communication in ELF is 'a form of intercultural communication characterised by cooperation rather than misunderstanding' (2000: 11). As the participants in her study came from 17 different first language backgrounds, the expected outcome would be a range of different communicative norms and practices in use in interaction which could contribute to problems of understanding or miscommunication; instead the participants displayed communicative behaviour not generally associated with their linguacultural backgrounds, resulting in talk that was cooperative and supportive in nature with few misunderstandings. Meierkord attributed the above to the participants' awareness of their interlocutors' different cultural backgrounds which motivated them to negotiate and jointly construct new communicative practices and norms.

The above views are to some extent shared by Firth (1990, 1996) and Gramkow (2001) who work within a conversation analysis framework. Although use of non-standard forms in addition to various other linguistic anomalies were displayed in their ELF data, open or overt misunderstandings were rare. The near absence of misunderstanding, however, cannot be attributed to the let-it-pass strategy, which the participants are said to employ to deal with ambiguities and problems of understanding (see also House, 2002). Firth (1996) explains 'let-it-pass' as a move by the ELF speaker to deliberately allow ambiguities and problems of understanding to pass without comment when these are adjudged to be irrelevant to the unfolding talk. However, as misunderstanding presupposes that the recipient lacks awareness of having misinterpreted the speaker's meaning, unless pointed out by the speaker in the next turn, it would be erroneous to suggest the conscious application of a strategy by the recipient to downplay the problem. The let-it-pass strategy may however explain the lack of overt displays of non-understanding by the recipient as non-understanding presupposes that the recipient is conscious of his or her inability or failure to understand, wholly or partially, the speaker's message and thus has the option of either making it known to the speaker or letting it pass.

Others who have observed few instances of misunderstanding in their ELF data include Mauranen (2006), who attributes this to efforts by the participants themselves to prevent or pre-empt such problems from the outset. In addition to self-repairs, other pre-emptive measures include the use of various interactional practices such as repetition, confirmation and clarification requests and the like, which allow the participants to check, monitor and clarify understanding (see also Kaur, 2009). A more significant finding than the non-prevalence of misunderstanding in Mauranen's data, however, relates to the source(s) of misunderstanding.

> I found no clear evidence of culture-based comprehension problems, at least not in the traditional sense of 'national culture'. Apart from the most surface-level misunderstandings concerning the linguistic meaning of items, the other types are not specific to lingua franca communication, but likely to occur elsewhere independently of the speakers' native languages. (Mauranen, 2006: 144)

While much of the early work in intercultural communication attributes misunderstanding to cultural difference, the above finding highlights the need to refrain from treating the link between cultural diversity and misunderstanding as a given.

Like Mauranen, House (1999) failed to find a causal link between cultural difference and the understanding problems she detected in her data. House, who specifically set out to test the hypothesis that 'misunderstandings in ELF interactions are largely caused by differences in L1-based cultural knowledge frames and interactional norms' (1999: 75), found no supporting evidence in her data. House noted that the participants' affiliation with their native language and cultural norms is never foregrounded in their interactions in ELF: 'In ELF interaction, national and native language and culture adherence is eclipsed' (1999: 84). As such, the misunderstandings that occur cannot be traced to cultural differences; rather, House attributed the participants' problems of understanding to their lack of pragmatic fluency due to turntaking and interactional mismanagement in the main. House's study however was exploratory in nature as it involved the analysis of a 30-minute interaction, which was elicited rather than authentic, involving only four participants.

The findings of the two aforementioned studies suggest that interaction in ELF, while constituting one type of intercultural communication, may have features that are unique to it that not only minimise the occurrence of misunderstanding but also cause some other factor to take precedence over cultural difference as the main source of misunderstanding. This is particularly so considering that studies that examine native speaker-non-native speaker interactions have found misunderstanding to be a common occurrence. To delve deeper into the nature of (mis)understanding in ELF, Kaur (2011) conducted a study to examine the sources of misunderstanding in intercultural communication in ELF by analysing naturally occurring ELF data within the framework of conversation analysis (CA).

Sources of Misunderstanding in ELF Communication

Kaur (2011) examined 15 hours of naturally occurring spoken-interaction in English as a lingua franca which had been audio recorded at an institution of higher education in Kuala Lumpur.[2] The 22 participants, who were mainly graduate students, came from 15 different linguacultural backgrounds and therefore used English as the main medium of communication (see Appendix 1). As the students were required to work on several group assignments for their various courses, discussions pertaining to the assignments that took place outside the classroom formed a large part of the data. Casual conversations between the participants were also included as they constituted a large part of the interactions that took place in this setting. The recordings, which were conducted over a 10-week period by the participants themselves without the presence of the researcher, were then transcribed using a slightly adapted version of the notation system developed by Jefferson (2004) for CA (see Appendix 2).

An analysis of the participants' own understandings, as they are displayed in the turn-by-turn development of their talk, reveals a total of 33 overt misunderstandings. Following CA, the participants' perspective is taken into consideration, namely, that the participants orientate to the talk as being problematic, or as Schegloff puts it, 'the parties themselves address the talk as revealing a misunderstanding in need of repair' (1987: 204). Misunderstandings thus come to light when the speaker is seen to make a move to correct the understanding arrived at by the recipient, as displayed in the response given by the recipient to an enquiry or in a request for confirmation of understanding put forward by the recipient. It is the repairs therefore that 'anchor the analysis as misunderstandings and ... show what the participants treat as sources of the misunderstanding as well' (Schegloff, 1987: 204). Also, by taking into account the participant's perspective, phenomena other than misunderstanding such as non-understanding, performance errors and the like can be excluded from the analysis. In line with the principles of CA, elements of the social context such as the participant's cultural background are not treated as givens in the analysis of data; rather, the participants must be seen to be attending to such elements in their talk for their relevance to the talk to be acknowledged. By ensuring that any misunderstanding that is attributed to cultural difference is in fact grounded in the actual verbal conduct of the participants, the analyst is prevented from applying preconceived notions of a causal relationship between misunderstanding and cultural difference to the data.

All instances of overt misunderstanding were then examined in detail to determine the source(s) of the problem. Frequently, several factors can be seen to contribute to the problem, each interacting with the other(s) in complex ways (see also Bazzanella & Damiano, 1999; House, 1999; Weigand, 1999). It is for this reason also that Bremer *et al.* suggest that 'a constellation of several causal factors' (1996: 38), rather than a single cause, be considered when investigating the data. Where a misunderstanding could be attributed to several possible causes based on the details of the talk, all contributory factors are taken into account; the misunderstanding is, however, categorised according to the factor that can be most clearly seen to impact the understanding of the participant. A CA approach to the data failed to reveal any misunderstandings that could be attributed to cultural differences between the participants. In no one misunderstanding is the cultural background of the participant(s) seen to be contributory based on what is observable in the talk.

Extracts from Kaur's (2011) analysis of the main sources of misunderstanding in her ELF data are provided below.[3] The four main sources of misunderstanding identified are ambiguity (n = 16), performance-related misunderstanding (n = 10), language-related misunderstanding (n = 5) and gaps in world knowledge (n = 2).

Ambiguity

A major source of misunderstanding in the data pertains to the ambiguity inherent in many of the speakers' utterances. This constitutes a common source of misunderstanding even in intracultural communication

(Bazzanella & Damiano, 1999). Ambiguity itself can be traced to various sources, but the most common is the lack of explicitness on the part of the speaker. Weigand explains that '[n]ot everything is explicitly said in communication ... because of time-economical reasons and because we are not always aware of every piece of information that would be necessary for clear understanding' (1999: 777). As a consequence, the recipient is often left to infer meaning and not infrequently may draw the wrong inference and misunderstand the speaker's utterance.

According to Schegloff, problematic reference constitutes 'a commonly recognized potential source of ambiguity' (1987: 205) in communication. For instance, failure to make the connection between a pro-term and its referent is likely to result in an 'interpretive error' (Schegloff, 1987: 205), which manifests itself as a misunderstanding. Besides ambiguous reference, misunderstanding can also result from ambiguous semantics. In the case of the latter, the meaning of an utterance is open to different interpretations. Misunderstanding results when the interpretation achieved by the recipient is not the one intended by the speaker. Some of the ambiguities that lead to misunderstanding can be attributed to the speaker's failure to provide sufficient detail or context in the first place. Given the lack of information provided, the recipient is left to infer meaning. Under-specified utterances are obviously open to various interpretations and can result in misunderstanding.

Extract 1 is an example of a misunderstanding that stems from ambiguous semantics. D (Indonesian), citing an article he had read, informs S (Korean), his coursemate, that most American students admit to plagiarising at least 'once' in their lifetime, which makes it a common practice among students the world over.

Extract 1

1　**D:**　er they say ...(1.4) most of a: american students
2　**S:**　yeah
3　**D:**　they admit they:: that they if- they- ...(0.6) once of their life time
4　**S:**　yeah
5　**D:**　cheats: in the school.
6　**S:**　wa-once [of what? once of what?=
7　**D:**　　　　　[cheat
8　　　　　=once of in their:: er: ...(1.3) in their educations
9　**S:**　yeah
10　**D:**　in their er::: school time

11	**S:**	yeah
12	**D:**	they cheat once.=
13	**S:** →	=you mean er they don't cheat really er a lot-a lot?
14	**D:**	no
15	**S:**	they
16	**D:**	the-just the- the facts that er …(0.6) it's common for
17		everybody that (yes)=
18	**S:**	=it's common for everyone to cheat?
19	**D:**	yes

D's remark that most American students claim to have cheated at least 'once of their life time' (Line 3) elicits a request for recapitulation in Line 6. In response, D substitutes 'life time' with 'educations' and 'school time' (lines 8 and 10, respectively) as a means of addressing S's displayed problem. In Line 13, S makes a move to check his understanding of D's comment; S it appears has understood D's utterance to mean that American students rarely cheat in school. This interpretation is clearly based on the point that D has made about the students cheating 'once' in their lifetime or school time. D's move to execute repair in lines 16 and 17, however, succeeds in disambiguating the meaning of his prior utterance. The message D was trying to get across, contrary to S's interpretation, pertains to the point about 'most' American students cheating in school, thus making it a common phenomenon. In seeking to verify the accuracy of his understanding of D's prior turn, S reveals his misinterpretation of D's claim, which subsequently leads to a repair sequence in which the problem is addressed.

Ambiguity in the speaker's utterance seems to be the main source of misunderstanding in the ELF data examined. As stated above, various factors contribute to this ambiguity, which include problematic reference, ambiguous semantics and lack of specificity. The resulting misunderstandings however are not specific to ELF communication for they occur regularly in all types of communication. Bazzanella and Damiano, who examine intracultural interactions in Italian, state that 'ambiguity seems to play a major role in generating misunderstanding' (1999: 818) and attribute 66% of the misunderstandings in their data to this factor while in Kaur's study, ambiguity contributes to 48% of the misunderstandings.

Performance-related misunderstanding

Some of the misunderstandings in the data are clearly the result of performance problems such as mishearing and slips of the tongue. Bremer *et al.*, however, caution that a misunderstanding which is attributed to faulty hearing may have been 'reinforced by another factor such as the utterance having been spoken quickly and/or unclearly' (1996: 38). This is certainly relevant in many ELF interactions where the participants speak different varieties of English with some variation in pronunciation and accent that can impinge on the clarity and intelligibility of sound segments (Jenkins, 2003). Inability to identify the phonological sequence of a word or phrase can cause the recipient to 'come to a false identification' (Weigand, 1999: 775) resulting in misunderstanding. Whereas mishearing constitutes a problem at the perception level, this translates into misunderstanding at the comprehension level (Dua, 1990, as cited in House *et al.*, 2003). Thus incorrect understanding is achieved on account of the incorrectly heard word or phrase.

In Extract 2, D (Indonesian) and M (Burmese), who are coursemates, are talking about a research proposal they have to write for a particular course. D hears the word 'gender' as 'general' and incorrectly understands the topic of M's research proposal to pertain to something 'general'.

Extract 2

1	**D:**	and how about the: Halimah ...(1.2) proposal [((mumbles))
2	**M:**	[uh no-no-no: idea at
3		all. it's quite difficult? so I was thinking I write gender
4		(1.5)
5	**D:** →	general:=
6	**M:**	=er gender
7	**D:**	oh uh gender?
8	**M:**	yeah gender issues

D's mishearing of the word 'gender' is displayed in the next turn, in Line 5, in what is meant to be a repeat of the word. D's (incorrect) repeat comes after a 1.5-second pause, which suggests that D finds the word 'gender' in M's prior utterance problematic. Since D appears to have heard the word 'general' instead of 'gender', '... I write (on) general' is syntactically incomplete as it is missing a noun following the attributive adjective 'general'. D orients to this incompleteness by withholding an immediate response. When M fails to produce additional talk, however, D takes up the next turn to repeat the prior incorrectly perceived word. The repeat, produced with a sound stretch, appears designed to elicit a clarification or a completion of the prior utterance but it also alerts M to the problem. M's repair in the form of a simple repeat of the problematic item in Line 6 is 'oh'-receipted by D in Line 7, which suggests 'a change of state of knowledge or information' (Heritage, 1984: 309) – in this case, a change in the understanding achieved. The questioning repeat that follows the particle 'oh' (Line 7) allows D to check that the understanding now achieved is in fact correct, which M confirms in the next turn.

The kind of misunderstanding examined above is to be expected in everyday speech regardless of whether the participants in interaction are monocultural or multicultural. While incorrect identification of the phonological sequence of a word, i.e. mishearing, is presumed to be more frequent in ELF talk, given the greater variation in pronunciation and accent, there is no evidence to support this in the data. Only 4 of the 33 misunderstandings identified could in fact be attributed to faulty hearing on the part of the recipient.

Language-related misunderstanding

Some of the misunderstandings found in the data can be attributed to language problems on the part of one or both of the participants in interaction. That some of the participants face problems in their use of the language is evidenced by the many ungrammaticalities and disfluencies detected in the data. For the most part, however, these linguistic anomalies do not pose an obstacle to achieving successful communicative outcomes. In fact findings from research into ELF show that non-native speakers of English are adept in their use of communication strategies and interactional practices to negotiate meaning and arrive at mutual understanding (see for example Kaur, 2010; Pitzl, 2005; Watterson, 2008). Nevertheless, some of the misunderstandings in the data can be traced to the speaker's non-standard use of lexical items while others are triggered by the lack of coherence in the speaker's utterances.

In Extract 3, D (Indonesian) is telling his coursemate, S (Korean), about a case of plagiarism he had read about on the internet. D's non-standard use of the verb 'make', as in 'make plagiarism', may have contributed to S's misunderstanding of D's utterance.

Extract 3

1	D:	and I found that …(1.1) in internet the::: …(1.5) the news about
2		…(2.5) a very: high level: case of …(0.8) plagiarism one of
3		assistant professor at harvard or something like that
4	S:	yeah
5	D:	er they say that they admit make a::
6	S:	plagiarism?
7	D:	yes

8	S: →	oh he-he allow plagiarism?
9	D:	no he o he he make- he-he do he do=
10	S:	=he-he-he did the plagiarism?
11	D:	he did the plagiarisms

In Line 5, D uses the expression 'they admit make a', which S correctly completes with the noun *plagiarism* (Line 6) when D displays difficulty in finding the relevant next word. Although D incorrectly uses the third person plural pronoun instead of the singular one, it is his use of the expression 'admit make a plagiarism' which is misinterpreted by S, as revealed in his request for confirmation in Line 8. S understands D's use of 'admit make' to mean 'allow'. That S's enquiry is 'oh'-prefaced seems to reflect S's own surprise at discovering this (incorrect) piece of news, namely, that an assistant professor had condoned the act of plagiarism. This suggests that S's use of the word 'allow' is a display of genuine misunderstanding and is not the result of an incorrect choice of word. D's switch to the word 'do' in Line 9 indicates that he is probably aware of the inadequacy of the verb 'make' in conveying his meaning; his use of the verb 'do' reflects an attempt to drive home the point that the lecturer concerned was in fact the perpetrator of the act.

Gaps in world knowledge

Some of the misunderstandings that occur in the data can be attributed to gaps in the recipient's knowledge of the world. Such misunderstandings thus pertain to content rather than language. However, as the example below shows, the speaker's lack of competence in the language can to some extent exacerbate the problem. Efforts to clarify meaning in such cases are not always successful as the speaker may lack not only sufficient knowledge of the topic in question but also the necessary linguistic resources.

In Extract 4, M (Burmese) informs her coursemates K (Cambodian) and S (Cambodian) that a lecturer who will be teaching them soon suffers from Parkinson's disease. M's attempts to explain the lecturer's medical condition however results in misunderstanding, as displayed in K's request for confirmation in Line 23.

Extract 4

1	M:	so whenever he er: he came here Tim: Tim help him because
2		he's got parkison, you know parkison disease?
3	K:	hu:h=

4	S:	=°what's that°?=
5	M:	= where he's shaking all the time
6	S:	uhhuh
7	M:	and then er before he: got up er: er Tim have to do timing
8		one: two: three and then pull him.
9	S:	oh
10	M:	really hhh
11	K:	( ) pull his hand?
12	M:	yeah er er you know he's shaking his muscle is shaking
13	K:	mm
14	M:	and: and then in the class for him er: er they have to arrange
15		microphone
16	K:	mm
17	M:	from different ...(0.6) different you know corner
18	K:	huh
19	M:	so: so that we can hear. ...(2.0) so he-he- i- he's coming in
20		february I think.
21	K:	february?
22	M:	yeah. =
23	K: →	= oh from from pakistan huh?
24	M:	er n-no no he's er not er: er pakistan ...(0.6) er parkison disease
25		he's having.
26	K:	mm
27	M:	mister sin- I think- I- I'm not sure where is- where is he from
28		...(1.1.) so huhhuhhuh=
29	K:	=very strange [teacher that we have here.
30	M:	[huhhuhhuhhuhhuh

The misunderstanding above can be attributed to various interacting sources. In the first place, M pronounces the word 'parkinson's' as 'parkison'. This does not appear to be a mere slip of the tongue as she consistently and systematically produces the word as such in Extract 4 (lines 2 and 24). In response to S's request for clarification in Line 4, M manages to describe only one physical symptom of the disease, i.e. 'he's shaking all the time'. Thus, in addition to K's and S's own lack of knowledge of the subject, M herself displays gaps in her knowledge of the matter; M fails to provide adequate clarification of the disease and its symptoms. In Line 23, K seeks confirmation that the lecturer in question is from 'pakistan'. K has clearly misunderstood 'parkison' to mean 'pakistan' in spite of the explanation provided by M following S's request for clarification. The repair that M performs following K's displayed misunderstanding does little to shed light on the matter. K's remark regarding the strangeness of the lecturer (Line 29) indicates that understanding has not been achieved. While there are several factors contributing to this misunderstanding, it is the lack of knowledge of the subject in question on the part of the recipient – and the speaker, to some extent – that is most significant.

In the extract above, mutual understanding seems not to have been achieved despite the attempts made to address the misunderstanding. This may be attributed to the fact that several factors can be seen to contribute to and complicate the misunderstanding. It appears that lack of world knowledge on the part of the recipient and gaps in the knowledge of the speaker can lead to misunderstandings that are irreparable. It is also possible that M may have been hampered in her efforts at clarifying meaning due to the lack of relevant vocabulary, as the disfluencies in the repair turn suggests. The hesitation markers in Line 24 in the extract above point to some form of trouble, in this case a possible word search in progress. The absence of hesitation in the earlier turns to the extent displayed in the repair turn, and the switch in topic following the unsuccessful repair attempt does seem to suggest difficulty in finding the words needed to clarify meaning. It is therefore conceivable that some limitations of vocabulary on the part of the M may have also contributed to her inability to successfully repair the misunderstanding.

Significance of Findings to Intercultural Communication Research

By taking into account the local context, i.e. the turns and the turns within sequences produced by the participants themselves, and the orientations of the participants as well as the repair moves that follow the displayed misunderstanding, Kaur (2011) reveals that the sources of misunderstanding in her ELF data, with the exception of the language-related one, have also been observed to contribute to misunderstanding in communication between people of the same linguacultural background. Ambiguity, mishearing and lack of world knowledge have been identified as common causes of misunderstanding in intracultural interactions (Weigand, 1999). Thus, although the participants communicating in ELF are of diverse cultural backgrounds, this does not seem to create any additional problems where the co-construction of understanding is concerned, at least in the case of the data in this study.

As stated previously, much of the early research conducted on intercultural and interethnic communication, regardless of whether it is from a cultural-anthropological perspective, an interactional-sociolinguistic perspective or a cross-cultural pragmatic perspective (see Sarangi, 1994), attribute the misunderstandings that occur to the differences in the participants' cultural backgrounds. The lack of shared assumptions and beliefs among the participants, together with their use of different discourse strategies and communicative styles, is said to render such communications difficult and problematic. Kaur's study, conducted within a conversation analysis framework, however, finds no evidence of the above. None of the misunderstandings in her data can be traced to differences in the participants' cultural background, a finding previously noted by House (1999) and Mauranen (2006).

The findings provide support for some of the new perspectives on intercultural communication and the issue of misunderstanding (see Buhrig & ten Thije, 2006; Piller, 2007). Hartog, for instance, at the outset of her paper, raises questions on whether 'the category of "misunderstanding" is discriminating and thus relevant for analysing intercultural communication' (2006: 176) and whether 'all communication [is] intercultural simply because members of different [national] cultures meet' (p. 175). Approaching both language and culture as social action and applying a functional-pragmatic discourse analysis method on a genetic counselling session between a German doctor and Turkish counsellees at a university hospital in Germany, Hartog (2006) found the institutional setting of the interaction to be contributory to what traditionally may have been interpreted as intercultural misunderstanding. Hartog further asserted the need to move away from conceptualising an interaction as 'intercultural' simply because the interactants are of different cultural backgrounds. Interestingly enough she found only one instance in the entire interaction she examined to be intercultural, that is, where the participants orientated to differences in their cultural backgrounds as relevant.

Fine-grained analyses of ELF data that take an emic perspective, as in the case of this study, have produced findings similar to that of Hartog (2006) and others like Rost-Roth (2006). Confining the analysis to the details of the talk on a turn-by-turn basis reveals that the participants misunderstand on account of factors that similarly affect the understanding of speakers in monocultural settings. The absence of culture-based misunderstanding in 15 hours of naturally occurring interactions in ELF is certainly noteworthy. In addition, the small number of misunderstandings identified in the data confirms that talk between people of different cultural backgrounds is hardly synonymous with misunderstanding in spite of previous claims made to this effect. House, who put forward 'the culture irrelevance hypothesis' to investigate 'the non-influence of ELF speakers' native linguaculture' (1999: 84) in

ELF interaction attributes the absence of adherence to native language and national culture to 'a focus on interpersonal and individual concerns' (House, 1999: 84). Kaur, however, offers an alternative explanation for this phenomenon, namely, a concern with achieving mutual understanding and accomplishing communicative goals in the lingua franca. It is this concern in all likelihood that underlies much of the participants' efforts at co-constructing new practices and procedures, negotiating and accommodating to each other, all of which have been widely documented in ELF research findings (see Jenkins et al., 2011).

The notion of 'third culture', which has been put forward 'to clarify the dynamics of communication in an intercultural setting' (Casmir & Asuncion-Lande, 1988: 294), may to some extent explain both the absence of culture-based misunderstanding and the overall small number of misunderstandings detected in ELF talk despite the diversity and variability present in terms of the variety of English spoken, level of linguistic competence and cultural background, amongst others. Conversely, findings from research into the use of ELF provide empirical evidence to support the idea of a third culture. As Casmir and Asuncion-Lande explain, a third culture is more than just the fusion of the interacting participants' separate cultures; rather it derives from 'the "harmonization" of composite parts into a coherent whole' (1988: 294). Participants in intercultural communication can surely be expected to be aware of and highly sensitive to any differences that exist between them with regard to norms, values and behaviour. It is conceivable that in the interest of achieving shared understanding, a prerequisite to accomplishing their communicative goals, these differences are put aside or suspended through 'temporary behavioural adjustments' (1988: 294) made in and through interaction as a means of converging in a cultural space that is shared between the participants. Casmir and Asuncion-Lande (1988) suggested that in adjusting and readjusting to each other, participants build upon commonalities that already exist between them. In ELF communication, the participants share the status of being non-native speakers of the language and possibly a 'shared incompetence' (Varonis & Gass, 1985: 71) in the language. As many of the examples above show, the threat of communication breakdown is a very real one when participants are compelled to use a medium of communication that is not their native language. It is possible then that the lingua franca context, perhaps more than any other context of interaction, causes participants to put aside cultural difference and seek out or create common cultural forms and practices that can contribute to shared understanding and successful communicative outcomes.

A study conducted by Meierkord (2002) to investigate the presence of culture in lingua franca communication provides some evidence of the workings of a third culture in ELF. Meierkord found very few instances in her ELF data where participants employed culture-specific practices when communicating in English and this too was confined to only two features, i.e. the use of proverbial expressions from the participant's native culture by two participants, and the use of first language norms when requesting by a number of participants. She explained that 'a large number of features that can be said to characterise lingua franca conversations in my corpus are not reflections of the participants' mother tongues' communicative norms' (2002: 117). For instance, turn management and pausing behaviour which are generally considered to be culture specific could not in fact be linked to the speakers' linguacultural background. In addition, laughter and pausing were used by the participants in novel ways, that is, to substitute verbal back-channels and to mark topic and phase boundaries, respectively. By suspending the use of norms and practices associated with their native culture and employing instead universal features known to all, e.g. laughter and pausing, to perform new functions, the participants may be seen to be creating third culture practices and procedures, which may contribute to minimising the incidence of misunderstanding, particularly culture-based ones.

Further evidence that participants in ELF communication are able to limit the incidence of misunderstanding, especially culture-based ones, by creating and adopting third culture practices comes from a more recent study by Baker (2009). Baker's study is motivated by an interest to gain deeper understanding of the relationship between language and culture in ELF. In addition to analysing ELF spoken data, he conducted interviews with some of the participants who were Thai speakers of English. These interviews are illuminating in that they shed light on what the participants perceive themselves as doing when communicating with people of other linguacultural backgrounds in ELF. Baker, in his comments on one of the participant's responses states the following: 'She has adapted them [English native speaker norms] to suit her own needs and purposes and arrived at a different place that is free from the conventions of any one particular culture' (2009: 580). The participants by their own admission refrain from falling back on the norms and practices of their native culture when communicating in an ELF setting. Likewise, English native speaker norms are never fully adopted in this context. Baker, in summarising his finding, asserts that communication in ELF occurs in a 'third place' (see also Kramsch, 1993) characterised by conventions and practices that are distinct from the participants' native culture as well as the culture of the native speaker of English.

Both Meierkord (2002) and Baker (2009) provide evidence that participants in ELF communication are inclined to suspend recourse to their native culture norms and practices when interacting, and instead, jointly seek out or create shared practices to facilitate communication in the lingua franca. Cultural differences between participants in such instances cease to be foregrounded during the course of the interaction as participants collaborate, negotiate and adapt to create meaningful communication that allows for communicative goals to be achieved. This would certainly account for the absence of culture-based misunderstanding in ELF as noted by House (1999), Mauranen (2006) and Kaur (2011).

Conclusion

Findings from research into the use of English as a global lingua franca by speakers of varied linguacultural backgrounds provide support for some of the new perspectives on the subject of misunderstanding in intercultural communication (Buhrig & ten Thije, 2006). There is mounting evidence to suggest that misunderstanding and miscommunication need not be the expected outcome when people engage in intercultural encounters. Nonnative speakers of English in international settings have shown themselves to be able to produce and interpret meaning successfully in the language, despite the diversity of the cultures in contact and the variability and lack of stability in the Englishes used. Findings in fact point to a form of intercultural communication that is 'characterized by a high degree of interactional robustness, cooperation, consensus-seeking behaviour and affiliation' (Firth, 2009: 149). This is not to say that ELF communication is devoid of problems; exchanges are not infrequently marked by speech pertubations and disfluencies but equally, participants in ELF communication have been observed to exert much effort in monitoring, adapting, negotiating and accommodating, utilising a great number of strategies designed to clarify and raise the explicitness of their utterances and to preempt problems in understanding.

In much of ELF research, the participant's perspective is paramount and findings are based on what the participants themselves orientate to as relevant in their communication. Cultural difference it appears is not what defines their interactions, rather it is a thing to be downplayed in the course of the interaction in favour of what is common and shared. Participants seek our commonalities and where there are none, jointly create practices and procedures to facilitate communication. With increasing criticisms against the approaches adopted in and the focus of intercultural communication research from within the field and the move to not only reassess current practices but also reconfigure basic notions such as 'culture' and 'intercultural' (e.g. Buhrig & ten Thije, 2006; Lavanchy *et al.*, 2011; Piller, 2007), findings from ELF research provide strong support for such developments.

Findings from ELF communication research also raise questions linked to pedagogical implications and practices. While the approach thus far has been to consider and attempt to devise effective means to incorporate cultural awareness raising in second/foreign language pedagogy, interactions in ELF reveal that participants are highly competent in handling diversity in intercultural communication. Having acquired a first language, and likely, a second and multiple other languages, at varying levels of proficiency, ELF users appear to have developed the skills and abilities required to negotiate and to adapt to the linguistic and cultural diversity and variability present in ELF contexts of interaction (cf. Canagarajah, 2007). As Baker says of the respondents in his study, 'many of the participants viewed cultures as mixed, hybrid, and open, and saw the need to adapt, interpret and mediate between different cultures' (2009: 585). Given the above, cultural awareness raising in second/foreign language pedagogy that is limited to inculcating in learners knowledge of one's own culture as well as the culture of the Other(s) is insufficient in preparing learners for the realities of present day global communication. Not only is it unrealistic to expect learners to have knowledge of all the cultures they are likely to encounter but it is equally impossible to predict the cultures they may come into contact with (Baker, 2012). Further, second/foreign language learners may have already acquired varying degrees of cultural knowledge and awareness through their first language.

House asserts that '[i]nstead of cultural knowledge, it is *linguistic knowledge* which is of prime importance in ELF interactions' (emphasis as in the original) (1999: 85). The assertion is certainly valid when one takes into account Piller's comment, based on the findings of numerous studies, that 'misunderstandings predominantly result from limited proficiency in one or more of the languages of the participants in the interethnic encounter' (2007: 218). Kaur's (2011) findings also show that some of the misunderstandings in her data could be traced directly to a language problem on the part of a participant and language inadequacies can exacerbate problems associated with (mis)hearing, ambiguity and lack of world knowledge. Knowledge of the grammar, vocabulary and phonology of the language is, albeit crucial, in itself insufficient to provide for successful communication in international settings. Similarly, heightened awareness and knowledge of the differences between national cultures is unlikely to be very helpful when boundaries are increasingly becoming blurred and culture takes on a more dynamic and fluid hue (Baker, 2011).

Although it is beyond the scope of this chapter to delve into how findings from ELF research can translate into concrete pedagogical practices (if indeed they can), what is certain is that developing in learners the skills – both linguistic and communicative – displayed and strategies employed by successful multilingual English speakers interacting in multicultural settings should be made an integral part of any second/foreign language programme.

Notes

(1) This chapter consists of a slightly revised version of 'Intercultural communication in English as a lingua franca: Some sources of misunderstanding', first published in *Intercultural Pragmatics* 8:1 (2011), 93–116.
(2) Details of the participants, the setting and the methodology employed are provided in Kaur (2011: 98–100).
(3) Other examples of how these four factors contribute to misunderstanding can be found in Kaur (2011: 100–111).

References

Baker, W. (2009) The cultures of English as a lingua franca. *TESOL Quarterly* 43 (4), 567–592.
Baker, W. (2011) Intercultural awareness: Modelling an understanding of cultures in intercultural communication through English as a lingua franca. *Language and Intercultural Communication* 11 (3), 197–214.
Baker, W. (2012) From cultural awareness to intercultural awareness: Culture in ELT. *ELT Journal* 66 (1), 62–70.
Bazzanella, C. and Damiano, R. (1999) The interactional handling of misunderstanding in everyday conversations. *Journal of Pragmatics* 31 (6), 817–836.
Bremer, K., Roberts, C., Vasseur, M.T., Simonot, M. and Broeder, P. (1996) *Achieving Understanding: Discourse in Intercultural Encounters*. London: Longman.
Buhrig, K. and ten Thije, J.D. (2006) *Beyond Misunderstanding: Linguistic Analyses of Intercultural Communication*. Philadelphia: John Benjamins.
Canagarajah, S. (2007) Lingua franca English, multilingual communities, and language acquisition. *The Modern Language Journal* 91, 923–939.
Casmir, F.L. and Asuncion-Lande, N.C. (1988) Intercultural communication revisited: Conceptualization, paradigm building, and methodological approaches. *Communication Yearbook* 12, 278–309.
Dua, H.R. (1990) The phenomenology of miscommunication. In S.H. Riggins (ed.) *Beyond Goffman: Studies on Communication, Institution and Social Interaction* (pp. 113–139). Berlin: Mouton de Gruyter.
Firth, A. (1990) 'Lingua franca' negotiations: Towards an interactional approach. *World Englishes* 9 (3), 269–280.
Firth, A. (1996) The discursive accomplishment of normality: On 'lingua franca' English and conversation analysis. *Journal of Pragmatics* 26 (2), 237–259.
Firth, A. (2009) The lingua franca factor. *Intercultural Pragmatics* 6 (2), 147–170.
Gramkow, K. (2001) *The Joint Production of Conversation*. Centre for Languages and Intercultural Studies, Aalborg University.
Hartog, J. (2006) Beyond 'misunderstandings' and 'cultural stereotypes'. In K. Buhrig and J.D. ten Thije (eds) *Beyond Misunderstanding: Linguistic Analyses of Intercultural Communication* (pp. 175–188). Philadelphia: John Benjamins.

Heritage, J. (1984) A change-of-state token and aspects of its sequential placement. In J.M. Atkinson and J. Heritage (eds) *Structures of Social Action: Studies in Conversation Analysis* (pp. 299–345). Cambridge: Cambridge University Press.
House, J. (1999) Misunderstanding in intercultural communication: Interactions in English as lingua franca and the myth of mutual intelligibility. In C. Gnutzmann (ed.) *Teaching and Learning English as a Global Language* (pp. 73–89). Tubingen: Stauffenburg.
House, J. (2002) Communicating in English as a lingua franca. In S. Foster-Cohen, T. Ruthenberg and M.L. Poschen (eds) *EUROSLA Yearbook* 2 (pp. 243–261). Amsterdam: John Benjamins.
House, J., Kasper, G. and Ross, S. (2003) Misunderstanding talk. In J. House, G. Kasper and S. Ross (eds) *Misunderstanding in Social Life: Discourse Approaches to Problematic Talk* (pp. 1–10). London: Longman (Pearson).
Jefferson, G. (2004) Glossary of transcript symbols with an introduction. In G. H. Lerner (ed.) *Conversation Analaysis: Studies from the First Generation* (pp. 13–23). Philadelphia: John Benjamins.
Jenkins, J. (2003) *World Englishes*. London: Routledge.
Jenkins, J., Cogo, A. and Dewey, M. (2011) Review of developments in research into English as a lingua franca. *Language Teaching* 44 (3), 281–315.
Kaur, J. (2009) Pre-empting problems of understanding in English as a lingua franca. In A. Mauranen and E. Ranta (eds) *English as a Lingua Franca: Studies and Findings* (pp. 107–125). Newcastle upon Tyne: Cambridge Scholars Publishing.
Kaur, J. (2010) Achieving mutual understanding in world Englishes. *World Englishes* 29 (2), 192–208.
Kaur, J. (2011) Raising explicitness through self-repair in English as a lingua franca. *Journal of Pragmatics* 43 (11), 2704–2715.
Koole, T. and ten Thije, J.D. (2001) The reconstruction of intercultural discourse: Methodological considerations. *Journal of Pragmatics* 33 (4), 571–587.
Kramsch, C. (1993) *Context and Culture in Language Teaching*. Oxford: Oxford University Press.
Lavanchy, A., Gajardo, A. and Dervin, F. (2011) Interculturality at stake. In F. Dervin, A. Gajardo and A. Lavanchy (eds) *Politics of Interculturality* (pp. 1–25). Newcastle upon Tyne: Cambridge Scholars Publishing.
Mauranen, A. (2006) Signaling and preventing misunderstanding in English as lingua franca communication. *International Journal of the Sociology of Language* 177, 123–150.
Mauranen, A. (2007) Hybrid voices: English as the lingua franca of academics. In K. Flottum (ed.) *Language and Discipline Perspectives on Academic Discourse* (pp. 243–259). Newcastle upon Tyne: Cambridge Scholars Publishing.
Meierkord, C. (2000) Interpreting successful lingua franca interaction. An analysis of non-native/non-native small talk conversations in English. *Linguistik Online* 5 (1). See http://linguistik-online.com (accessed 21 October 2004).
Meierkord, C. (2002) 'Language stripped bare' or linguistic masala'? Culture in lingua franca conversation. In K. Knapp and C. Meierkord (eds) *Lingua Franca Communication* (pp. 109–133). Frankfurt am Main: Peter Lang.
Piller, I. (2007) Linguistics and intercultural communication. *Language and Linguistic Compass* 1 (3), 208–226.
Pitzl, M.-L. (2005) Non-understanding in English as a lingua franca: Examples from a business context. *Vienna English Working Papers* 14, 50–71. See http://www.univie.ac.at/Anglistik/Views0502mlp.pdf (accessed 28 September 2008).

Rost-Roth, M. (2006) Intercultural communication institutional counseling sessions. In K. Buhrig and J.D. ten Thije (eds) *Beyond Misunderstanding: Linguistic Analyses of Intercultural Communication* (pp. 189–215). Philadelphia, PA: John Benjamins.
Samovar, L.A. and Porter, R.E. (1991) *Communication between Cultures*. Belmont, CA: Wadsworth.
Sarangi, S. (1994) Accounting for mismatches in intercultural selection interviews. *Multilingua* 13 (1–2), 163–194.
Schegloff, E. (1987) Some sources of misunderstanding in talk-in-interaction. *Linguistics* 25 (1), 201–218.
Scollon, R. and Scollon, S.W. (1995) *Intercultural Communication*. Oxford: Blackwell Publishers.
Scollon, R. and Scollon, S.W. (2001) Discourse and intercultural communication. In D. Schiffrin, D. Tannen and H. Hamilton (eds) *The Handbook of Discourse Analysis* (pp. 538–547). Oxford: Blackwell.
Seidlhofer, B. (2011) *Understanding English as a Lingua Franca*. Oxford: Oxford University Press.
Varonis, E. and Gass, S. (1985) Non-native/non-native conversations: A model for negotiation of meaning. *Applied Linguistics* 6 (1), 71–90.
Watterson, M. (2008) Repair of non-understanding in English in international communication. *World Englishes* 27 (3–4), 378–406.
Weigand, E. (1999) Misunderstanding: The standard case. *Journal of Pragmatics* 31 (6), 763–785.

Appendix 1

Table 6.1 Participants according to ethnicity, mother tongue and role (Kaur, 2011)

	Ethnicity	Mother Tongue	Role	No.
1.	Burmese	Burmese	Student	1
2.	Cambodian	Cambodian	Student	2
3.	Filipino-Chinese	Chinese	Lecturer	1
4.	Indonesian	Indonesian	Student	1
5.	Italian	German	Research Student	1
6.	Korean	Korean	Student	2
7.	Laotian	Lao	Student	1
8.	Malaysian-Malay	Malay	2 Students, 1 Lecturer	3
9.	Malaysian-Chinese	Chinese	3 Students, 1 Research Student	4
10.	Malaysian-Indian	Tamil	Research Fellow	1
11.	Nigerian	Igbo	Student	1
12.	Spanish	Spanish	Lecturer	1
13.	Sri Lankan	Sinhala	Student	1
14.	Thai	Thai	Student	1
15	Vietnamese	Vietnamese	Student	1

Appendix 2

The transcription notations (Jefferson, 2004) used in this chapter are as follows:

[	a left square bracket marks the onset of overlap
]	a right square bracket marks the end of overlapping talk; this feature, however, is only indicated when it can be accurately discerned
=	an equals sign marks latching
–	a hyphen marks a cut-off
...(0.6)	a numeral placed within parentheses following three dots marks a pause of 0.6 seconds and above
:	a colon marks a stretched sound
?	a question mark marks rising intonation
.	a full stop marks falling intonation
,	a comma marks continuing intonation
.hhh	a series of 'h's preceded by a dot marks audible inhalation
hhh	a series of 'h's not preceded by a dot marks audible exhalation
°soft°	degree signs mark speech that is relatively softer than the surrounding talk
(done)	words within parentheses mark the transcriber's uncertainty of the actual words produced
( )	empty parentheses represent segments of talk that could not be transcribed
((sighs))	double parentheses enclose the transcriber's comments

7 Finnish Engineers' Trajectories of Socialisation into Global Working Life: From Language Learners to BELF Users and the Emergence of a Finnish Way of Speaking English

Tiina Räisänen

Introduction

English as a lingua franca, ELF, is *the* world language and thus the inevitable communicative medium of choice for many speakers of different first languages. This is the starting point most often adopted for the exploration of both ELF and BELF, i.e. English as a business lingua franca (Louhiala-Salminen *et al.*, 2005; Seidlhofer, 2011: 7). In the study of ELF, it is also important to consider how its users, ELF speakers, embody different communicative repertoires (Räisänen, 2013) and linguacultural backgrounds (Risager, 2010) and the ways in which such a background is constructed in communication. When ELF speakers communicate, they always bring their unique repertoires, background assumptions and expectations into locally constructed interactions in different ways (see also Baker, 2009; Jenkins, 2007: 43; Jenkins *et al.*, 2011; Seidlhofer, 2006: 43). An individual's communicative repertoire refers to the package of all the resources available to them and used by them to communicate meaning (Blommaert & Backus, 2011: 7). Repertoire development is influenced by one's unique trajectories of socialisation and access to community memberships and interactions. The same applies to an individual's linguaculture which, as Risager (2010: 8) argues, develops as a result of, on the one hand, membership in communities (i.e. the collective aspect) and, on the other, the person's history and biography (i.e. the individual aspect). Linguaculture is tied first of all to the language(s) one first acquires, and it develops further as the individual learns additional languages. One's communicative repertoire and linguaculture form the basis for the identification of the self; thus, they are important in the study of ELF users' discursive identity construction.

This chapter investigates the ways in which a group of Finnish engineers discursively construct their language user identities by drawing on their collective and individual backgrounds. It illustrates a trajectory in their discursive identity construction and their enregisterment of Finnish ways of speaking English over time. It elaborates on my co-authored paper with Professor Tarja Nikula (Virkkula & Nikula, 2010), which investigated discursive identity construction among Finnish ELF users as revealed in interviews with seven engineering students aged 22–26 years both before and after a stay abroad, in Germany, in 2003. After that, the participants were again interviewed during their employment in an international company in Finland from 2008 to 2010. This data is added to the analysis to show the ways in which identity work and processes of enregisterment change as individuals gain experience in intercultural encounters and are socialised into new ways of speaking during their global employment. The findings also illustrate how ideas of culture and nationality become more and more important for people in making sense of lingua franca interactions and of themselves as users of English.

This chapter focuses on discursive identity work in interviews as individuals talk about themselves as English language learners and users. This chapter extends the discussion in the earlier paper by exploring how cultural and intercultural dimensions feature in discursive identity construction, particularly in working life proper, where the study participants communicate with people from various backgrounds. Consequently, this chapter addresses a gap in research which to date has largely overlooked the cultural and intercultural dimensions in ELF users' identity construction. By taking a non-essentialist and post-constructionist stance to questions of identity, this chapter focuses on the ways in which identities emerge, are locally negotiated and discursively constructed in interviews.

The present participants are viewed as drawing on discourses (or Discourses; Gee, 2005) related to English in their talk, such as discourses of language proficiency, Finnishness and global working life. Simultaneously, individuals position themselves as certain kinds of people (Davies & Harré, 1990), or construct a certain kind of identity for themselves. Over time, as the participants become mobile globally, their discursive identity construction changes and begins to incorporate more cultural and intercultural aspects. For example, the participants focus on the challenges they meet in intercultural interactions, and their feelings and emotions attached to those interactions; they foreground and question stereotypes; and they begin to accept new ways of doing and being, and to assess their earlier assumptions about nationalities. Such processes can be seen as part of the development of intercultural competence, which has been defined, for example, as a relational ability to manage intercultural interactions (Spitzberg & Changdon, 2009: 7, as cited in Holmes & O'Neill, 2012: 708). In the interviews, the participants foreground the notion of 'culture' in discussing their intercultural experiences. Discursive manifestations of culture of this kind have been defined as being of central interest in discussion of the intercultural dimensions of communication in the age of globalisation (Piller, 2011).

The present chapter is organised as follows: first it introduces the longitudinal study, the participants and the theoretical approach adopted in the study. Next, the chapter presents the dichotomy between the language learner and language user identity as foregrounded in the earlier study (Virkkula & Nikula, 2010). In particular, the chapter illustrates the ways in which a language learner identity emerges out of the Finnish schooling system, but is later reconstructed and seriously challenged when the participants engage in intercultural encounters during their stay abroad in Germany and in working life proper. In their identity construction as users of English, the participants assign value to linguistic features and differentiate them from the rest of the language. In these enregisterment processes (Agha, 2007), culture and nationality are discursively attached to ways of speaking. This becomes even stronger in working life. Finally, the chapter ends with a discussion and conclusion.

The Study and the Participants

This chapter focuses on Oskari, Pete, Risto, Simo and Tero (pseudonyms), who were interviewed three or four times during the period 2003–2010. The participants' first language is Finnish; they were born between 1977 and 1981 and they have lived in Finland all their lives. Each of them studied English for seven years at junior and secondary school, and for three years in either high school or vocational school. In total, they studied English as a school subject for 10 years, and took a few courses at their polytechnic (now officially called a university of applied sciences). The participants carried out an internship of four to six months in Germany in 2003 when, for the first time, they used English extensively as a lingua franca. I, as a researcher and a student of German, also carried out my own language practice period abroad, accompanied the participants to Germany, and lived in the same student hall of residence for five months. This situation enabled me to gain an ethnographic, insider's perspective of the participants' lives in Germany and of the kinds of communicative situations they encountered. They interacted with German, Greek, Chinese and Indian students living in the same hall of residence. At work, they communicated with their colleagues, who were mostly of German or Portuguese origin. English was the principal lingua franca. The participants also used some German in their workplace, because according to company policy, interns were encouraged to learn German rather than use English, because German was the only language known to many of the German employees.

The participants were interviewed in Finnish first at the beginning of their stay, and then they were interviewed again at the end of the stay or after the stay was over. The first interviews concentrated on the participants' views of foreign language proficiency in general, their own proficiency in particular, and their feelings about using English. Prior to their internship in Germany, these students saw the use of English principally in terms of speaking. None of them had travelled abroad earlier for more than two weeks, and many mentioned the lack of opportunities to speak English in Finland. Interestingly, research has discovered that Finnish people in general now encounter and appropriate English through various forms of new media, information technologies and through products of popular culture (cf. Leppänen & Nikula, 2007; Leppänen et al., 2011). However, the participants encountered English more than spoke it; they referred to the school context and occasional encounters with tourists when describing their experience of speaking English. In addition to the themes of the first interviews, the second interviews emphasised the participants' actual experience of being abroad and the effects it had on them and their skills as foreign language users. In particular, the interviews focused on the participants' encounters with people in English and their perceptions of these encounters.

After the period abroad, the engineering students returned to Finland, completed their studies in two years and were either already employed or almost immediately received a job in sales, project engineering or project management in an international company based in Finland. Their employer companies had English as either the official or the working language – hence, the participants began to use English in more varied ways for professional purposes. The longitudinal ethnographic research project continued in 2008. The participants were followed at work in Finland and in some of their work trips abroad (in the US and China), their work-related interactions were audio- or video-recorded and they were interviewed for a third round (once or twice, 2008–2010) about their experiences of working life English and possible changes in their conceptions of themselves as English users since 2003 (for more information about the ethnographic study, see Räisänen, 2013).

Discursive approach to ELF users' identity construction

Virkkula and Nikula (2010) and, similarly, I in this chapter adopt a discursive approach to ELF users' identity construction because such an approach makes it possible to tackle participants' own understandings and points of view, i.e. the discourses they draw on. This chapter also utilises perspectives belonging to the sociolinguistics of globalisation, in which ethnographic approaches (e.g. drawing on Hymes, 1996) have gained more ground with the aim of gaining a holistic understanding of what language does to people and what people do to language (Blommaert, 2010).

When people communicate and interact, they draw on discourses which, according to Gee (1990: 143), are 'socially accepted association[s] among ways of using language, of thinking, feeling, believing, valuing and of acting that can be used to identify oneself as a member of a socially meaningful group or "social network", or to signal (that one is playing) a socially meaningful "role"'.

Discourses are thus representations of knowledge from a particular point of view (see also Gee, 2005). They offer, in a way, tools for identification of the self and the other (Georgakopoulou, 2007). For example, when individuals construct a sense of themselves as users of English, they draw on pre-existing discourses about English, language proficiency and communication, which they have learned and into which they have become socialised during their lives. A discursive approach is necessary for exploring cultural and intercultural aspects of language use because it is often beneath the surface that we witness the kind of reality participants construct, reject, embrace and reconstruct, i.e. layers of hidden discourses (Dervin, 2011). By uncovering such discourses one is able to trace the ways in which individuals construct identities in relation to intercultural encounters and their linguistic and discursive choices when talking about their experiences.

Such a discursive approach forces the researcher to critically examine his/her own biases, assumptions and understandings, which have a direct influence on the interview interaction, questions asked and replies given (Dervin, 2011: 47). In other words, interviews should be seen as interactions, and analysis should consider the interviewer's word choices and points of view, which have a direct impact on the way the interviewee answers the questions and talks about the topics. If we are to properly analyse intercultural encounters and understand them, the very method of data analysis should also consider aspects of interculturality, interaction and the co-construction of knowledge between the interviewer and the interviewee. As a result of such analysis, we can witness a unique perspective on the one hand (occurring only in that moment, at that time) and a co-constructed perspective on the other hand (the interviewer and the interviewee making sense of the world with their own repertoires and linguacultures).

In the present study, the participants and the researcher shared a very similar linguaculture, similar trajectories of socialisation into Finnish discourses and common experiences during the stay abroad. Thus, this shared background should be acknowledged when interpreting the participants' accounts of themselves as language users, their descriptions of good language proficiency, and their labelling of and judgments about their own and other people's ways of speaking and communication. These co-constructed metapragmatic typifications provide information about the kinds of ways of speaking being enregistered and about how cultural and intercultural dimensions are part of such enregisterment work. Importantly, which discourses individuals have access to depends on their linguaculture and intercultural experiences. By implication, access to discourses is unequal among different individuals, and this inherently characterises intercultural communication, which is 'typically between people who have starkly different *material, economic, social and cultural resources* at their disposal' (Piller, 2011: 173, italics added).

Discussion of research findings

The linguistic identity that emerges out of the Finnish schooling system

In ELF-related research, two main identity options are identified for users of English as a foreign language: those of a language learner and a language user (Jenkins, 2007; Jenkins *et al.*, 2011: 307–308; Virkkula & Nikula, 2010). They are seen to orient to language use in different ways. While the learner's ultimate goal would, ideally, be to approximate as closely as possible to native speaker skills, the language user is less preoccupied by such considerations; instead, he or she is more focused on language for communication. Of course, in the context of schooling and foreign and second language education, teachers approach pupils foremost as learners. Hence, learners are socialised into discourses of schooling which function as powerful resources in students' discursive identity construction. We (Virkkula & Nikula, 2010) found this in our earlier study with Finnish engineering students.

In Virkkula and Nikula (2010), my co-author and I showed how the participants responded to the question of whether they thought they were good at English. Although such a question about good language skills already evokes a particular discourse (i.e. evaluation), the participants evaluated their skills as lacking something, not being particularly valuable, and thus highlighted their shortcomings in language proficiency. The participants explained that they had had very little experience of using English with others before their stay abroad, so their views were restricted to the experiences they had had, i.e. learning English at school, using it only receptively and a little outside school. Therefore, from the perspective of their linguacultural background, they understandably constructed learner identities.

The 'ELF experience' affecting identity construction

When approaching users of English from the perspective of communication and interactional abilities rather than the evaluation of linguistic proficiency, individuals' performance is seen as legitimate in their own right (e.g. Jenkins, 2006). Moreover, ELF speakers can be viewed as affiliating with members of different groups and different ELF users in various ways: they may wish to create their own shared, temporary membership; to bring their earlier assumptions and discourses into their ELF interactions; or to reinvent their current identities by blending into other linguacultural groups (Baker, 2009 and this volume; Jenkins *et al.*, 2011). At other times, these speakers may very strongly hold on to their identities as constructed through primary and secondary socialisation in their previous contexts – hence rejecting what an ELF situation has to offer (i.e. new identities). Thus, neither ELF interactions nor ELF user identities are static; rather, they are changing and fluid and emerge as such especially when investigating individuals' trajectories across contexts and over time. Identities that have been constructed earlier do not disappear but gain new meanings when individuals engage in new intercultural encounters. Such multiple, fluid and negotiable identities characterise post-constructionist understandings of what identity is (e.g. Pavlenko & Blackledge, 2004).

Virkkula and Nikula (2010) show how Finnish engineering students began to see themselves as legitimate (Norton, 2000) users of ELF in relation to other ELF speakers with whom they interacted abroad. They also learned to recognise and use English in new ways and assign different values to English and their own ways of speaking it. In the interviews, they constructed new identities related not only to language but also to nationality and group membership. Hence English used as a lingua franca enabled them to engage with realities other than their own and thus to develop intercultural competence (Piller, 2011: 53). Example 1 (please see Appendix 1 for transcription conventions) captures the positive effect of their stay abroad very well:

Example 1

Tiina: so how did it make you feel when you were able to say what you really wanted
Tero: well yes it felt quite good and there was a sort of a feeling of success

As Example 1 illustrates, a period abroad can generate powerful emotional effects (see also Jackson, 2008; Kinginger, 2004; Kinginger & Belz, 2005). The effects for the participants in the present study were both positive and negative; on the one hand, their stay abroad contributed to raising self-confidence in their English skills in certain contexts, but on the other hand, they found the period emotionally demanding and it aroused feelings of anger and frustration, either because the desired effects of the stay abroad were not reached (see also Gallucci, 2013) or because the participants experienced communicative challenges, for example, at work or in public offices. However, rather than constructing identities as incompetent language learners and linguistic identities with concerns about coping with specific skills, they constructed identities as competent language users and communicators who could survive with their repertoires in daily life. Finally, a collective identity as Finnish speakers of English as a lingua franca emerged more strongly than in the first interviews, conducted before they left for Germany or at the beginning of the stay, as will be shown in the following section.

A strengthening sense of Finnishness

In addition to changes in the individuals' discursive positions from learners to users, the engineering students began to talk about themselves from within a more macro perspective, i.e. not only as individual users of English, but also as Finns in relation to other speakers of English. Thus the collective aspect of linguaculture strengthened in their identity work as a result of staying abroad: the participants constructed identities as Finnish people and engaged in enregistering Finns' English as a distinct way of speaking with either negative or positive value for them, depending on the discourse drawn on. This is how nationality and national culture emerged as resources for identity construction. Example 2 illustrates the growing sense of being a Finnish speaker of English.

Example 2

Risto: well I think that if you compare Finns themselves then maybe it is a bit better the sort of general level [---] well I've had that impression also before but I've noticed it here as well that other people aren't terribly good at English either

Here Risto is asked to evaluate himself on a European scale as a speaker of English. He acknowledges the fact that other people for whom English is not a native language do not know English terribly well either and that Finnish people perhaps possess 'a bit better' skills in general. 'Finnish English' (my own label) was associated by the participants either with one's own way of using English or with Finns' ways of speaking in general, the point of comparison being either a native-speaker of English, or a speaker of English as a foreign language or as a lingua franca. In Example 3, Simo introduces the notion of a Finnish way of speaking which is not nice to hear, especially when evaluated by a native speaker.

Example 3

Simo: it's [my speaking] (.) basic Finnish [---] well the way Häkkinen also speaks (.) pronunciation is probably not [---] it isn't nice to hear (.) when (.) if an English person hears it or (2.0) people from any country for that matter (.) it really is distinguishable (.) [---] maybe it's like childish for Finns to pronounce it in a fancy way or something like that but of course you try to speak as clearly as possible (.) you wouldn't dare to pronounce them in any way you like (*miten sattuu* in Finnish)

In this example, Simo evaluates his pronunciation as 'basic Finnish' and likens it to the English of another Finn, the former Formula 1 driver Mika Häkkinen, who was often interviewed in English in the international media. Furthermore, Simo contrasts Finnish and native speaker pronunciation by valuing the latter more and assigning authority to English people to judge his Finnish-style speech. Interestingly, Simo seems to consider non-native speakers' adherence to native speaker pronunciation to be 'childish' and 'fancy', and he assumes this is why Finnish people do not pronounce like native speakers. Hence, rather than being unable to pronounce English correctly, Finns, according to Simo, possess agency to select their own way of speaking. Moreover, Simo seems to resist the power of native speakers by aligning himself with those Finns for whom native-like language use carries overtones of acting in a fancy way, i.e. not being true to oneself and others. This is how

Simo discursively constructs an identity as a Finnish speaker of English, distinguishing different ways of speaking English and assigning values to them.

Furthermore, the way Häkkinen speaks functions as a model for Simo to recognise both Finnish and his own way of speaking. It is common in enregisterment processes to establish such a model and associate a way of speaking with a person (cf. Goebel, 2010: 172). Therefore, although Simo understates his own pronunciation skills, his Finnish way of speaking is a powerful cultural resource for constructing a language user identity. This relates back to the personal and collective aspects of linguaculture (Risager, 2010) discussed earlier: even though Simo describes his individual way of speaking, by drawing on a shared discourse of Finnishness, he is able to justify his peculiarities in speaking. Last, Simo's attempt to pronounce as clearly as possible and his statement 'you wouldn't dare to pronounce them in any way you like' indicates his awareness of appropriate behaviour and sensitivity in intercultural encounters.

As discussed in Virkkula and Nikula (2010), the participants describe Finns' speaking competence in more favourable terms than that of Germans and other users of English as a foreign language. This finding should be situated in the context in which the participants lived and interacted: they could use little English with the native speakers of German at work, partly due to company policy and partly because most of their German colleagues were not proficient in English. These factors probably influenced the participants' discursive construction of most Germans as 'reluctant to speak English', preferring German instead. Such a discourse about Germans may partly explain why the participants embraced Finns' English skills. A study by Dervin (2013) confirms that ELF users often opt for comparing their performance to that of others. Furthermore, the Erasmus students in Finland and France he studied evaluated Finns' English skills positively. In the present study, the positive value ascribed by the participants to a Finnish way of speaking is based on: (1) the Finnish educational system, praised by the participants for its emphasis on foreign language studies; (2) the participants' own Finnish way of pronouncing English, which is seen as clearer than, for example, Indians' pronunciation (see Virkkula & Nikula, 2010: 267); and/or (3) the simple notion that other people, particularly Germans, are not terribly good at English either (266).

Perhaps comparing oneself to others is safer collectively, particularly if one's own group is seen in a more positive light. This is shown in Example 4, in which Pete is asked to discuss what features of his own English skills, on the one hand, helped him cope in Germany and which, on the other hand, prevented him from doing so. Instead of answering from his personal point of view, he chooses to talk about language proficiency in Finland and Finns' skills in general.

Example 4

Pete: [---] [in Finland] everybody studies English today (.) almost [---] you're not probably as nervous about it as Germans are [---] maybe Finns have a lower barrier to speaking

Risto (Example 2) also thought that Finns' skills were a bit better than those of other Europeans and conceded that other people are not terribly good at English either. These all point towards raising awareness of local ways of speaking English and a shared sense of their Finnish nationality. Contrasting 'Us' and 'Them' can, obviously, lead to national stereotyping, but in this case adopting a collective identity as 'we Finns' and relating this to other groups also serves as a way of putting into perspective participants' earlier concerns about speaking English fluently, as also other people are seen to share similar shortcomings. Again, intercultural encounters affect one's identity construction and in this case have contributed to the engineering students drawing on a discourse of Finnishness which, clearly, is an important discursive resource for defining the self (and the other) as a speaker of English (for a discussion on nationality as an interactional resource, see Jenks in this volume).

However, these analyses and discussions focus on a rather narrow sense of identity, i.e. that related to language proficiency. Moreover, had the engineering students lived in another country, their experiences and views would likely have been very different. For a holistic understanding of the influence of a stay abroad on identity construction, one should also consider the intercultural dimensions of identity work and the processes of acquiring and developing intercultural competence. Questions worth asking are, for example, do the participants foreground stereotypes, move beyond opposing 'Us' and 'Them' and challenge their own views about cultures? How do they manage intercultural encounters? By considering these aspects, we can find evidence of more complexity than was found in the earlier focus on language and language proficiency in Virkkula and Nikula (2010).

To illustrate the intercultural experience further, there are one or two other points worth mentioning. The participants were at first very excited about their forthcoming period abroad, but their adjustment to Germany involved many ups and downs. The 'downs' were particularly due to adjusting to German culture. German culture was constructed in various ways in the interviews. It was seen, for example, as rigid, a conclusion reached from the various difficulties they experienced in interactions with officials and the hierarchical company structure in the workplace, which prevented the students from handling issues smoothly. Then again, some participants were not satisfied with their job at the factory and saw it as a waste of their time because it was not demanding enough for them; some of them left Germany a month earlier than initially planned because of this. By contrast, other participants were more open and tolerant, able to adjust to the circumstances, and enjoyed every new possibility they encountered during their stay. Judging by the engineering students' stories, their stay abroad also contributed to widening their worldview and their appreciation of Finland as a home country. Thus, feelings of national belonging and patriotism strengthened, but also awareness and understanding of the other.

As a result of their stay abroad, the participants became more aware of cultural differences and engaged in the process of foregrounding stereotypes, such as that Finns are silent and Germans are rigid. Such stereotypes were also challenged, and individual differences acknowledged. In the post-stay interview Tero, for example, explicitly said how he would not have expected Finnish and German cultures to be so different. When I asked what he meant by that, Tero (Example 5) explained.

Example 5

Tero: it is a bit different to do business in stores and everything in general those offices and then also people behave differently in a certain way [...]

Tiina: where does it show does it show when you speak with someone or in general handle things?

Tero: well it is for example handling things for example in offices it just doesn't seem to work I don't know if it is because of the language barrier or what but (.) the culture is a bit different

Here, Tero and I are constructing a sense of how handling everyday matters in Germany is different from in Finland. For Tero, encounters with German people have contributed to his view of cultural differences (his last line, 'the culture is a bit different'), with daily interactions as an example of where 'it just doesn't seem to work'. Tero's notion of the widely used term 'language barrier' points to a learned discourse which is often introduced to explain communication difficulties between people speaking different languages. Tero provides two explanations for the difficulties in Germany: the language barrier, and different cultures.

Later in the interview, when I asked if anything in particular had made Tero's adjustment to Germany difficult, he mentioned Germans' unwillingness to speak English. He thus referred to language problems due to the other. Because the participants knew little German, they encountered difficult situations at work and were unable to defend themselves in conflicts.

The German language hence functioned as a powerful tool in the workplace with which the hosts could rule the visitors (cf. Dervin & Layne, 2013). Those situations were described as frustrating by the participants and as forcing them to manage their emotions. Tero illustrates his rising awareness of Germans' distinct way of communicating compared to Finns: he explained that Germans use their hands more, and use facial expressions and different tones of voice to make a point.

The emergence of a Finnish BELF user identity

As the first two interviews showed significant changes, it is not surprising to find even more changes after the participants had moved into professional life. For example, the participants now described their progress with English in terms of a specialised vocabulary and being able to 'talk business', but they also felt regression because of their sometimes limited ability to use English at work (Räisänen, 2013). Moreover, their identity as a Finnish user of English had strengthened even further, had gained new meanings and had become a crucial factor for the participants in how they defined their professional communication in English. This part of the analysis focuses on the discursive construction of a Finnish BELF user identity and the enregisterment of a Finnish way of speaking in working life proper.

As the analysis of post-stay abroad interviews (the second set of interviews) showed, experiences in lingua franca situations contributed to the emergence of counter discourses and a trajectory of values assigned to a Finnish way of speaking. In working life proper, as illustrated in the third set of interviews, the constructed discourse of Finnish English (i.e. that there is something special in the Finnish way of speaking and using English) becomes even more valuable for the participants and a resource for constructing a BELF user identity. Example 6 shows how Oskari assigns great value to the way Finnish people speak and know English. Such appreciation has to do with Oskari forgiving himself for the shortcomings in his own pronunciation.

Example 6

Tiina: do you think there have been changes in your language proficiency [---]?

Oskari: the fear to speak is probably completely gone [---] I sort of know that I (.) cannot speak as well as- that I have forgiven myself (.) in pronunciation and the like as I have really noticed even more (1.0) how well Finns speak English and know and understand it compared to what I have encountered in the world and that there is no reason to feel humble about it

This example first illustrates the changes that Oskari has experienced over time and with his increasing intercultural encounters: his own hesitation about speaking has vanished, he has noticed that he can cope with the English he knows, and his self-confidence as a user of English has grown. Yet Oskari discursively frames this realisation as being possible after noticing his own and Finns' good English skills. In particular, the example illustrates ethnocentrism, as Oskari highlights and praises Finnish people's language proficiency as opposed to others. It is not certain what Finns are particularly good at in Oskari's opinion, but Finns' competence is particularly highlighted because Oskari does not want Finns to feel ashamed of their language skills – as is usually the case. This finding is common throughout the study.

Leppänen et al.'s (2011) findings on Finns' perceptions of different ways of speaking English suggest that Finns' admiration of native speakers' skills influence their typifications. In the present study, the participants gradually begin to appreciate Finns' English skills and modify their earlier assumptions about appropriate language use and communication. This implies that national culture and nationality are indeed important in using English as a lingua franca, and while people use and talk about ELF, they strongly construct their identities in relation to both their own nationality and culture, and to their intercultural encounters. Oskari above focuses mostly on language, but in some other cases (see the following example), the participants might reinforce their regional or professional identities. A mere linguistic identity, i.e. that of a language learner or language user, is too narrow for conceptualising identity in using English as a lingua franca.

In working life, the participants used English for various purposes with people from different linguacultural backgrounds. Some common, identifiable features characterise a Finnish way of business communication: discourses of Finns as not very talkative and as direct communicators explicitly emerge in the interviews. In Examples 7 and 8, both Risto and Tero describe themselves as typically Finnish – again, nationality emerges as a discursive resource in constructing a sense of self.

Example 7

Tiina: how does your small talk go?
Risto: well my [small talk] is sort of taciturn – typically Finnish but then again as I gradually gain more confidence about being able to talk lightly and my speaking flows better so that I no longer have to translate sentences and words in my head before speaking it is much easier and more natural too

Example 8

Tiina: what observations about language did you make in the US [---]?

Tero: people start talking more easily than for example in Finland for example they may start talking to you in an elevator and that scares a kind of Ostrobothnian guy like me heheh

In Example 7, Risto first describes his small talk as 'taciturn – typically Finnish' (*suomalaisittain jäyhää* in Finnish), i.e. as not talkative at all, but then with the word choice 'but' he makes a move to describing how through gaining confidence his speaking has become easier and more natural. Further, Risto brings the stereotype of Finns as 'taciturn' into question as he distances himself from this constraining stereotype by stating that his discursive resources are much richer than the stereotype conveys. However, these evaluations provide this way of speaking English a somewhat negative value because of a lack of confidence and of fluency. Risto also describes how he has to 'translate sentences and words in his head before speaking', suggesting that the mental process of translating speech from Finnish to English hinders a Finn like Risto from speaking well. Although this behaviour may not be unique to Finns, it is discursively framed as Finnish, and nationality is introduced by the participant as an explanatory factor.

In Example 8, Tero implicitly refers to Finns' lack of confidence to speak ('people start talking more easily than for example in Finland') when compared to 'talkative' Americans. He thereby reinforces stereotypes, and by conforming to Finnishness and Finns' quietness (also elsewhere in the interview), he is able to justify his own behavior in an encounter with a native speaker of English. This is a clear example of the discursive power difference constructed between an NS and an EFL speaker of English: discourses of speaking English in an American way (i.e. the native speaker) include the notion of talkativeness and small talk, whereas discourses of Finns speaking English (i.e. the EFL speaker) include the requirement to learn native speaker habits, such as small talk.

Tero also explicitly characterises himself as 'a kind of Ostrobothnian guy like me' (*tämmönen pohjalainen* in Finnish) which is implicitly associated with the stereotypically untalkative and 'silent Finn'. These findings are in line with Sajavaara and Lehtonen's (1997) well-known arguments about Finns' national perception of self as untalkative and coming from the north, which from the geohistorical point of view can be seen as a remote periphery (Tero's reference to *pohjalainen*, i.e. a person from Ostrobothnia (Nurmi, 2006)). Ostrobothnia refers to a historical province in the west and north of Finland, mostly to the regions by the Gulf of Bothnia (Hakulinen, 2006; Nurmi, 2006). In particular, southern Ostrobothnians are characterised in Finnish society as having a particularly strong sense of themselves, for example as descendants of a rustic culture and having a particular sense of entrepreneurship (Zimmerbauer, 2002). However, we can also see that Tero is playing with these stereotypes as signalled in his laugher at the end of the extract.

Returning to Tero's example (8), it should be noted that from the observer's point of view (as a researcher I accompanied Tero, a sales manager, on his work trip with a group of Finnish colleagues to a large convention in San Diego). Tero, however, was quite active in discussions and not at all 'silent' as a user of English, except perhaps when first meeting new people. Hence, from a researcher perspective, Finnish silence is not, after all, as prominent a discourse in interactions as it is from the participant perspective as brought out in the interview. Could it be, then, that discourses of Finnishness are learned and rooted in our stories (our linguaculture), and that we draw on them to justify our sense of our own behavior, such as silence in Tero's case, although they were not 'true' in interactions? Examples 9 and 10 further illustrate the cultural resource of Finnishness for the participants as they view Finns as using English in their own way in business.

Example 9

Pete: in general I've tried as in Finnish not to write unnecessary poetry but to tell the issue heh as it is [--]

Pete's example (9) is part of his description of himself as a user of English at work. As he illustrates, he typically goes straight to the point and does not use small talk, which he chooses to describe with the word 'poetry'. After this, he continues with the topic, explaining how there are differences in cultures in the way, for example, email messages are formulated. Pete has noticed that Finnish people are typically direct communicators. Oskari introduces the same characteristics in Example 10. Oskari was working as a project manager in a Finnish company which has a subsidiary in China, where Oskari was travelling frequently at the time of the interview. He had therefore gained experience of communicating with his Chinese colleagues. In many of the meetings Oskari attended, a Chinese interpreter was present.

Example 10

Oskari: I have noticed that in meetings when we negotiate a Chinese person [--] goes around the topic for example start with the person's personal characteristics saying for example @you as an intelligent person understand your best interest in this matter@ and so forth. at times it feels like (.) if the translations are correct [--] it is almost like telling a story [--] if I for example say that @you should deliver this within a week@ and it's after all only about the subject matter but then they coat it

Oskari constructs a difference between 'we', himself and a Chinese person who, according to him, 'tells a story' and 'coats' the message (*kuorruttaa* in Finnish). This example shows how Oskari views the differences between his communicative style and that of a Chinese professional, and how this affects communication: his message is no longer the same when related by the interpreter from the Chinese point of view. While Oskari has learned about these differences and developed his awareness, he seems to be somewhat confused by them, judging by his comment that his command 'You should deliver this within a week' is 'after all only about the subject matter'. Nevertheless, such a simple command is, according to Oskari, loaded with additional expressions anyway. This example suggests that an awareness of differences does not necessarily mean respect for them, since Oskari seems to give his approval to his own way of focusing on the subject matter. This is a good example of how cultural differences are discursively constructed.

It should also be noted that although Oskari mentions 'we' (i.e. Finns) and a Chinese person, and thus indicates the existence of two distinct national groups, he could also be referring to a clash between different organisational cultures (see Angouri, 2010). Elsewhere in the interview (Example 11), Oskari shows that he knows about the Chinese face-saving communicative culture to which he has had to adjust in his work; this admission may indicate that earlier he was also constructing difference between 'imagined' national cultures.

Example 11

Oskari: the message does not come across [via interpreters] in the same way as it has been presented by us apparently strong filtering occurs and somehow they don't want to cause a difficult situation and a loss of face

This example clearly shows Oskari's rising awareness of the communicative challenges involved in working in China: he describes how Chinese interpreters do not translate word-for-word but rather filter the message, which he has noticed since the message has not come across in the intended way. Oskari also evidently knows about the notion of 'face' as part of Chinese communicative culture, as he explicitly mentions the term. Adjusting to such an environment has been a central part of Oskari's job. Apparently, communicative differences create visible tension at the local level of interaction and need to be locally negotiated in the workplace. For Oskari, managing such differences has been important, and he characterises his workplace communication with the notion of simplicity, directness and without any redundancies (Räisänen, 2013: 114). Although the notion of saving face applies to all communicative situations (Brown & Levinson, 1987), it is a feature that explicitly emerges in the participants' accounts of workplace communication with Chinese people. By implication, the importance of culture and nationality is foregrounded again when individuals characterise and understand ELF interactions.

The third interviews thus shed further light on the Finnish engineers' identities as BELF users. A collective Finnish BELF user identity is growing and is being typified in more specific ways, i.e. with directness and untalkativeness as discursively ascribed to the way of speaking, a theme also discussed in earlier studies (e.g. Sajavaara & Lehtonen, 1997; Louhiala-Salminen *et al.*, 2005; Kankaanranta & Lu, 2013). Moreover, the data also shows some deviation of this stereotype too, as some participants do not perceive themselves as conforming to the stereotype. All in all, the discursive and enregisterment work by the engineers becomes more complex as a result of their socialisation into working life.

Discussion and Conclusion

This chapter has traced a group of Finnish engineers' discursive identity construction, first, as engineering students, and later, as professionals, for over six years. The participants moved from the local, educational Finnish context to global working life in which English functioned as an essential communicative resource for professional lingua franca communication. In this process, discourses of deficiency were replaced by discourses of legitimacy, which allowed the participants to construct identities as successful ELF and BELF users, and discourses of complexity which began to question some common stereotypical attributes given to Finns as quiet or 'taciturn'. In addition, experiences in intercultural encounters gave rise to specific resources for identity construction, such as group membership, nationality and culture.

Before their stay abroad, participants' identity construction focused on the individual level. After the participants gained experience in intercultural encounters, during both work experience and in working life proper, they subscribed more strongly to having particularly Finnish features, in ways that suggested both acceptance of these features and some questioning of them, as well as reluctance to fully identify with models learned earlier. Hence, a complex Finnish speaker identity emerged and participants seemed to gain power as *Finnish* ELF users, and also in ways that challenged existing stereotypes. As Jenkins (2007: 201) argues, power relations exist among ELF speakers in that ELF varieties are seen as hierarchical. Indeed, some of the present participants felt more powerful with their own 'ELF variety', or rather, ELF ways of speaking, than others (i.e. non-Finns). The Finnish engineers' self-ascribed power may be a reflection of the current prestige enjoyed by the Finnish education system, as also mentioned by the participants. Moreover, the contrasts between 'Us' and 'Them' reflect a somewhat controversial image of these individuals' linguacultures and intercultural competence. Discourses of evaluation acquired in the earlier stages of socialisation persisted over the years of this study and the collective aspect of linguaculture was evident in the participants' discursive identity construction. These findings suggest that these individuals have become socialised to ethnocentric and judgmental discourses at home and do not explicitly foreground what has been considered essential for genuine intercultural dialogue, i.e. mutual negotiation and the co-construction of new ways of speaking and being (Dervin & Layne, 2013).

However, some of the data revealed the participants' strong orientation to discourses of Finnishness. This suggests that they are imposing upon themselves the identity of a silent Finn as a speaker of English, but over time challenged this position. In their discursive work describing their intercultural experiences and the challenges they experienced in working life, the participants often introduced the notions of culture and nationality. It seems as if culture functioned as an explanatory factor for them in their understanding of individual differences in linguistic proficiency and communicative competence, and in their misunderstandings and gaps in intercultural communication (see also Angouri, 2010; Piller, 2011). Silence and directness were attributed to discourses of Finnishness and gradually became more like questions of pride than of shame (cf. Dervin, 2013; and Jenks' findings in this volume), and national identity seemed to be the key way in which, as professionals, they constructed an understanding of ELF interactions at work. Similar to Angouri's (2010: 210) findings, macro-level discourses of national culture prevailed in everyday working life and were drawn on by employees to explain work-related problems in situations involving people from different cultural backgrounds.

This chapter has illustrated how ELF experiences contribute to recognising intercultural differences and reconstructing identities as language users and communicators. Evidently, the Finnish engineers have learned to do their jobs in global working life and the interview excerpts analysed here show that the participants have not only developed but also actively sought to develop an understanding of foreign business practices and cultures, and of themselves and others as users of English. Across their trajectories, they have faced complexity, begun to assess and accept new ways of doing, and found ways to manage cultural conflicts at work. As I have shown in an earlier study (Virkkula-Räisänen, 2010), Tero, for instance, has developed his intercultural competence in managing intercultural interactions in a meeting between Finnish and Chinese colleagues.

Nevertheless, experiences of ELF situations may not help individuals overcome ethnocentric views of the self or move beyond the construction of stereotypes. The present findings suggest that ELF carries a lot of inequality, which partly relates to differences in language proficiency (i.e. the linguistic aspect), but to a large extent, links to power relations and individuals' unequal access to resources (Blommaert, 2010; Piller, 2011; Räisänen, 2013). ELF is by no means a neutral medium of choice and does not necessarily trigger any intercultural awareness; it can, instead, reinforce stereotypes and ethnocentrism.

As this chapter has aimed to show, ELF users' identity work and intercultural development is an ongoing process as individuals actively negotiate their sense of themselves and communication in the age of globalisation. This chapter has demonstrated that identity is a central matter when using English as a lingua franca and, extending the discussion in Virkkula and Nikula (2010), it has shown that ELF user identity is more than a 'learner' or a 'user' identity, but is to a great extent a 'communicator' identity (Gao, 2014). As Gao (2014: 72–73) notes, different identities can exist within the same individual, and have variations and combinations for different situations, being determined in interaction between the social and the individual. Intercultural and cultural dimensions are essential for our understanding of English used as a lingua franca and its users.

Acknowledgements

I wish to respectfully thank Wiley for granting permission to republish parts of an article that first appeared in the *International Journal of Applied Linguistics* 20, 2 (Virkkula & Nikula, 2010). In addition, I want to thank the editors of this volume for their constant support and insightful suggestions for improving the arguments in this paper. Finally, I wish to thank Eleanor Underwood for proofreading the text.

References

Agha, A. (2007) *Language and Social Relations*. Cambridge: Cambridge University Press.
Angouri, J. (2010) 'If we know about culture it will be easier to work with one another': Developing skills for handling corporate meetings with multinational participation. *Language and Intercultural Communication* 10 (3), 206–224.
Baker, W. (2009) The cultures of English as a lingua franca. *TESOL Quarterly* 43 (4), 567–592.
Blommaert, J. (2010) *The Sociolinguistics of Globalization*. Cambridge: Cambridge University Press.
Blommaert, J. and Backus, A. (2011) Repertoires revisited: 'Knowing language' in superdiversity. *Working Papers in Urban Language and Literacies* 67. See http://www.kcl.ac.uk/sspp/departments/education/research/ldc/publications/workingpapers/67.pdf (accessed 10 March 2014)
Brown, P. and Levinson, S. (1987) *Politeness: Some Universals in Language Usage*. Cambridge: Cambridge University Press.
Davies, B. and Harré, R. (1990) Positioning: The discursive production of selves. *Journal for the Theory of Social Behaviour* 20 (1), 43–63.
Dervin, F. (2011) A plea for change in research on intercultural discourses: A 'liquid' approach to the study of the acculturation of Chinese students. *Journal of Multicultural Discourses* 6 (1), 37–52.
Dervin, F. (2013) Politics of identification in the use of lingua francas in student mobility to Finland and France. In C. Kinginger (ed.) *Social and Cultural Aspects of Language Learning in Study Abroad* (pp. 101–125), Amsterdam: John Benjamins.
Dervin, F. and Layne, H. (2013) A guide to interculturality for international and exchange students: An example of hostipitality? *Journal of Multicultural Discourses*, DOI: 10.1080/17447143.2012.753896
Gallucci, S. (2013) Emotional investments during the year abroad: A case study of a British ERASMUS student in Italy. *Apples: Journal of Applied Language Studies* 7 (2), 17–37.
Gao, Y. (2014) Faithful imitator, legitimate speaker, playful creator and dialogical communicator: Shift in English learners' identity prototypes. *Language and Intercultural Communication* 2014, 14 (59).
Gee, J.P. (1990) *Social Linguistics and Literacies: Ideology in Discourses, Critical Perspectives on Literacy and Education*. London: Falmer Press.
Gee, J.P. (2005) *An Introduction to Discourse Analysis*. New York: Routledge.
Georgakopoulou, A. (2007) *Small Stories, Interaction and Identities*. Amsterdam: John Benjamins.
Hakulinen, K. (2006) *Paikannimet (Names of places)*. Helsinki: WSOY.
Holmes, P. and O'Neill, G. (2012) Developing and evaluating intercultural competence: Ethnographies of intercultural encounters. *International Journal of Intercultural Relations* 36 (5), 707–718.
Hymes, D. (1996) Ethnography, *Linguistics, Narrative Inequality: Toward an Understanding of Voice*. London: Taylor & Francis.

Jackson, J. (2008) *Language, Identity and Study Abroad: Sociocultural Perspectives*. London: Equinox Publishing Ltd.
Jenkins, J. (2006) Points of view and blind spots: ELF and SLA. *International Journal of Applied Linguistics* 16 (2), 137–162.
Jenkins, J. (2007) *English as a Lingua Franca: Attitude and Identity*. Oxford: Oxford University Press.
Jenkins, J., Cogo, A. and Dewey, M. (2011) Review of developments in research into English as a lingua franca. *Language Teaching* 44 (3), 281–315.
Kankaanranta, A. and Lu, W. (2013) The evolution of English as the business lingua franca: Signs of convergence in Chinese and Finnish professional communication. *Journal of Business and Technical Communication* 27 (3), 288–307.
Kinginger, C. (2004) Alice doesn't live here anymore: Foreign language learning and renegotiated identity. In A. Pavlenko and A. Blackledge (eds) *Negotiation of Identities in Multilingual Contexts* (pp. 219–242). Clevedon, UK: Multilingual Matters.
Kinginger, C. and Belz, J.A. (2005) Sociocultural perspectives on pragmatic development in foreign language learning: Case studies from telecollaboration and study abroad. *Intercultural Pragmatics* 2 (4), 369–421.
Leppänen, S. and Nikula, T. (2007) Diverse uses of English in Finnish society: Discourse-pragmatic insights into media, education and business contexts. *Multilingua* 26 (4), 333–380.
Leppänen, S., Pitkänen-Huhta, A., Nikula, T., Kytölä, S., Törmäkangas, T., Nissinen, K., Kääntä, L., Räisänen, T., Laitinen, M., Pahta, P., Koskela, H., Lähdesmäki, S. and Jousmäki, H. (2011) National survey on the English language in Finland: Uses, meanings and attitudes. *Studies of Variation, Contacts and Change in English* 5, http://www.helsinki.fi/varieng/series/volumes/05/evarieng-vol5.pdf (accessed 10 December 2015).
Louhiala-Salminen, L., Charles, M. and Kankaanranta, A. (2005) English as a lingua franca in Nordic corporate mergers: Two case companies. *English for Specific Purposes* 24 (4), 401–421.
Norton, B. (2000) *Identity and Language Learning. Gender, Ethnicity and Educational Change*. Harlow: Pearson Education Ltd.
Nurmi, T. (2006) *Nykysuomen keskeinen sanasto (Central Vocabulary of Modern Finnish)*. Jyväskylä: Gummerus.
Pavlenko, A. and Blackledge, A. (eds) (2004) *Negotiation of Identities in Multilingual Contexts*. Clevedon: Multilingual Matters.
Piller, I. (2011) *Intercultural Communication: A Critical Introduction*. Edinburgh: Edinburgh University Press.
Räisänen, T. (2013) Professional communicative repertoires and trajectories of socialization into global working life (PhD thesis). *Jyväskylä Studies in Humanities* 216. See http://urn.fi/URN:ISBN:978-951-39-5470-3 (accessed 10 December 2015).
Risager, K. (2010) The language teacher facing transnationality. Paper presented at the First EUNoM Symposium, 7–8 September 2010, University of Udine, Italy. See http://in3.uoc.edu/opencms_in3/export/sites/in3/webs/projectes/EUNOM/_resources/documents/Karen_Risager_The_Language_Teacher_Facing_Transnationality_posted.pdf (accessed 10 March 2014).
Sajavaara, K. and Lehtonen, J. (1997) The silent Finn revisited. In A. Jaworski (ed.) *Functions of Silence* (pp. 263–283), Berlin: Mouton de Gruyter.
Seidlhofer, B. (2006) English as a lingua franca in the expanding circle: What it isn't. In R. Rudby and M. Saraceni (eds) *English in the World: Global Rules, Global Roles* (pp. 40–50). London: Continuum.

Seidlhofer, B. (2011) *Understanding English as a Lingua Franca*. Oxford: Oxford University Press.
Virkkula, T. and Nikula, T. (2010) Identity construction in ELF contexts: A case study of Finnish engineering students working in Germany. *International Journal of Applied Linguistics* 20 (2), 251–273.
Virkkula-Räisänen, T. (2010) Finnish manager as a mediator in a multilingual meeting. Linguistic repertoires and semiotic resources in interaction – a Finnish manager as a mediator in a multilingual meeting. *Journal of Business Communication* 47 (4), 505–531.
Zimmerbauer, K. (2002) Etelä-Pohjanmaan imagon jäljillä. [In search of the image of southern Ostrobothnia]. *Maaseudun uusi aika*. *Maaseutututkimuksen ja- politiikan aikakauslehti* 2 (2002). See http://www.mua.profiili.fi/SIRA_Files/downloads/Arkisto/MUA_lehti/2002/2_02_zimmerbauer.pdf (accessed 19 January 2015).

Appendix 1

Transcription conventions

[—]   omitted text
[text]   added text to aid understanding
-       cut-off word
@   animated voice
(.)   a micro pause
(1.0)   silence marked in tenths of seconds
(xxx)   unclear speech/transcriber's interpretations

8 The Local Purposes of a Global Language: English as an Intracultural Communicative Medium in China

Eric S. Henry

Introduction

As a populous, rapidly developing nation with a keen interest in acquiring English fluency, but without a core population speaking it as a first language (L1), China appears to be ripe for an investigation of the English as a lingua franca (ELF) phenomenon. ELF can be defined as 'any use of English among speakers of different first languages for whom English is the communicative medium of choice, and often the only option' (Seidlhofer, 2011: 7) and ELF studies typically explore the broad range of English use in contexts where the language exists as a common medium among non-native-speaking users. Seidlhofer (2011: 9) further argues that use of the term 'ELF' highlights the role of English among second language (L2) users who 'should be accorded the right to take an active role in the development of the language, and to be taken seriously as legitimate users.' In China, English is everywhere: on television, radio and billboards; in schools and examinations; and at work. Levels of communicative competence can vary greatly, ranging from those speakers who have near-native levels of fluency – often the product of study abroad – to individuals with only a few half-remembered language lessons from school. Nonetheless, English has become a common medium of communication in a range of educational, business, retail and entertainment contexts (Bolton, 2003; Gil & Adamson, 2011; Pan, 2009).

Chinese educational policy documents, such as the English curriculum standards published by the Ministry of Education in 2001, stress that English is 'of growing importance in a world of information technology and economic globaliz ation,' and that 'in the basic educational development strategies of most countries, teaching English has become a major component of educating quality citizens' (Ministry of Education, 2001; also Adamson, 2004; Cheng, 2011; Hu, 2005; Hu & McKay, 2012).[1] Students receive formal English as a foreign language (EFL) education from the third grade of primary school to the end of high school. Whereas pedagogical practices in the twentieth century tended to be teacher-centred, emphasising strict grammatical norms and minimising communicative interaction among students, today there are a host of ongoing efforts to introduce communicative and task-based language teaching practices into the curriculum with the aim of increasing communicative competence and developing intercultural awareness (Mao & Yue, 2004; Zheng & Davison, 2008). Although the success of these efforts has been uneven, the focus of foreign language education has been to train a generation of interculturally competent global citizens, fluent in English and capable of successfully engaging (and competing) with foreigners on the world stage (Kipnis, 2011).

Despite this intercultural goal, most English speakers in China have few opportunities to converse with non-Chinese. Outside of large cosmopolitan cities such as Beijing and Shanghai, foreigners can be a rare sight and opportunities for communicative interaction are limited. Although some Chinese individuals, particularly those with upper-middle-class wealth and government connections, are now able to study abroad and business trips outside China are becoming more common, the vast majority of Chinese citizens have infrequent contacts with native speakers of English (NSE) or other foreigners who might share English as an L2. A contrast therefore exists between the ostensible aims of EFL education in China, which focus on successful intercultural communication, and the realities of actual English use, for which opportunities are scarce.

In this chapter I develop an ethnographic examination of ELF phenomena in Shenyang, a large metropolitan centre in China's northeastern region. I argue that, in practice, the status of English as a global lingua franca is juxtaposed in China with very different, and very important, domestic concerns. The tension between local forms of identity and global aspirations within ELF use has also been noted in Higgins' (2009) recent ethnographic work on English in postcolonial Tanzania and in the study of other developing nations (e.g. Billings, 2009; Canagarajah, 2006; Schneider, 2007; Sung, 2014b). Similarly, I argue that despite the global and intercultural associations of the language, in Shenyang English is equally if not more importantly directed at immediate and localised discursive concerns such as producing cultural capital, negotiating status, establishing authority, signalling identity and a host of other objectives in interactions with other native speakers of Chinese (NSC). In other words, while ELF in China may be useful for producing intercultural understanding, it is also an arena for intracultural imaginings of, for instance, modern or cosmopolitan identities.

Methodology: Collecting data in Shenyang, China

The data in this chapter are drawn from 14 months of ethnographic fieldwork in English language schools in Shenyang, combining participant observation of classrooms and conversational events with interviews of teachers, students and administrators. To serve a population of more than seven million, there are hundreds of public and private English language schools, most of which operate as small single-teacher businesses unregulated by the government. Larger schools, which must be certified by the Ministry of Education, may have multiple branches and thousands of students. Fieldwork was conducted in a range of educational institutions, including public schools ranging from elementary to university level, and private schools specialising in childhood EFL education. In total, I visited 18 different schools in Shenyang: two universities, two middle schools, two elementary schools, three private adult language education centres, and eight private children's schools. I chose to concentrate on five of these schools (one university, one elementary school and three children's schools) by spending at least a full week at each location. During this time, I observed classes taught by multiple teachers and took note of teacher-student interactions, pedagogy, methods, textbooks, technology and other teaching materials.

I also interviewed more than 50 English language teachers (both foreign and Chinese) as well as students, parents and school administrators to ascertain their understandings of English, the role it plays in Chinese society and their own relationship to the language. These semi-structured interviews ranged from only a few minutes to, in one case, four hours in length. I typically asked several initial questions concerning subjects such as the respondent's biography, family background, educational experiences and impressions of language use. However, I gave respondents great latitude to direct the conversation and to provide extended narratives on topics they believed relevant to the issue of English language use in China. The interviews were audio-recorded where possible, although some individuals felt uncomfortable being recorded; in these cases, notes were made by hand.

Interviews were conducted in the respondent's language of choice, although this was not made explicit at the outset. Instead, I allowed respondents to negotiate and set the boundaries and conditions of language use in the course of our interaction. If an interviewee chose to speak in Chinese, I responded in kind, although many actively discouraged me from speaking Chinese in order to practice their English. Other respondents chose, although not always consistently, to employ extensive code-mixing in their speech repertoires. In the following sections, all responses in quotations were spoken in English except where indicated. In the latter cases, I offer both the original language and my own translation.

New Theoretical Orientations?

Attention to the local purposes of English in China calls for some re-evaluation of dominant trends in ELF research. Herein, I would like to focus on two broad areas of priority: the intercultural as opposed to the intracultural, and intelligibility over indexicality. I have already indicated that ELF might benefit from closer attention to the uses of L2 English among speakers who share a similar L1. In terms of the second contrast, most ELF research is concerned with intelligibility, where the primary purpose of ELF usage is assumed to be the successful communication of referential knowledge. But this is only a fraction of the information conveyed to listeners through language choices. ELF discourse also has an indexical component; this includes the way varied forms of referential (demonstratives, pronouns, tense) and non-referential (accent, stance, style, etc.) content become linked with or 'point to' particular forms of speaker identity (Agha, 2007; Hanks, 2000; Silverstein, 2003). This is not to claim that research focused on questions of the intercultural or intelligibility are wrong in any sense, but that they act as assumptions that in some ways limit the scope of current and future research programs.

Intracultural communication and language varieties: Discourse and imagination

ELF research tends to stress the potential for intercultural communication among multilingual users operating in diverse global settings. The intercultural is a component of most definitions of ELF in the literature, such as the definition given by Seidlhofer (2011; also Friedrich & Matsuda, 2010; Meierkord, 2006). Recently, emphasis has also been placed on the idea that ELF users need not necessarily all be L2 speakers (Jenkins et al., 2011: 283); in addition, speakers from Kachru's Inner Circle (Kachru, 1985) have been found to use many of the same communicative strategies as conventional lingua franca users when in conversation with Expanding Circle representatives. But English usage among L2 English speakers who share a common L1 (i.e., who think of themselves as sharing a culture) also displays many of the same strategies and functions as conventional ELF.

It may be tempting to posit that definitions of ELF should merely add the word 'intracultural' as a remedy to this observation, but I think we can go further. Baker (2009) has pointed out that the concepts of intercultural and intracultural, among other boundary-related terms in applied linguistics (e.g. Inner and Outer circles, native and non-native speakers, etc.), are ill-defined and imprecise, but function as necessary shorthands in the field (see also Seidlhofer, 2011: 42–61). Nevertheless, these concepts also function as ideologically constructed perceptions of sameness and difference that are salient to speakers; this salience may also explain their indispensability. As Holliday (2011) shows, echoing a rich tradition in anthropology, cultural description is never a neutral practice but rather is bound up in political discourses that negotiate the meanings and boundaries of individual and society, self and other.

The very idea of communicative competence was traditionally premised on the notion of a coherent speech community with shared goals and interests; however, such groups can only be created through the social act of discourse and the work of speakers to define their boundaries and qualifications for membership (Bucholtz, 2003: 400–403; Kramsch, 2011). Therefore, when I say that ELF can be used for intracultural imaginings, I mean that such interpretations of the meaning of words are predicated upon ideological notions of 'Chineseness' and associated emotional qualities of national belonging, cultural homogeneity and perceived sameness, rather than upon any objective or essentialist cultural similarities between the interactants. The speakers feel that they belong to the same culture, and this feeling affects how they orient themselves to the conversation and to each other. I therefore argue that ELF can also be used to understand language use among individuals who base their communicative interaction on the premise of cultural similarity rather than difference, but nonetheless choose to use English despite the fact that another communicative resource – namely, their native language – is available.

I employ a similar logic when I talk about 'varieties' of English further on in this chapter. Most ELF researchers have rejected the notion that English or other languages can be sorted into distinct varieties that are 'essentially fixed, predetermined, [and] tied to a restricted number of geographic centres' (Dewey, 2007: 346; see also Jenkins *et al.*, 2011: 296–297). In contrast, ELF tends to be highly fluid and hybridised, and to draw upon multiple linguistic resources that are both global and local in scope, to construct novel speech forms. 'Standard' forms of the language have been rightly criticised as ideological constructions based upon structures of institutional power and authority. Elsewhere, I have shown how stigmatised forms of English in China, labeled 'Chinglish,' are identified less through the actual form of speech than through the relative social positionings of the interactants (Henry, 2010). Like Standard English, the precise form of which is tied to factors such as national origin, social class and regional accent of the individual evaluating it as such, Chinglish is a complex and hybrid language pattern which constantly shifts depending upon the perspectives and purposes of speakers and listeners.

Agha (2007) calls the ideological work of identifying and delimiting both the content and value of particular language forms 'enregisterment' and shows how social knowledge of these speech forms is sedimented over time through everyday discursive practices. Chinglish is, in this manner, a cardinal organising concept for the evaluation of English speech in highly charged discursive contexts in China, such as examinations and job interviews. In classrooms and examinations, teachers praise students by saying their English is very 'standard,' and criticise others as speaking 'Chinese English' or 'Chinglish.' Therefore, when I refer to varieties of English herein, it is with the knowledge that these are not categories based on language form, but in truth are emergent social categories based on what particular speech patterns mean in the context of the Chinese speech community.

Indexicality: Language choices and social meaning

Intelligibility is perhaps the most fundamental concept in ELF research. We assume that the primary purpose of ELF is the successful exchange of referential information and that the major barriers to successful communication are phonological, lexical and syntactic forms of variation (Firth, 1996; Jenkins, 2000; Kaur, 2011; Pickering, 2006). More recently, Jenkins et al. (2011: 296) have detected a shift from the goal of describing the particular forms of language used by speakers to an appreciation of the flexible and fluid nature of ELF talk. ELF users 'exhibit substantial linguistic variation in their interactions for a range of purposes, including the projection of cultural identity, the promotion of solidarity, the sharing of humor and so on, rather than (primarily) to promote intelligibility between speakers from different first language groups or as a result of interlocutors' different levels of proficiency.' These elements of discourse are not mutually exclusive – indeed, most speech is used for purposes of both intelligibility and performing identity. However, to date most ELF research has sought to answer how communication succeeds despite communicative barriers, rather than examining the work of identity involved in speaking.

In my research with ELF users in China I quickly learned that English is often used in spite of, and occasionally because of, problems with intelligibility. According to my observations, occasionally the purpose of English use was to successfully communicate information – as in the case of professionals employing technical vocabulary in English rather than Chinese – but far more commonly the purpose of ELF was indexical (i.e. how particular choices about register, style, accent and lexical usage signalled to other speakers desirable identities, stances, attitudes and forms of belonging). In China, English is associated with cultural activities of global scope, and use of ELF represents this association to listeners.

For instance, many Chinese English language teachers I observed in classes gave instructions to their students in English and then repeated the utterances in Chinese (e.g. 'Okay, now open your books, page forty-two. *Tongxuemen dakai shu, sishi er ye* [Students open your books to page forty-two]'). In interviews, these teachers told me that ideally they would speak only in English, but the students' limited comprehension skills made this impossible, even at advanced levels. For the most part, students told me that they ignored the English half of the ongoing talk from their teachers, confident that the full content would also be delivered in Chinese. This was especially relevant for complex discussion of grammatical rules or pragmatic norms, where the English language component of the explanation was superfluous to the goal of the interaction, which was full comprehension of the lesson.

Compare this practice to Firth's (1996) description of the 'letting it pass' strategy for communicative intelligibility. Firth argues that ELF users in conversation frequently ignore words or phrases they do not comprehend, confident that they can work out the general meaning as the conversation continues. Interactants can thus achieve the practical end of successful communication while only in possession of partial fragments of the full code. In the present study, however, students 'let it pass' not because they intended to work out the meaning later, but because they knew the meaning would follow in their native language. Yet both teachers and students agreed that English was a necessary presence in the foreign language classroom. It created, in the words of one teacher, an 'English language environment that the students can know more about the sounds and the words.' This idea of an English language environment was important, she continued, 'because Chinese who study or live abroad in the United Kingdom or United States have the language around them every day. In China, we can't have that so we make the classroom an English zone.' The combination in this rationale of linguistic familiarity, ties to foreign countries and the benefits that accrue to individuals who achieve this level of fluency (foreign degrees, international travel, etc.) are all represented through the act of simply using English, regardless of intelligibility, which in turn sanctions the language classroom as a culturally globalised space.

The linkages between language and larger social formations, or speech and the contexts within which speech is produced, can be identified as relations of indexicality. An index is a relationship based on the logical connection between two elements, such as smoke indicating fire or shadow indicating sunshine. As applied to language, particularly in the work of Silverstein (2003), speech contains clusters of linked indexes which, taken together, allow interactants to make sense of the context surrounding their discourse. At a primary level, this can include certain discourse markers that index the level of formality in a conversation, such as *tu/vous* in French: *vous* can index a more formal, public or socially distant conversational frame and *tu* a more informal, private, relaxed or comfortable one (Silverstein, 2003: 204–211; also Goffman, 1974). But conversation also contains higher-level indexical orders such as accent, code-mixing, dialect choice and so on, that can reference more complicated contextual information. For instance, Besnier (2004) has noted how English is used as a lingua franca in Samoan urban markets not simply because of its ability to bridge communicative gaps, but also because it allows sellers to competitively position their goods as originating from authentic international sources. Their use of a New Zealand-inflected English accent indexes this fashion-forward location as the source of their wares and associates the speaker with the cosmopolitan authenticity of the outside world.

Indexicality is one of the principal means of constructing the negotiated and hybrid forms of identity that are of current interest to applied linguists and ELF researchers. Increasingly, identity has come to be understood as a 'relational and sociocultural phenomenon that emerges and circulates in local discourse contexts of interaction rather than as a stable structure located primarily in the individual psyche or in fixed social categories' (Bucholtz & Hall, 2005: 585–586; also Block, 2007; Gu *et al.*, 2014; Pavlenko & Blackledge, 2004). Blommaert (2005: 74) has argued that because certain speech forms come to 'mean' certain things to certain speakers in certain contexts, 'there is always identity work involved, and the orientations towards orders of indexicality are the grassroots displays of "groupness".' As speakers perform various speech styles or registers that are indexed to particular forms of identity, they assert powerful claims of belonging to these groups. Conversely, their speech may result in them being ascribed to particular marginalised groups by institutional forces or by authoritative representatives of standardised linguistic norms, e.g. teachers, educators or employers. Indexicality embodies the ideological work that takes place in valuing some linguistic codes over others – the very work of linguistic standardisation which has vexed many ELF scholars (Jenkins, 2007: 31–59; Seidlhofer, 2011: 42–61). Evaluative utterances such as those that classify speech as 'heavily accented' or 'nonsensical' mask the naturalisation of social marginality by displacing status differences between speakers onto perceived deviations from an already constituted 'standard' form (Agha, 2007: 190–232).

To summarise my argument thus far, ELF research has (for the most part, although not exclusively) focused on English speakers in situations of intercultural contact and, as a consequence, has emphasised intelligibility as the primary goal of discursive interactions; this is generally true in the majority of cases. I have indicated that in China these are assumptions that might actually limit our understanding of how English is used as a lingua franca: that it is, in fact, primarily used intraculturally among groups of people who imagine themselves to be linguistically homogeneous and culturally similar. Their use of English is not solely directed at intelligibility but may also be used to signal to listeners indexical information about the speaker, specifically membership in a class of globally competent Chinese citizens as signified through English fluency.

The role of ethnography in research on indexicality

How do we investigate indexicality? If intercultural intelligibility is the primary focus, a range of potential approaches to ELF research, ranging from data-driven corpora studies to detailed analyses of conversational extracts, can and have been employed. One limitation of these methods is that the linguist's conclusions must be based on the referential content of speech, since evaluating the indexical content requires access to the speaker's intentions and interpretations. I have already described my research methodology; however, the merits of the previous theoretical discussion also invite consideration of the suitability of ethnography to ELF research on indexicality. Specifically, I propose that ethnography can provide a means of investigating and describing the interpretive facets of communication.

Ethnography draws on a long-term engagement with people in a given location to facilitate a nuanced understanding of how culture and language are understood in that context. The approach also encourages practitioners to pay attention to local interpretations. Ethnographic researchers may bring their own analytical frameworks to the process of fieldwork, but ultimately they listen to how their informants interpret the meaning of their own activities and ideas. The knowledge produced in ethnography is coconstructed with the participation of research subjects and is based on their categories, experiences and understandings.

Ethnography is also an ongoing process in which collection of data begins with an interaction but continues long afterward. In this way, the researcher's own impressions or conclusions are constantly tested and revised with the input of the participants themselves. All these features are conducive to understanding the largely implicit cultural knowledge of indexical meanings in language use, where the goal is to articulate the intentions underlying talk rather than to provide a strictly objective description of linguistic forms.

Ethnography challenges assumptions about the ideological underpinnings of research design and data collection (Creese, 2008; Tusting & Maybin, 2007). Although it is becoming more popular in applied linguistics, some concerns have been raised in terms of its objectivity and reproducibility (Hammersley, 2006). In the field of anthropology, however, the ethnographic method is inextricably tied to an encompassing vision of culture and the means of understanding it. Anthropological notions of culture are commensurate with recent trends in ELF, notably the shift in emphasis from culture as congruent with nations or ethnic groups to culture as a resource for constructing flexible and hybridised forms of identity (Baker, 2009; Norton, 2000). Ethnography therefore has great potential in ELF research and, in particular, is suited to an examination of localised intracultural ELF usage and its indexical meanings, such as I present here.

My use of the ethnographic method is crucial to understanding the material that follows. For instance, I tried to follow up with participants after recording interviews or conversations to gauge their metalinguistic interpretations of the events. This was achieved by asking questions about how they understood the interaction and the relative stances of other interactants. Such conclusions were often the result of multiple consultations and interviews over the course of my field research. I therefore present not only the interactions themselves but also how various speakers evaluated their participation and that of others in the event itself.

English as an Intracultural Communicative Resource

With my conceptual and methodological apparatus in place, I now turn to some of the ethnographic data that highlights the intracultural utility of ELF in China. Most uses of English among Chinese L1 speakers are unmarked and pass without much comment. At times though, English becomes the medium through which conversational stances are actively contested and negotiated. One of the clearest examples from my observations was recorded during a business English class at Washington English – a large, private, language school (Extract 1; please see Appendix 1 for transcription conventions).² Washington charges very high fees for small-enrollment classes which ensure intensive teacher-student interactions. This particular class involved four students: two were very proficient female Chinese students and the other two remained silent during this exchange (and, in fact, throughout most of the class). Also present were myself, recording the class but outside of the interactional field, and the male foreign teacher, an American NSE in his late twenties who had only a rudimentary ability in Chinese.

At the beginning of the class, as the foreign teacher gave handouts to the students covering new vocabulary, exercises and a conversational script for the students to practice together, one of the students complained to the teacher that the lessons were out of order. This student, Naomi, was in her late thirties, had travelled abroad several times on business, and was hoping to improve her English in order to secure a promotion within her company. Comparing the lesson to her schedule, she noted that the topic for that day was to be covered in the fourth class, but this was only her second class. Appearing exasperated, she rose from her seat and left the room, returning less than a minute later with Mei, a slightly younger woman who supervised the Chinese teachers at the school.

Extract 1

(N - Naomi; S – Unnamed Student; M - Mei)³

N: *Ni kan* (Look). ((shows M the class handout)) The lesson here is wrong. Today is 'checking in' but the lesson here is 'customs.'

M: This, yes... okay, this is just lesson plan.
The teachers, they use this just make the lesson.

N: But the lesson plan and our class,
they should be... *yizhi* (consistent), [yes↺]

S: [Match,] they should match.

M: But... mm, yes, but teachers, they prepare the lesson and then... the lesson, that is an extension of the scripts.

N: *Shenme yisi* (What does that mean)↺

M: The lesson is an extension of the scripts. [Okay↺]

N: [*Buzhidao* (I don't understand).]
M: *Zhe liang zhang ye shi di gei xuesheng. Zhe liang zhang shi wei laoshi beike. Zhidao ma?* (These two pages are given to the students. These two pages are for the teacher to prepare for class. Understand?)
N: The class today, we have four day class, four day plan. We should—
M: Your teacher—((gestures towards foreign teacher))
N: *Ta buzhidao. Ta shenme dou buzhidao.* (He doesn't understand. He doesn't understand anything.)
M: ... The problem is not so serious. You should follow the teacher teaches you. ((to foreign teacher)) Please begin class again.

My analysis of this interaction is informed by the subsequent interviews with two of the participants: Mei, the head teacher, and Naomi, the student. I also discussed the incident with the foreign teacher, but he did not understand the nature of the dispute. The conversation began in English, a choice made by Naomi, and continued until Mei employed a word ('extension') that the students did not understand. Naomi, who felt frustrated by this, told me that Mei was trying to force the students into a subordinate status position by using 'big' words. Mei would not confirm this accusation, but she did pride herself on her extensive lexical knowledge. In another interview, Mei described how she felt students looked down on her because she was a L2 English teacher. 'You look my face, "Oh, you're a Chinese? What do you know?" But I'm teaching here six years. I'm a teacher too.' Mei appears to have strategically used her lexis in cases like this to impress others and assert her own expertise and authority.

After Naomi's objection Mei initially only repeated herself in English, which led to a further request for clarification. She then switched into Chinese to explain her interpretation of how the pages shown to her by Naomi were to be used. Naomi then switched back into English to protest, along the lines of her original objection. When Mei pointed towards the foreign teacher, presumably to assert his responsibility for the class, Naomi switched the conversation into Chinese again and objected that he 'doesn't know anything.' Her choice of Chinese here was informed by the desire to avoid insulting the teacher, whom she said she liked but also felt did not understand the situation. Mei finally switched back into English and, after a short pause, ended the conversation by asking the foreign teacher to begin teaching again.

Implications of language choices

All of the participants in Extract 1 spoke Chinese as a first language. Even though there were two native speakers of English present (myself and the foreign teacher), we were not addressed during the conversation. Whereas in most everyday disputes of this nature the participants would likely use Chinese, the setting within the English school and the specific claims to conversational authority (Naomi had been abroad; Mei was the school's head English teacher) influenced the decision to conduct the conversation in English, at least initially. Naomi told me that she felt comfortable using English to complain about the school's mistake because she had used similar conversational strategies to complain to airlines and hotels in foreign countries. Although perhaps less conversationally fluent, Mei by contrast possessed a much larger vocabulary and could use this strategically to assert a kind of conversational control; in this way, she employed her superior lexical knowledge to force Naomi to switch into Chinese. Language choices were thus used here indexically to negotiate boundaries and statuses between the participants.

The dispute between Naomi and Mei is also embedded within a larger cultural framework that informs their relative statuses, beliefs and approaches to language learning. Despite a limited technical knowledge of English grammar, Naomi had travelled abroad and successfully navigated foreign countries with her conversational language abilities. She graduated from a technical school with a degree in business and was working her way up from an entry-level position in a company specialising in foreign trade, but still needed a high TOEFL score for promotion. In contrast, Mei had never been abroad, but held a master's degree in English from a prestigious provincial-level university. Although less capable than Naomi in conversational interaction, she had achieved very high scores on college-level English exams which helped secure her position as head teacher. Other teachers frequently consulted her on questions of grammar and lexis, and she was widely respected by other Chinese members of the teaching and administrative staff. In other words, Naomi and Mei embody two different approaches to linguistic capability in the Chinese foreign language context, one based on communicative competence and the other on academic success – measured, in China's competitive educational environment, in examination scores and other quantitative metrics (e.g. number of words memorised).

Naomi's communicative skill is rooted in an ELF approach: she uses her knowledge of English to communicate successfully in intercultural contexts. In contrast, Mei's exacting and highly technical knowledge of English is the product of both China's examination-dominated academic system and standardising ideologies which leave little room for creativity or error (Cheng, 2008). Traditionally, EFL classrooms in China employed the grammar-translation method almost exclusively. Teachers emphasised close textual reading, memorisation and detailed knowledge of lexical items and grammatical rules (Cortazzi & Jin, 1996; Hu, 2002; Zheng & Davison, 2008).

Educational reforms in the 1990s initiated some pressure to incorporate greater use of communicative language teaching (CLT) in public school EFL classrooms, along with task-based teaching and enhancing the ability to use language in diverse settings (Hu, 2005). High school English teachers reported to me, however, that despite the reformed curricular plans, students spent every minute of their final year preparing for discrete-point language assessments, especially the National College Entrance Examination. A foreign language such as English is one of three required subjects (along with Chinese and mathematics); since results of the examination determine university admissions and, thus, future opportunities, all effort is directed at preparing students to achieve high scores.[4] China's ELT efforts therefore exhibit opposed and contradictory pressures: national foreign language curricular policies encourage CLT, but also demand from students a breadth of textual and technical knowledge that can only be obtained through non-CLT forms of instruction.

Students appreciate this dichotomy. Boshan, a university student I interviewed, characterised it as a difference between the 'oral English' he learned at private foreign-language schools and the 'mute English' he was taught in public school. He explained that public school English is mute because the students only learn to read and write instead of learning to speak. In contrast, private schools teach conversational English, often with direct instruction from L1 speakers. The nature of these two forms of English also differs: whereas mute English demands close attention to linguistic form, oral English values extemporaneous production. Mute English is therefore more exacting and more beholden to standardising linguistic ideologies, while oral English is flexible and practical. In mute English the goal is to answer examination questions correctly; in oral English the goal, as in ELF, is to be understood.

My point here is that the exact nature of Naomi's and Mei's dispute is not inherent to the transcript itself. Their argument was embedded within a larger cultural context and their linguistic choices in that interaction reflected that context. It was also clear from our discussions that they knew the meanings of those choices would be clear to other locally oriented L2 English users – that is, culturally similar interactants – and opaque to non-local users or even native speakers who were excluded from the conversation. The use of ELF in this instance illustrates how interaction was shaped by an intracultural imaginary that links Naomi and Mei into a common world of discourse.

English and identity

The value ascribed to mute and oral forms of English depends upon the context, whether one is attempting to secure entrance to a good university or attempting to communicate with a NSE. As I noted previously, however, these two varieties are not categorically different; after all, they are both English and many students employ overlapping strategies to achieve multiple competencies. Yet through the indexical associations embedded in Naomi's and Mei's speech styles, we can see them asserting and countering various forms of identity based on particular language strengths – with the ultimate goal of claiming control of the conversation. English can therefore be used quite creatively and strategically, and can act as an additional linguistic resource to the standard repertoire of Chinese (Gu *et al.*, 2014; Sung, 2014a). Speakers play with various stances and personae in their speech, indexed through language choice, word choice, accent, register and other factors. In other words, language is used to index, and thus construct, particular identities.

This type of identity work was common in English usage, as for instance when Ellen, a thirty-year-old English instructor at a local university, described to me how she felt speaking English:

> In English, myself will be more logical. But in Chinese, you know, more emotional, not logical. English is, I think, more *mingxi de, qingxi de* (distinct, clear), but Chinese is not this kind of language. It can have this feeling, *mohu de* (blurry) feeling. If I use English to describe something in society, some really existed thing, it is okay, but cannot do this in Chinese.

We might interpret Ellen's code-switching in this excerpt as a response to lexical gaps when, for instance, she wants to express the feeling of indistinctness. But note also her categorisations of English and Chinese; English can be used for things which are logical, but Chinese for things which are emotional and/or unclear. It is precisely at the points where she expresses emotional attachments to language (distinct, clear, blurry) that she switches into Chinese. In other words, her code-switching reflects a language ideology (Schieffelin *et al.*, 1998) that partitions logic and emotion between two languages and indexes shifts in her own perception of social identity as she moves back and forth between them. Chinese is the language of emotion,

English the language of logic, and her discursive choices emphasise these contrasting aspects of her sense of self.

Other than logic, English in Shenyang is also, and perhaps most importantly, associated with identities that are international in orientation; these are configured as Western, cosmopolitan or global. Jeff, another English teacher at a city-level university in his late twenties, used English to assert an identity he explicitly described as 'Western.' While discussing his students, he explained what he perceived as differences between Chinese and English communicative styles:

> Chinese people tend to communicate in, like a group kind of a way. So we want to start our sentence 'we', 'you' as in plural, and 'they,' whereas Westerners, I guess, are paying attention a lot to the individuality of a person, like, who is this person? Even by naming the dog, you guys will say 'she' or 'he,' but we will just call it *ta* (it) and like, that's it... In English, like, you personalise everything, you know, come on, take care of me first.

Note here that these styles are laminated with particular forms of identity, one Western and the other Chinese.[5] For Jeff, it is not merely the linguistic codes themselves that are important, but also how they connote opposed attitudes or worldviews. Once he had established these relations for me, Jeff continued: 'In speaking, well me, I'm Westernised, I will look you in the eye. But most Chinese, will tend to look at their fingers, at the ceiling, outside at the window.' Jeff's own use of English underwrites his claim to membership in the second group of people – those Westerners who 'personalise' everything, who value individuality and want to be 'taken care of' first. There is a tremendous fluidity in these forms of identification, as Ellen and Jeff move back and forth between competing forms of identification embedded in English and Chinese speech. By code-switching between them, they highlight the hybridity inherent in ELF users' sense of self as positioned between global and local forms of identity (Canagarajah, 2006; Dewey, 2007; Sung, 2014a).

Conclusion

I have presented in this chapter several examples of English use in China in order to highlight two components of ELF research that I believe have been largely overlooked: the significance of intracultural usage, and the importance of indexicality for understanding the construction of identity.

I have explained the role that ethnography plays in anthropological research as a way of producing situated and collaborative knowledge about the meanings of linguistic choices made in context, and have attempted to show how ethnographic material from my research in Shenyang can illustrate the discursive production of identity in practice.

These forms of identity cannot be neatly delineated as either Western or Chinese, just as the speakers' interactions cannot be clearly categorised as intercultural or intracultural. Instead, the speakers I have depicted herein use English as an indexical resource for shifting among different identities; at times they express membership in a localised group of culturally similar Chinese speakers and at other times they affiliate with globally expansive cultural others. English can represent a gateway, grounded in ideological claims to its lingua franca status, to broader forms of global social belonging that Chinese citizens may take advantage of by becoming conversationally fluent, as illustrated by Boshan's notion of 'oral English.' At the same time, 'mute English' operates as a kind of gatekeeping mechanism, necessitating hours of study on non-conversational linguistic knowledge to be able to obtain success in education or employment. This is the paradox of global languages: They are potentially international in scope, but also shape local forms of social interaction (Higgins, 2009). Culture is thus understood not as a fixed set of attributes, but as a larger context that allows interactants to make sense of the significance of these linguistic choices.

If we take seriously Jeff's claim to cosmopolitanism, studies of ELF must, in turn, take account of the power of language's indexical content in order to accurately comprehend how that language is deployed in interaction, especially in the context of the globalisation of English that underlies so much of today's research (Dewey, 2007; Ives, 2010). Expanding the field of study beyond solely intercultural interactions predicated on ideological perceptions of cultural difference and questions of intelligibility to intracultural interactions and questions of indexicality can illuminate undercurrents of power, inequality, ideology and, ultimately, the understandings of the speakers using that lingua franca. This can serve, as Seidlhofer (2011: 73) envisions, to shift our focus from 'how far forms of language conform to *codified norms*, [to] how they *function* as the exploitation of linguistic resources for making meaning.' These functions can include more than simply the goal of communicating information clearly to other English users.

As I have argued in this chapter, the communicative function of English, particularly in apparent cases of ELF use, should be combined with culturally specific understandings of the indexical function of discourse styles. In this way, we can see how English is a performative enactment of particular identities or claims to authority which are salient to the speakers themselves. The stances language users occupy vis-à-vis each other are just as important as the actual referential content of their speech. In the context of intercultural communication, these indexicalisations may not be apparent to intercultural listeners, such as NSEs, and can lead to significant forms of misunderstanding or non-understanding. By examining the shared meanings that exist in lingua franca use as a form of intracultural communication, researchers can possibly extrapolate the intentions and understandings of L2 English speakers beyond the local context into more global frames of discursive interaction.

Notes

(1) All translations of both textual and spoken materials are my own.
(2) All named research participants, as well as the names of schools and businesses, have been altered to maintain confidentiality. Almost all urban Chinese under the age of 30 have an English name, either self-chosen or assigned by a teacher, but not all regularly use this name in English interaction. In providing pseudonyms, I followed the language preferences of my informants – English pseudonyms for English names, and Chinese pseudonyms for Chinese names.
(3) Transcription conventions are as follows:

.	full stop
,	pause
¿	rising intonation/question
...	longer pause (over 0.2s)
[ ]	overlapping speech
( )	translation from Chinese
(( ))	contextual information
—	truncated/interrupted speech

(4) The exact form of the test is subject to ongoing educational reforms and to minor regional variations.
(5) Both Ellen and Jeff were speaking directly to me, an NSE, during the interview, with no-one else present. Although we might interpret these instances as based on presumed intercultural rather than intracultural relations, in their classes with Chinese students Ellen and Jeff built upon these statements: Ellen frequently discussed the 'logical' quality of English grammar with her students, while Jeff's classes were rambunctious performances of his Western identity.

References

Adamson, B. (2004) *China's English: A History of English in Chinese Education*. Hong Kong: Hong Kong University Press.

Agha, A. (2007) *Language and Social Relations*. Cambridge: Cambridge University Press.
Baker, W. (2009) The cultures of English as a lingua franca. *TESOL Quarterly* 43 (4), 567–592.
Besnier, N. (2004) Consumption and cosmopolitanism: Practicing modernity at the second-hand marketplace in Nuku'alofa, Tonga. *Anthropological Quarterly* 77 (1), 7–45.
Billings, S. (2009) Speaking beauties: Linguistic posturing, language inequality, and the construction of a Tanzanian beauty queen. *Language in Society* 38 (5), 581–606.
Block, D. (2007) *Second Language Identities*. New York: Continuum.
Blommaert, J. (2005) *Discourse*. Cambridge: Cambridge University Press.
Bolton, K. (2003) *Chinese Englishes: A Sociolinguistic History*. Cambridge: Cambridge University Press.
Bucholtz, M. (2003) Sociolinguistic nostalgia and the authentication of identity. *Journal of Sociolinguistics* 7 (3), 398–416.
Bucholtz, M. and Hall, K. (2005) Identity and interaction: A sociocultural linguistic approach. *Discourse Studies* 7 (4/5), 585–614.
Canagarajah, S. (2006) Negotiating the local in English as a lingua franca. *Annual Review of Applied Linguistics* 26, 197–218.
Cheng, L. (2008) The key to success: English language testing in China. *Language Testing* 25 (1), 15–37.
Cheng, X. (2011) The 'English curriculum standards' in China: Rationales and issues. In A. Feng (ed.) *English Language Education Across Greater China* (pp. 133–150). Bristol: Multilingual Matters.
Cortazzi, M. and Jin, L. (1996) English teaching and learning in China. *Language Teaching* 29 (2), 61–80.
Creese, A. (2008) Linguistic ethnography. In K.A. King and N.H. Hornberger (eds) *Encyclopedia of Language and Education* (2nd edn, vol. 10), *Research Methods in Language and Education* (pp. 229–241). New York: Springer.
Dewey, M. (2007) English as a lingua franca and globalization: An interconnected perspective. *International Journal of Applied Linguistics* 17 (3), 332–354.
Firth, A. (1996) The discursive accomplishment of normality: On 'lingua franca' English and conversation analysis. *Journal of Pragmatics* 26 (2), 237–259.
Friedrich, P. and Matsuda, A. (2010) When five words are not enough: A conceptual and terminological discussion of English as a lingua franca. *International Multilingual Research Journal* 4 (1), 20–30.
Gil, J. and Adamson, B. (2011) The English language in Mainland China: A Sociolinguistic Profile. In A. Feng (ed.) *English Language Education Across Greater China* (pp. 23–45). Bristol: Multilingual Matters.
Goffman, E. (1974) *Frame Analysis*. Cambridge: Harvard University Press.
Gu, M., Patkin, J. and Kirkpatrick, A. (2014) The dynamic identity construction in English as lingua franca intercultural communication: A positioning perspective. *System* 46, 131–142.
Hammersley, M. (2006) Ethnography: Problems and prospects. *Ethnography and Education* 1 (1), 3–14.
Hanks, W. (2000) Indexicality. *Journal of Linguistic Anthropology* 9 (1–2), 124–126.
Henry, E. (2010) Interpretations of 'Chinglish': Native speakers, language learners and the enregisterment of a stigmatized code. *Language in Society* 39 (5), 669–688.
Higgins, C. (2009) *English as a Local Language: Post-colonial Identities and Multilingual Practices*. Bristol: Multilingual Matters.

Holliday, A. (2011) Cultural descriptions as political cultural acts: An exploration. *Language and Intercultural Communication* 10 (3), 259–272.
Hu, G. (2002) Recent important developments in secondary English language teaching in the PRC. *Language, Culture, and Curriculum* 15 (1), 30–49.
Hu, G. (2005) English language education in China: Policies, progress, and problems. *Language Policy* 4 (1), 5–24.
Hu, G. and McKay, S.L. (2012) English language education in East Asia: Some recent developments. *Journal of Multilingual and Multicultural Development* 33 (4), 345–362.
Ives, P. (2010) Cosmopolitanism and global English: Language politics in globalisation debates. *Political Studies* 58 (3), 516–535.
Jenkins, J. (2000) *The Phonology of English as an International Language*. Oxford: Oxford University Press.
Jenkins, J. (2007) *English as a Lingua Franca: Attitude and Identity*. Oxford: Oxford University Press.
Jenkins, J., Cogo, A. and Dewey, M. (2011) Review of developments in research into English as a lingua franca. *Language Teaching* 44 (3), 281–315.
Kachru, B.B. (1985) Standards, codification, and sociolinguistic realism: The English language in the outer circle. In R. Quirk and H. Widdowson (eds) *English in the World: Teaching and Learning of Language and Literature* (pp. 11–30). Cambridge: Cambridge University Press.
Kaur, J. (2011) Intercultural communication in English as a lingua franca: Some sources of misunderstanding. *Intercultural Pragmatics* 8 (1), 93–116.
Kipnis, A. (2011) *Governing Educational Desire: Culture, Politics and Schooling in China*. Chicago: University of Chicago Press.
Kramsch, C. (2011) The symbolic dimensions of the intercultural. *Language Teaching* 44 (3), 354–367.
Mao, L. and Yue, M. (2004) Foreign language education in the PRC: A brief overview. In M. Zhou and H. Sun (eds) *Language Policy in the People's Republic of China: Theory and Practice Since 1949* (pp. 319–330). Boston: Kluwer.
Meierkord, C. (2006) Lingua franca communication past and present. *International Journal of the Sociology of Language* 177 (1), 9–30.
Ministry of Education (PRC). (2001) *Yingyu kecheng biaozhun* [English language curriculum standards]. Beijing: Beijing Normal University Publishing House.
Norton, B. (2000) *Identity and Language Learning: Gender, Ethnicity and Educational Change*. Harlow: Longman.
Pan, L. (2009) Dissecting multilingual Beijing: The space and scale of vernacular globalization. *Visual Communication* 9, 67–90.
Pavlenko, A. and Blackledge, A. (eds) (2004) *Negotiation of Identities in Multilingual Contexts*. Clevedon: Multilingual Matters.
Pickering, L. (2006) Current research on intelligibility in English as a lingua franca. *Annual Review of Applied Linguistics* 26, 219–233.
Schieffelin, B., Woolard, K. and Kroskrity, P. (eds) (1998) *Language Ideologies: Practice and Theory*. Oxford: Oxford University Press.
Schneider, E. (2007) *Postcolonial Englishes*. Cambridge: Cambridge University Press.
Seidlhofer, B. (2011) *Understanding English as a Lingua Franca*. Oxford: Oxford University Press.
Silverstein, M. (2003) Indexical order and the dialectics of sociolinguistic life. *Language and Communication* 23 (3–4), 193–229.

Sung, C.C.M. (2014a) English as a lingua franca and global identities: Perspectives from four second language learners of English in Hong Kong. *Linguistics and Education* 26, 31–39.

Sung, C.C.M. (2014b) Hong Kong university students' perceptions of their identities in English as a lingua franca contexts: An exploratory study. *Journal of Asian Pacific Communication* 24 (1), 94–112.

Tusting, K. and Maybin, J. (2007) Linguistic ethnography and interdisciplinarity: Opening the discussion. *Journal of Sociolinguistics* 11 (5), 575–583.

Zheng, X.M. and Davison, C. (2008) *Changing Pedagogy: Analysing ELT Teachers in China*. London: Continuum.

Part 3
Commentary

9 Intercultural Communication and the Possibility of English as a Lingua Franca

John O'Regan

Historical Prolegomena

To which marts, that English men call fayres, Ech nation oft maketh her repayres: English, and French, Lombardes, Jennoyes, Catalones, thedre they take her wayes: Scots, Spaniards, Irishman there abides, With great plenty bringing of sale hides. (Richard Haklyut, 1589/1927, *The Principal Navigations Voyages Traffiques and Discoveries of the English Nation*, vol. 1: 187)

When hailed by another ship, pirates, who were multinational in origin, usually answered that they came 'from the seas,' not from any particular country. Some pirates explained to captives that they had 'sold their nation' for booty. They made the point with brutal clarity after the declaration of war against Spain ... in March 1719, when the British admiralty and royal officials throughout the Americas desperately hoped that pirates would come in, accept the King's commissions, and go back to sea as privateers. (Marcus Rediker, 2004, *Villains of all Nations: Atlantic Pirates and the Golden Age*: 8)

Multiethnic and multinational crews had to work together and fight together in spite of language differences; Spaniards had to be interrogated, used as pilots and traded with; and Indians were needed as guides and allies: all things were hindered without clear communication. For the buccaneer, the addition of another tongue was as natural and necessary as knowing the difference between taking in, casting off, and letting go.

(Benerson Little, 2007, *The Buccaneer's Realm. Pirate Life on the Spanish Main, 1674–1688*: 150)

Now every body, excepting those situated in and near the windows, began to grow outrageous, and many delirious. *Water, Water* became the general cry. And the old Jemmautdaar, before mentioned, taking pity on us, ordered the people to bring some skins of water, little dreaming, I believe, of its fatal effects. This was what I dreaded. I foresaw it would prove the ruin of the small chance left us, and essayed many times to speak to him privately to forbid it being brought; but the clamour was so loud, it became impossible, and the water appeared. (John Zephaniah Holwell, 1764, *A Narrative of the Deplorable Deaths of the English Gentlemen who were Suffocated in the Black Hole in Fort William, at Calcutta, June 1756*: 395)

For a laugh, our captors would tell us every now and then: 'It'll be two or three days, or a week, and then you'll be free in Italy.' It was just to see our desperation when they added the word *"Inshallah"* (God willing). It was their way of lying without seeming to lie. (Dominico Quirico, the *Observer*, 15 September 2013: 30)

ELF and the Adequacy of a Concept

I see my role here in the nature of an intervention within a set of sociolinguistic positions, arguments, assumptions, procedures, instruments and practices which have been lexicalized in the study of applied linguistics as 'English as a lingua franca', or ELF; a concept which has been expressed in this book variously as 'a new field of research that accounts for an empirically based and theoretically informed understanding of how English is used today in an increasing number of contexts' (Holmes & Dervin, 2016: 4); 'a communicative situation dominated by people who don't have the language in question as their first or early second language' (Risager, 2016: 37); 'a construct that refers to mutual engagement, joint enterprise and shared repertoire' (Bjørge, 2016: 116); 'a contact language spoken by interactants that do not share a common L1' (Jenks, 2016, 97); 'the dynamic and fluid manner in which form, function and context are constructed in intercultural communication' (Baker, 2016: 70); and a phenomenon which is 'highly fluid and hybridized, and [drawing] upon multiple linguistic resources that are both global and local in scope, to construct novel speech forms' (Henry, 2016: 184). Let me begin with two questions. The first is, What would the world have to be like for ELF to be possible? This is a question which is qualitatively different to a second question, which is, What would the world have to be like for lingua franca Englishes to be possible?). I believe that the answers to these two questions are different, and that they lead to different conclusions about the history and dissemination of English(es) in the world. This is the subject which I wish to address in this chapter.

The reader will have noticed that the term ~~ELF~~ is here purposely placed 'under erasure' (Spivak, 1976: xvii), with a line drawn through it. This is in order to signal how this term is not just provisional, but inadequate in relation to the sociolinguistic complexity of global and local uses of 'English' in the world. As intimated in the last sentence, the same can also be said of the term 'English', a term which not only hides a multitude of varieties within it (Blommaert, 1998), but in a world increasingly acknowledged to be populated by 'Englishes' (Kachru, 1985), and with an entire 'World Englishes' field dedicated to their research, has long been seen as erroneous and problematic. The same can also be said for the word 'culture'. There is evidently a wider discussion to be had – and which is being had – about the adequacy of all these terms (see Blommaert, 1998, 2010; Holliday, 2010; Pennycook, 2007; Rajagopalan, 2012), but in the space I have here I will confine myself to ~~ELF~~, and so in this chapter, only this term will appear with a line drawn through it.

On the one hand, ~~ELF~~ is an hypostatization (O'Regan, 2014); that is, its very use implies something fixed and stable – having the property of concreteness – and notwithstanding the widespread statements of ~~ELF~~ supporters disputing this. On the other hand, when persons of different linguistic and community or cultural backgrounds meet together for whom 'English' is not a mother tongue, they are evidently not speaking 'English', as this too suggests something which is uniform, or 'centripetal', in relation to an implied hegemonic norm (Rajagopalan, 2012). Instead, it might be more accurate to say that they are speaking Englishes together, or something more 'centrifugal' (Rajagopalan, 2012); which is to say, that rather than speaking ~~ELF~~ (or even, as is sometimes claimed, 'in ~~ELF~~'), or faithfully reproducing standardized native-like inner-circle norms (Gao, 2014), which on the face of it are also 'Englishes' (American, Welsh, Irish, Australian, etc.), they are speaking one or other forms of L1-inflected English (here still a problematic term). Although that is not to deny that a certain amount of modelling of imagined native speaker (NS) norms may be in process amongst the speakers as well, with greater or lesser degrees of success and, depending on the subjective judgment of the hypothetical hearer, whether native or not. But here again as I write these sentences I am conscious in the very inscription of the word of the problem which makes ~~ELF~~, like the sign, 'that ill-named t~~hing~~' (Derrida, 1976: 19). For in contradistinction to its supporters' claims about the plurilithicism, hybridity and originality of their object of knowledge, '~~ELF~~' is introduced into this complexity as an hypostatized form – reified, settled, resolved, fixed, sedimented, cemented, and finally stamped onto the page: an inked sign in a white landscape.

Much of the foregoing critique rests upon an acceptance that speakers of 'English' in intercultural settings are in fact speaking qualitatively different forms of English to one another, depending on their lifeworld experiences of the language known as 'English' and the individual linguacultural as well as personal backgrounds from which they speak, e.g. Japanese, Italian, Korean, Chinese, Arabic, Portuguese, Spanish or even English. It is an entirely subjective decision as to whether you accept non-native speaker 'English' as a type or style of English, or not. For some, English is a term which must infer an abstracted authority which is able pronounce on what is or is not legitimate English. So that when non-native speakers (NNSs) are said to be speaking 'English', the signified of which their speech is the signifier seems by implication to be a recognized native-speaker norm. So if a Japanese and a Greek are said to be speaking 'English' to one another, the implied signified for this is the native-speaker form of the language. But we could equally say instead that the Japanese speaker is speaking 'English' (that term again) with Japanese characteristics and the Greek is speaking English with Greek characteristics, and if we did accept this, then it could be argued that the speakers are speaking Englishes of slightly – or possibly very – different kinds. Or we might even say that they are speaking lingua franca Englishes or LFEs, but it would be apocryphal to claim that they are speaking ELF: a language variety with no NSs. In the term ELF a different order of signification is in play, and it is one which mimics the type of signification which applies to the term 'English'. That is, as the inscription ELF appears as a trace on the page, ELF becomes hypostatized as a thing-in-itself and thus simultaneously the universal signified for L2 intercultural communicative encounters.

In drawing attention to the hypostatization of ELF, and also of English, and by presenting it in this way, I am concerned with a figure which is absent. Namely, the world which would have to be assumed for ELF to be possible – the implied ontology for ELF (Bhaskar, 2008). In relation to this, I wish to maintain a critical stance towards ELF. My objective is not a sedimented mode of enquiry, that is, one which takes ELF as a given object of knowledge and proceeds from that premise; rather, it is an enquiry into the very nature of that sedimentation. The metaphor of sedimentation is appropriate to this discussion when one considers that it infers a settling, fixity, substantiality, density, materiality and, by dint of this, emergence into some form of completeness and permanence – of ELF as 'an emerging English that exists in its own right' (Jenkins, 2007: 2). The capacity of ELF supporters to slide seamlessly between 'ELF with its emphasis on hybridity, innovation and accommodation' (Dewey & Jenkins, 2010: 76) to speaking and writing 'in ELF' in 'ELF settings' which are populated by 'ELF speakers' (e.g. House, 2012: 285; Jenkins, 2013: 38; Jenkins et al., 2011: 302; Mauranen & Metsä-Ketelä, 2006: 6) is worthy of comment and arises from an underlying weakness within ELF theory. This weakness proceeds from the reduction of ontology (reality) to epistemology (what can be observed) so that what is presumed to be real is interpreted and understood – or misrecognized – primarily in terms of what is observed.

In other words, in ELF, the mere fact of intercultural communication in 'English' amongst speakers of different L1s is taken as a sufficient basis to be able to speak of an entity that is ELF and to take this as a self-affirmed starting point.

The mythologization of ELF

The mythologization of ELF proceeds from the implication, in much of the discourse related to it, that non-native speakers (NNSs) of Englishes in the world are in the process of evolving a new variety of English – ELF – with accompanying pragmalinguistic strategies to which these users are incrementally contributing, whether consciously or unconsciously (cf. Cogo & Dewey, 2012; Jenkins et al., 2011; Seidlhofer, 2011). This implication explains why such great emphasis is placed upon observed empirical linguistic-pragmatic innovations and conjunctions of events in the discourse of speakers engaged in communication in inter- or cross-cultural settings. Building on this perception is the presumption that innovative language forms and creative accommodation techniques are travelling in a consistently uniform and incremental manner from one intercultural setting to another, such that it becomes possible to begin to map the emergence of ELF and its intercultural pragmatics. The assumption of ELF is self-legitimizing and rests on a mythologization in which intercultural encounters in English magically coalesce into communities of shared practice and repertoire (Seidlhofer, 2009) and where speakers, it is claimed, 'skillfully negotiate and co-construct English for their own purposes, treating the language as a shared communicative resource within which they innovate, accommodate and code-switch, all the while enjoying the freedom to produce forms that NSEs (native speakers of English) do not necessarily use' (Jenkins et al., 2011: 297).

My feeling is that such views both exaggerate and oversimplify matters, and that the innovative continuities which are implied as travelling between contexts are projected onto intercultural encounters from an overriding desire to uncover them. If anything, such encounters are marked by linguistic and pragmatic discontinuity – and real-world inequality – so that no one encounter is identical to another (Blommaert, 1998); and that where commonalities are observed across settings (e.g. dropping of the third-person 's' or apparently innovative or playful negotiated meaning construction between L2 speakers), these are indicative not of creative and imaginative realizations of ELF, or of shared repertoire, but are examples of variants typical of L2 production and also of coincidences between L1 lexico-grammars which are then realized in intercultural interactions in the L2. They are, in addition, examples of what Phipps (2007) has called 'the human struggle to make meaning' (19). Accommodation on this account is not simply the privileged domain of L2 speakers of Englishes in the world, or indeed of speakers of ELF. The hermeneutic and analytic traditions in philosophy and in linguistics (Gadamer, 1989; Grice, 1975; Habermas, 1984) have shown how accommodation and cooperation are basic to all human communication and action. As Habermas has argued,

> The concept of communicative action presupposes language as the medium for a kind of reaching understanding, in the course of which participants, through relating to a world, reciprocally raise validity claims that can be accepted or contested ... For both parties the interpretive task consists in incorporating the other's interpretation of the situation into one's own in such a way that in the revised version 'his' external world and 'my' external world can – against the background of 'our' lifeworld – be relativized in relation to 'the' world, and the divergent situation definitions can be brought to coincide sufficiently. Naturally, this does not mean that interpretation must lead in every case to a stable and unambiguously differentiated assignment. *Stability and absence of ambiguity are rather the exception in the communicative practice of everyday life.* (Habermas, 1987: 100; my emphasis)

To claim that there is something special, emergent and unique about the way L2 speakers of Englishes communicate with one another in intercultural encounters is to idealize a practice which is basic to human communication, as well as to the interactions observed. In addition, as the above passage indicates, human communication is rarely stable and unambiguous, perhaps more so in the case of lingua franca settings, and processes of communication are forever being constructed anew. A similar point has been made by Pennycook (2010a) and Canagarajah (2007) in relation to what they refer to as 'lingua franca English' (LFE). Pennycook (2010a) argues that the distinction between English as a lingua franca and lingua franca English is important because 'the former tends towards an understanding of a pre-given language that is then used by different speakers, while the latter suggests that LFE emerges from its contexts of use' (2010a: 684). He then cites Canagarajah as saying that 'LFE does not exist as a system out there. It is constantly brought into being in each context of communication' (Canagarajah, 2007: 91, cited in Pennycook, 2010: 684). In the mindful words of Blommaert (1998),

> If 'cultures meet', they usually do so under rather grim socioeconomic circumstances, with a clear societally sanctioned power difference between the various parties involved. It is, from that perspective, also useful to point at the abnormality of many studies of intercultural communication that focus on elite forms of interaction such as business negotiations, technological cooperation, international management or diplomacy [...] In sum, 'culture' in all its meanings and with all its affiliated concepts, is situational. It depends on the context in which concrete interactions occur. *Studying speech conventions of certain groups of people, and then contrasting them with those of other groups of people, is of little use to the study of intercultural communication.* (http://www.cie.ugent.be/CIE/blommaert1.htm; my emphasis)

If such enquiry is of little use to the study of intercultural communication, it is also of little use in the study of intercultural interactions which are taken to be realizations of ELF. We should also in this connection remind ourselves that accommodation and cooperation are present in the rejection, oppression and disparagement of the other (cf. Holliday, 2010; Jenks, 2012; Ladegaard, 2012; Phipps, 2014). It has often been presupposed in much of the writing about ELF and about intercultural communication that the objective is what Phipps (2007) has referred to as 'some nirvana of toleration and harmony' (19). Despite this assumption, however, the brute fact remains that around the world people are accommodating and cooperating in the marginalization, oppression and annihilation of one another, and that this is not new but rather has a long history. It is therefore possible to kill the other in ELF while being accommodating at the same time, as demonstrated by the Westgate shopping mall massacre in Nairobi in 2013 and the mass suffocation of 125 members of the multinational East India Company garrison in the 'Black Hole' of Calcutta in 1756. To these events we may add the kidnappings and summary executions of foreign nationals by jihadists in Iraq and Afghanistan over several years and the recent killing of an 'Afghan insurgent' by a British Royal Marine, who dispatched his victim with the words 'There you are. Shuffle off this mortal coil, you cunt. It's nothing you wouldn't do to us' (Mark Townsend, *The Guardian*, 9 November 2013). In addition, we might also note that the Norwegian white supremacist and mass murderer Anders Behring Breivik wrote his online *European Declaration of Independence* in ELF and would be classed as a proficient ELF user.

Ontological realism and lingua franca Englishes

A further distinction which this discussion raises is that the ELF concept is based on an historical narrative (or ontology) in which ELF is misrecognized as original and new. In brief, the narrative is that since 1945 the world has entered a new transformational era of international communication ensuing from globalization, decolonization and the diffusion of the knowledge economy, and that the lingua franca of international communication is a newly emergent, hybridized, plurilithic and deterritorialized form of English which is especially suited to this new era (Dewey, 2007; Dewey & Jenkins, 2010; Jenkins, 2013; Jenkins *et al.*, 2011; Seidlhofer, 2011). Another aspect of this narrative is that it is often implied that learners of English globally are, without exception, all users, and it is on this basis that NNSs of English outnumber NSs. This may well be so, but its extent depends on the criterion of use that is applied, as not all learners become users. Nevertheless, the assumption in ELF that learners and users are synonymous not surprisingly provides the numerical basis for questioning the legitimacy of standard NS inner circle Englishes as the ideal models for English in classrooms around the world, a point I shall return to below.

The misrecognition which attends ELF is the perception that lingua franca situations in which 'English' (that term again) is selected by participants as the medium of communication are somehow original and new. In ELF, globalization and the specifics of ELF discourse are, in the words of Blommaert (2010), presented as, 'shockingly new things – as if the world we now live in is a totally new one. It is not' (2010: 16). A perusal of the ELF literature shows that the historiography of ELF is almost entirely confined to the recent past, and mostly since the mid-1990s. To read about ELF is thus to gather the impression that in previous decades and centuries when speakers of different L1s spoke to one another in 'English', they were not speaking ELF. Indeed, it seems that they were not speaking at all. The neglect of the historicity of English and its intertwinement in the globalization of a capitalist world system that dates to at least the 1600s (Wallerstein, 2004) is a fundamental flaw in an ELF narrative which barely scratches the surface of intercultural uses of 'English' historically. A more diachronic historical perspective shows that LFEs, as I am calling them, have been around for a very long time.

When the English naval explorer Francis Drake commenced his circumnavigation of the globe in 1557, the crew he took with him was multinational, but the language of the ship was what the sailors knew as 'English'. In the 'golden age' of Caribbean and Atlantic piracy from the 1650s to the 1730s, multinational, multi-ethnic and multilingual crews were the norm, and a number of these were commanded by English captains for whom

Spanish and English would have been shipboard lingua francas. The soldiers who fought in Cromwell's armies during the 'pacification' of Ireland in the 1650s were in part Irish mercenaries whose first language was Irish but who were led by native English-speaking commanders. The English East India Company (EIC) army of the 1600s and 1700s had large numbers of mercenary soldiers amongst its ranks, including Sepoys, French, Dutch and Portuguese. These fought alongside British EIC recruits and under English officers, and were essential to the establishment of British rule in India. The American Revolutionary War of 1775–1783 was fought on both sides in several languages, including English. The language of trade along the China coast from 1750 to at least 1850 was Canton Pidgin English, spoken not only between foreigners and local Chinese in the treaty ports but also between Chinese from different regions of China (Bolton, 2003; Van Dyke, 2005). What this historical sketch shows is that the concept of English, or better still Englishes, being used for lingua franca purposes amongst speakers of different L1s is not in any sense original, creative or especially new; lingua franca Englishes have been in existence for centuries. They are certainly not simply the progeny of a narrow range of modern-day bilingual elites in globally rarefied international business, education, research and leisure domains as appears to be the case in ELF (see Breiteneder, 2009; Ehrenreich, 2011; Kalocsai, 2009; Kankaanranta & Planken, 2010; Mauranen, 2012).

That these are lingua franca Englishes is key, because speakers of different L1s from different parts of the world carry their lexico-grammars and their lifeworlds with them when they are speaking other languages. That is, if they wish to speak at all, they intend to mean something and to receive meaning in return, and are willing to commit to the struggle to make meaning, regardless of how messy this process may be. These speakers speak and will often write in a form of English which is marked to a greater or lesser extent by their local L1 knowledge and experience, and when they come together in communication with speakers of other L1s, the result is lingua franca Englishes (LFEs), not ELF. Thus we may say that lingua franca Englishes when used in intercultural communication encounters are historical, contemporary, personal and often messy, and that the linguistic pragmatics of LFEs are created anew from one context to another, and not according to an *a priori*, emergent or incrementally evolving plan. LFEs are necessarily plural, not singular, because the contexts where LFEs are present are plurilingual (i.e. more than one variant or type of English is present). They are also differentiated and stratified in terms of class, race, gender, economy and religion. That is to say that encounters involving LFEs are not confined to globalized and largely White elites in international business, diplomacy and research contexts. The poor, the disenfranchised, the ethnically marginalized, and the exploited – the 'McWorkers' of neoliberal economies – are also users of LFEs in intercultural settings. In the world of ELF research, however, these speakers appear to have no voice.

Another reason for preferring LFEs over lingua franca English (LFE) is that 'LFE' is unable to capture simultaneously the singular and the plural of intercultural encounters where more than one variant of English is present, which also includes the personal imprint which each speaker brings to the variant they select. Every encounter is a personal one for each participant in respect of the English he or she chooses to speak – as a variant and idiolectally – as well as a multiple one in respect of the different Englishes drawn upon by all of the participants together. In this manner 'LFE' potentially suffers from the same problem as ELF. It follows from this that if terms such as 'LFE' or 'LFE context' are to be employed, the double meaning of 'LFE' needs to be somehow taken into account and foregrounded.

A similar argument might have been made for ELF, but it is already too late for that. The term has been inscribed into text and formulaic compound neologisms a million times and more, and so what remains is the darkening cloud of the hypostatized form only: 'ELF speakers', 'ELF settings', 'ELF encounters', 'ELF users', 'ELF interactions', 'ELF accommodation', 'ELF creativity', 'ELF innovation', 'written ELF', 'spoken ELF', 'ELF error', and so on. The term has slid into the linguistic collective consciousness and now, in Marx's words, 'weighs like a nightmare on the brains of the living' (Marx, 1978 [1852]: 595).

The supposed radicalism of the ELF project is similarly overstated. The ELF case proceeds from a liberal-idealist rationalism and acquiescence to the geo-capitalist status quo, which issues from its incapacity to critique, or even name, capitalism as a primary agent in determining the global distribution of economic and linguistic resources, and thus individuals' life chances as well. Instead, the world system is taken as given, and economic, gendered, racial, religious and class inequalities within and between the populations of nation states are discounted in favour of a focus on lingua franca forms as ideologically neutral and self-emancipating and, less promisingly, as geo-culturally Eurocentric and the property of cosmopolitan bilingual elites. ELF as a political project thus provides a pillar of support to mobile capital in the reproduction of global class stratifications along linguistic lines. To put this another way, those who have most access to intercultural lingua francas and the most opportunity to use them are those with the highest quotients of economic, social, cultural and linguistic capital (Bourdieu, 1986).

It is therefore not surprising to find that the NNSs who have the most native-like lexico-grammars in the L2 are from this group. This may appear contradictory, given that a principal focus of ELF research is to champion the claims of the NNS in the face of the hegemony of NS norms. The problem here lies in the kinds of groups such research prefers to champion. As I have indicated, these are not the 'ordinary' or the marginalized of the world, but elites (albeit stratified), as the ELF research data regularly shows. Some of these users may be entirely satisfied with their non-standard and 'non-native like' modes of articulation in speaking (but possibly less so in writing). However, capital dictates that this is an insufficient basis for gaining access to the higher echelons of international global power – whether in education, business, finance, philosophy or diplomacy. To reach this level of access, nothing less than standardized (and mythologized) native-speaker-like English will do.

> When I saw [Christine] Lagarde speak last week, she was wearing a scarf tied in a perfect geometric circle, holding her glasses in one hand as a prop, and standing as erect as you'd expect from a former member of France's synchronized swimming team. But the salient fact about her is her English, absorbed over 25 years in the US. Lagarde was an exchange student at a Maryland private school, interned on Capitol Hill, and eventually ran the law firm Baker & McKenzie. Her English is key to why everyone almost instinctively turned to her to replace Dominique Strauss-Kahn at the IMF. *The Economist*, house magazine of the global Anglophone elite, called her "a superb communicator, a good negotiator and, by all accounts, an excellent manager". Note which phrase came first. Lagarde is a woman for our times. To make it very big nowadays, speaking English usually isn't enough. You need perfect English. (Simon Kuper, 'Something in the way she speaks...', *The Financial Times*, 24 June 2011)

Quite apart from the preoccupations of senior officials in the IMF and their admirers, worldwide, people who have access to English, and who care about this, believe that their life chances and those of their children will be affected by the kind of English that they learn, and, despite widespread and well-documented local appropriations in such diverse areas such as hip hop and online chat rooms (Pennycook, 2007, 2010b; Jenks, 2012), usually care little about the democratising niceties of speaking local or hybridized Englishes, much as this may be welcomed by those of us who write about these things. Similarly, their governments believe this too. This is why there is such a clamour for NS models of English around the world; why tests based on NS models predominate in school and university examinations; why international testing systems such as IELTS, TOEIC and TOEFL (which are based on NS models) are aggressively promoted; why husbands and wives have been separated so that their children can move to an Anglophone country and acquire native-like competence; and why NS teachers continue to be favoured over NNS locals, particularly by parents who can afford to make the choice for their children – notwithstanding the ELF argument that the globalized spread of English puts into question the legitimacy of NS Englishes as the ideal models in English language classrooms around the world. That this is a result of the capitalist world system appears to be lost on ELF advocates, and this would explain the absence of any critique to this effect.

By utilizing Bhaskar's division of reality into the real, the actual and the empirical (Bhaskar, 2008) and applying it to ELF, it becomes apparent how ELF operates with an ontology which misses the real causal mechanisms (of globalized capital) which are responsible for the actual events (worldwide social and class distributions of Englishes) as well as the empirical experiences (uses of LFEs in intercultural contexts) which make up the three domains. ELF does so by a reduction of the real and the actual to the empirical (epistemic fallacy – interpretation of being in terms of knowing) such that reality is misrecognized by means of data gleaned from empirical observations. In other words, the empirical becomes the lens according to which the real world is distorted, and an imaginary world free of ideology and capital is set in its place. The act, in ELF, of making the empirical take ideological precedence over the domains of the actual and the real thus leads to a form of transcendental idealism or idealist rationalism (Bhaskar, 2008) in which the researched intercultural encounters of ELF are fetishized and the reality of Englishes in a structurally inegalitarian world is obscured. Until ELF theory is able to overcome this reduction, and recognizes the misrecognition, the prospect that through its arguments alone there ever could be a significant redistribution of language resources and capital away from elites in the world system towards those systematically disadvantaged as well as linguistically disparaged by it seems illusory.

Concluding Remarks

It is evident even in the writing of this text that there is a problem with terms such as 'English' and 'culture' as well as with 'ELF' in the interconnected domains of applied linguistics and intercultural communication, and that writing about them is always fraught with ambivalence. Perhaps all three terms ought to have been placed under erasure. I have not done so, and this lack is an anomaly in this text. Derrida (1978) makes the point that in order to critique the sign there is no getting away from using the sign, even as it is 'that ill-named thing'. In the same way, it seems difficult as well as impractical – for historical reasons – to move away from talking about 'English' and 'culture(s)' and much else in human experience in a way that does not also simultaneously invoke an essentialist and transcendental signified. It seems a necessary complicity to perform this invocation, even as we recognize its incommodity.

If this is the case, then why spend time deconstructing the signifier that is E̶L̶F̶? One good reason is that the twin concepts of 'English' and 'culture' have been the subject of much intense deliberation and critique with regard to the essentialisms which they have historically set in train, as the work of many authors in applied linguistics and intercultural communication have shown. Not so with the construct that is E̶L̶F̶, which seems to have become its own self-affirming principle. It is unfortunate – and indicative of a seeming wider paranoia – to note that such is the apparent gorgon-like hold of E̶L̶F̶ on the collective consciousness that those who agitate in its favour appear simply to view those who do not as enemies, reactionaries, unbelievers, wilful misinterpreters and spoilers – a reaction not dissimilar to that which is delivered up to those who question the motives of cults and other fundamentalist groups. In addition, due at least in part to the necessary complicity already mentioned, E̶L̶F̶ has also inevitably become present in the discourse of its retractors, as well as of those such as language teachers and students who find themselves simply confronted with the term. Hence my decision in this chapter to place it under erasure so that its provisional and sociolinguistically inadequate nature can be clearly signalled and explored. In this way, in the act of making this mark, perhaps we may for a while free our thought from its heavy inscriptional form and so, as Derrida (1976: 158) suggests, open a new reading.

References

Baker, W. (2016) Culture and language in intercultural communication, English as a lingua franca and English language teaching: points of convergence and conflict. In P. Holmes and F. Dervin (eds) *The Cultural and Intercultural Dimensions of English as a Lingua Franca* (pp. 70–92). Bristol: Multilingual Matters.

Bhaskar, R. (2008) *A Realist Theory of Science*. London: Verso.

Bjørge, A.K. (2016) Conflict talk and ELF communities of practice. In P. Holmes and F. Dervin (eds) *The Cultural and Intercultural Dimensions of English as a Lingua Franca* (pp. 114–133). Bristol: Multilingual Matters.

Blommaert, J. (1998) Plenary lecture, *Lernen und Arbeiten in einer international vernetzten und multikulturellen Gesellschaft*, Expertentagung Universität Bremen, Institut für Projektmanagement und Witschaftsinformatik (IPMI), 27–28 February 1998. See http://www.cie.ugent.be/CIE/blommaert1.htm (accessed 19 November 2013).

Blommaert, J. (2010) *The Sociolinguistics of Globalization*. Cambridge: Cambridge University Press.

Bolton, K. (2003) *Chinese Englishes: A Sociolinguistic History*. Cambridge: Cambridge University Press.

Bourdieu, P. (1986) The forms of capital. In J. Richardson (ed.) *Handbook of Theory and Research for the Sociology of Education* (pp. 241–258). New York: Greenwood.

Breiteneder, A. (2009) English as a lingua franca in Europe: An empirical perspective. *World Englishes* 28 (2), 256–269.
Canagarajah, A.S. (2007) The ecology of global English. *International Multilingual Research Journal* 1 (2), 89–100.
Cogo, A. and Dewey, M. (2012) *Analysing Engish as a Lingua Franca: A Corpus-Driven Investigation.* London: Continuum.
Derrida, J. (1976) *Of Grammatology.* Baltimore: Johns Hopkins University Press.
Derrida, J. (1978) *Writing and Difference.* London: Routledge.
Dewey, M. (2007) English as a lingua franca: An interconnected perspective. *International Journal of Applied Linguistics* 17 (3), 332–354.
Dewey, M. and Jenkins, J. (2010) English as a lingua franca in the global context: Interconnectedness, variation and change. In M. Saxena and T. Omoniyi (eds) *Contending with Globalization in World Englishes* (pp. 72–92). Bristol: Multilingual Matters.
Ehrenreich, S. (2011) The dynamics of English as a lingua franca in international business: A language contact perspective. In A. Archibald, A. Cogo and J. Jenkins (eds) *Latest Trends in ELF Research* (pp. 11–34). Newcastle upon Tyne: Cambridge Scholars.
Gadamer, H-G. (1989) *Truth and Method.* New York: Crossroad.
Gao, Y. (2014) Faithful imitator, legitimate speaker, playful creator and dialogical communicator: Shift in English learners' identity prototypes. *Language & Intercultural Communication* 14 (1), 59–75.
Grice, H.P. (1975) Logic and conversation. In P. Cole and J.L. Morgan (eds) *Syntax and Semantics.* London: Academic Press.
Habermas, J. (1984) *The Theory of Communicative Action: Reason and the Rationalisation of Society* (vol. 1). London: Heinemann.
Habermas, J. (1987) *The Philosophical Discourse of Modernity.* Cambridge: Polity Press.
Haklyut, R. (1589/1927) *The Principal Navigations Voyages Traffiques and Discoveries of the English Nation* (vol. 1). London: J. M. Dent & Sons.
Henry, E.S. (2016) The local purposes of a global language: English as an intracultural communicative medium in China. In P. Holmes and F. Dervin (eds) *The Cultural and Intercultural Dimensions of English as a Lingua Franca* (pp. 180–202). Bristol: Multilingual Matters.
Holliday, A. (2010) *Ideology and Intercultural Communication.* London: Routledge.
Holmes, P. and Dervin, F. (2016) Introduction – English as a lingua franca and interculturality: beyond orthodoxies. In P. Holmes and F. Dervin (eds) *The Cultural and Intercultural Dimensions of English as a Lingua Franca* (pp. 1–32). Bristol: Multilingual Matters.
Holwell, J. Z. (1764). A narrative of the deplorable deaths of the English gentlemen who were suffocated in the black hole in Fort William, at Calcutta, June 1756. In J. Z. Holwell and Friends (eds) *India Tracts* (pp. 252–276). London: T. Becket & T. A. de Hondt.
House, J. (2012) (Im)politeness in cross-cultural encounters. *Language and Intercultural Communication* 14 (4), 284–301.
Jenkins, J. (2007) *English as a Lingua Franca: Attitude and Identity.* Oxford: Oxford University Press.
Jenkins, J. (2013) *English as a Lingua Franca in the International University.* London: Routledge.
Jenkins, J., Cogo, A. and Dewey, M. (2011) Review of developments into research into English as a lingua franca. *Language Teaching* 44 (3), 281–315.
Jenks, C. (2012) Doing being reprehensive: Some interactional features of English as a lingua franca in a chat room. *Applied Linguistics* 33 (4), 386–405.
Jenks, C. (2016) Talking cultural identities into being in ELF interactions: an investigation of international postgraduate students in the United Kingdom. In P. Holmes and

F. Dervin (eds) *The Cultural and Intercultural Dimensions of English as a Lingua Franca* (pp. 93–113). Bristol: Multilingual Matters.

Kachru, B. (1985) Standards, codification and sociolinguistic realism: The English language in the outer circle. In R. Quirk and H.G. Widdowson (eds) *English in the World: Teaching and Learning the Language and Literatures* (pp. 11–30). Cambridge: Cambridge University Press.

Kalocsai, K. (2009) Erasmus exchange students: A behind the scenes view into an ELF community of practice. *Journal of Applied Language Studies* 3 (1), 25–49.

Kankaanranta, A. and Planken, B. (2010) BELF competence as business knowledge of internationally operating business professionals. *Journal of Business Communication* 47 (4), 380–407.

Kuper, S. (2011) Simon Kuper, Something in the way she speaks..., *The Financial Times*, 24 June 2011.

Ladegaard, H. (2013) Beyond the reach of ethics and equity? Depersonalisation and dehumanisation in foreign domestic helper narratives. *Language & Intercultural Communication* 13 (1), 44–59.

Little, B. (2007) *The Buccaneer's Realm. Pirate Life on the Spanish Main, 1674–1688*. Washington: Potomac Books.

Marx, K. (1978/1852) 18th Brumaire of Louis Bonaparte. In R.C. Tucker (ed.) *The Marx-Engels Reader* (pp. 594–617). New York: Norton.

Mauranen, A. (2012) *Exploring ELF: Academic English Shaped by Non-native Speakers*. Cambridge: Cambridge University Press.

Mauranen, A. and Metsä-Ketelä, M. (2006) Introduction. *Nordic Journal of English Studies Special Issue: English as a Lingua Franca* 5 (2), 1–8.

O'Regan, J.P. (2014) English as a lingua franca: An immanent critique. *Applied Linguistics* 35 (5), 533–552.

Pennycook, A. (2007) *Global Englishes and Transcultural Flows*. London: Routledge.

Pennycook, A. (2010a) 'The future of Englishes: One, many or none?' In A. Kirkpatrick (ed.) *The Routledge Handbook of World Englishes* (pp. 673–688). London: Routledge.

Pennycook, A. (2010b) *Language as a Local Practice*. London: Routledge.

Phipps, A. (2007) *Learning the Arts of Linguistic Survival: Languaging, Tourism, Life*. Clevedon: Channel View Publications.

Phipps, A. (2014) 'They are bombing now': 'Intercultural dialogue' in times of conflict. *Language & Intercultural Communication* 14 (1), 108–124.

Quirico, D. (2013) My 150-day ordeal as a hostage of Syria's rebels. *The Observer*, 15 September.

Rajagoplan, K. (2012) 'World English' or 'World Englishes'? Does it make any difference? *International Journal of Applied Linguistics* 22 (3), 374–391.

Rediker, M. (2004) *Villains of all Nations: Atlantic Pirates and the Golden Age*. London: Verso.

Risager, K. (2016) Lingua francas in a world of migrations. In P. Holmes and F. Dervin (eds) *The Cultural and Intercultural Dimensions of English as a Lingua Franca* (pp. 33–49). Bristol: Multilingual Matters.

Seidlhofer, B. (2009) Common ground and different realities: World Englishes and English as a lingua franca. *World Englishes* 28 (2), 236–245.

Seidlhofer, B. (2011) *Understanding English as a Lingua Franca*. Oxford: Oxford University Press.

Spivak, G.C. (1976) *Translator's Preface*, in J. Derrida, *Of Grammatology*. Baltimore: Johns Hopkins University Press.

Van Dyke, P.A. (2005) *The Canton Trade*. Hong Kong: Hong Kong University Press.

Wallerstein, I. (2004) *World Systems Analysis: An Introduction*. Durham and London: Duke University Press.

Index

accommodation 208, 209
agency 5
ambiguity 137, 140–142, 147, 152
anthropology 4

BELF 157
BELF user 157, 169, 174
biography 158

capital 212
China 180–197
   education policy 180–181, 186, 193
   English 185
   identity, see identity, Chinese
   pedagogy 181
   schools 182, 190–191, 193
   Shenyang 182–183
citizenship 34, 46, 48
code-switching 35, 183, 186, 194
collective identity 164, 167, 174
common core 53
Common European Framework of Reference 3
communicative competence 53, 71, 77–78
communicative goals 135, 149, 151
communicative repertoire 157, 158, 162
communities of practice 75, 114, 116, 118, 127, 129
conflict talk 114, 116, 118, 127–128
constructionist 116
context 15, 17, 25
conversational analysis 21, 137, 139, 148
creoles 35
critical awareness 34, 46, 48
criticality 71, 79–80, 83, 84

cross-cultural communication 52
crossing 35
cultural
   awareness (generic and specific) 63
   backgrounds 54, 56, 30
   content 56
   difference 4, 9, 15, 135–136, 138–140, 149, 151
   experiences 56
   flows 33, 35, 44
   hybridity 115, 127, 129
   identity 2, 53, 56, 60
   (and linguistic) homogeneity (assumed) 60, 61
   misunderstanding 7, 15
   performance 53
culture 6–7, 8, 12, 13, 16, 17, 158, 159, 160, 164, 167, 168, 170, 172, 173, 174, 175, 176
   and language 71–77
culture-bound 53
'culture-free' teaching 52
'culture-work' 63
Culture Irrelevance Hypothesis 148

directness 114–116, 118–119, 128–129
discourse 8, 13, 14, 15, 20, 21, 33, 39, 42, 43, 158, 159, 161–164, 166–172, 174, 175, 184–187
   markers 187
discourse strategy 115–116
discursive flows 42, 44
discursive identity construction 158, 159, 161, 162, 174, 174
diverse diversities 10

Index   219

early second language 36
ELF-user identity/ies 57
emergence 74, 77, 86
encounters 2, 11, 21, 25, 26
epistemic fallacy 214
English
  as a global language 55
  as an international auxiliary
    language 52
  as an international and intranational
    language 52
  as an international language 51, 52,
    55, 61, 62
  as a world language 51
  for intercultural communication 55
  for intercultural competence 53
  for specific purposes 51, 55, 63
  postcolonial 181
English as a lingua franca 50, 70–71,
  74–77, 78, 80–83, 84–85, 114–116,
  118, 127–129
  cultural and intercultural aspects of
    51, 52, 54, 63
  educational aspects of 50, 51, 54
  (inter)cultural aspects of 50
  linguistic aspects of 50, 51, 63
  pedagogic aspects of 51, 63
English language competence 52
English language teaching (ELT) 70–72,
  77–78, 83–85
English language user spectrum 57
enregisterment 22, 158, 159, 162, 166,
  169, 174
erasure 205, 215
essentialism 7, 10, 71–72, 115–116,
  129, 215
ethnography 14, 15, 188–189
Expanding Circle (Englishes and related
  paradigms) 57, 61, 63
explicitness 141, 151

first language 33, 36, 40
fluidity and fixity 74
foreign language 33, 36, 37
Foreign Language Education (FLE) 56

ghettoisation 60
global flows 73, 75

globalisation 56, 210
'good English' 3, 26
Greece/Greek context 50–59

high context communication 114–115
hybridity 13, 14, 16
hypostatization 205, 206, 212

identity 3, 6, 9, 10, 11, 13, 14, 15, 16, 18,
  21, 23, 26, 74–76
  Chinese 184
  in ELF 185–187, 194–195
identity dimension 40
ideology 11, 13
IELTS 3, 18
implications, pedagogical 152
indexicality 13, 23, 183, 185–189,
  194–197
indirectness 114–116, 118
Inner Circle (Englishes and related
  paradigms) 57, 62, 63
intelligibility 183, 185–188, 196
intercultural 44
  awareness 18, 21, 54, 71, 80–83, 84
  communication 53, 54, 55, 63,
    70–71, 72–74, 78, 80–81, 83–85
  communicative competence 20, 54,
    71, 78–79, 80–81, 83
  competence 25, 52, 54, 60, 71, 77–78,
    79, 80, 81, 84, 159, 167, 176
  dialogue 25, 60
  discourse 60
  education (rhetoric vs practice)
    59, 60
  (and interlingual) mediator 61
  schools 60
  skills 63
interculturalism 60
interculturality 2, 4, 5–6, 9, 10, 11, 12,
  15, 18, 19, 21, 25, 26, 50, 54, 59,
  61, 94–95
  renewed 2, 6
interdisciplinarity 4
international communication 50, 52, 54,
  55, 63, 64
international English 50, 58
International Forum 59, 62
international intelligibility 52

internationalisation 34
intersectionality 10
intersubjectivity 3
interview 158–165, 167–170, 172–174, 176
intracultural 184, 193–196
intracultural communication 10, 16, 23
intranational communication 52, 55, 63, 64
intranational English 58

L1 ←→ L1 57
L2 ←→ L1 57
L2 ←→ L2 57
language awareness 63
language-culture debate 53
language hierarchisation 35
language hierarchy 35
language learning trajectories 57
language learner 158, 159, 162, 164, 170
language learner identity 159
language user identity 159, 166
late second language 36
learner beliefs 56
let-it-pass 137–138
lingua franca 2, 4–5, 12
    English(es) 211, 212
    use 51
linguaculture 12, 19, 23, 26, 33, 39, 40, 41, 42, 43, 44, 158, 162, 164, 166, 172, 175
linguistic competence 53
linguistic flows 33, 34, 39, 44
linguistic fluency 53
linguistic identities 57
linguistic landscape 36
linguistic performance 53
linguistic resources 11, 19
low context communication 114

marginalisation 60
Marxism 14, 24, 25
meaning 44
methodology 14, 25
    appropriate 56, 63
metrolingualism 2
migration 33, 38, 46, 47
miscommunication 134, 136–137, 151

misrecognition 207, 210, 214
misunderstanding
    culture based 138, 148–151
    language-related 140, 144–145, 147
    overt 137–140
    performance-related 140, 142–144
    sources of 138–140, 147
mitigated disagreement 114, 116–119, 121, 128–129
mobility 33, 34, 38, 39, 46, 47
monolingualising ideology 60
mother tongue 51
multicultural awareness 20, 50, 63
multiculturalism 19, 50, 52, 60
multilingualism 52, 74, 78, 81, 83–84
mutual understanding 136, 144, 147, 149

national culture 115, 127, 129, 132–133
national identities 94–96, 99–101, 103–104, 106, 109–111
national paradigm 34
nationality 158, 159, 163, 164, 167, 170, 171, 174, 175
native/non-native 51, 53, 59, 63
native English 50
native language 34
native-like 53
nativeness/non-nativeness 56
native norms 53, 59
native speaker 5, 18, 19, 51
    models 54, 63
    norms 52
negotiation breakdown 116, 119, 128
negotiation process 116, 119, 128
non-understanding 136, 138, 140
norm(s)
    common core 53
    educated 53
    native 53
    native-speaker 52, 53

ontology 206, 210, 214
othering 8, 11, 21
Outer Circle (Englishes and related paradigms) 57, 63

pedagogy 11, 12, 14, 16, 17, 18–19, 20, 22
pidgins 35

poetic dimension 40
politeness 114–115, 121
post-TEFL (possibilities, challenge etc) 54, 61, 62, 64
pragmatic competence 4
pragmatic strategies 81, 84
power relations 6, 10, 11, 13, 17, 26

rapport management 116, 118–119, 121–122, 128–129
reflexivity 11
repair 138–140, 142, 146–147
repositioning (English language teaching) 62
researchers 11

second language 33, 36
semantic-pragmatic dimension 40
social construction 13, 24
speech community 184
stay abroad 158, 159, 162–164, 167–169, 175
stereotype 8, 23
symbolic competence 21, 80, 82

teacher awareness 64
teacher beliefs 56
teacher identity/ies 56
Teaching English to Speakers of Other Cultures (TESOC) 53

teaching paradigm 56, 62, 64
technology-mediated (English-based) communication 56, 59
textbook advice 114–116, 118, 121, 128
trajectory of sosialisation 157, 158, 162, 163, 176
transcultural flow 115
translingual flows 42
third culture 136, 149–150
third space 13, 136, 150
transnational 33, 34, 37, 38, 39, 45, 46, 47
and global flows 52, 59

unmitigated disagreement 114, 116–129
use of English
    intercultural use 51
    international use 51

variability 136, 149, 151–152
variety of English
    educated non-native speaker 54
    standard educated native speaker 54

way of speaking 158, 159, 162–167, 169–171, 174, 175
world Englishes 52, 55
world language 34

For Product Safety Concerns and Information please contact our EU Authorised Representative:

Easy Access System Europe

Mustamäe tee 50

10621 Tallinn

Estonia

gpsr.requests@easproject.com

www.ingramcontent.com/pod-product-compliance
Lightning Source LLC
Chambersburg PA
CBHW070603300426
44113CB00010B/1382